WHAT THEY DON'T LEARN
in SCHOOL

Colin Lankshear, Michele Knobel,
Chris Bigum, and Michael Peters
General Editors

Vol. 2

PETER LANG
New York • Washington, D.C./Baltimore • Bern
Frankfurt am Main • Berlin • Brussels • Vienna • Oxford

WHAT THEY DON'T LEARN in SCHOOL

Literacy in the Lives of Urban Youth

Edited by JABARI MAHIRI

PETER LANG
New York • Washington, D.C./Baltimore • Bern
Frankfurt am Main • Berlin • Brussels • Vienna • Oxford

Library of Congress Cataloging-in-Publication Data

What they don't learn in school: literacy in the lives of urban youth /
edited by Jabari Mahiri.
p. cm. (New literacies and digital epistemologies; v. 2)
Includes bibliographical references and index.
1. Literacy—Social aspects—United States. 2. Education,
Urban—Social aspects—United States. 3. Minority
youth—Education—United States. I. Mahiri, Jabari. II. Series.
LC151 .W44   302.21′244′0835—dc21   2002010500
ISBN 978-0-8204-5036-0
ISSN 1523-9543

What they don't learn in school : literacy in the lives of urban youth /
ed. by Jabari Mahiri. –New York ; Washinton, DC/Baltimore ; Bern ;
Frankfurt am Main ; Berlin ; Brussels ; Vienna ; Oxford : Lang.
(New literacies and digital epistemologies ; Vol. 2)
ISBN 0-8204-5036-7

Cover photo by Kahlil Jacobs-Fantauzzi
Cover design by Sophie Boorsch Appel

The paper in this book meets the guidelines for permanence and durability
of the Committee on Production Guidelines for Book Longevity
of the Council of Library Resources.

For Nina Luna Mahiri
– the first –

Table of Contents

Figures

Acknowledgments

I would like to acknowledge the following people for their important contributions to this book. First I want to thank the authors of each of the chapters. They have gone from graduate school to take significant positions as faculty and professionals in education. It was a pleasure working with them individually and as a group, and each one is now a valued colleague. I also want to thank the respondents to each of the chapters. Each is a friend and scholar whose work I admire, and from whom I have learned a lot. They all took time from busy schedules to write their responses, which have definitely added to the merit of this work. Additionally, I want to say thanks to James Paul Gee and Keith Gilyard for their generous back cover comments. Jim Gee particularly has provided selfless support for every phase of my career as a college professor. Colin Lankshear and Michele Knobel, editors for the series in which this work appears, went well beyond the call in their invaluable help in getting this work to publication. Beyond my heartfelt thanks to them, I have truly enjoyed becoming friends in the process. Finally, I want to thank Susan Roberta Katz for her advise and critique throughout the process of completing this book.

Permissions

We wish to thank the following for permission to use material for which they hold copyright as follows. Kahlil Jacobs-Fantauzzi for the cover photo. The editors of Social Justice for permission to reprint chapter 2 which first appeared in volume 24 (4), published in 1997. Stephenie MAZE/NGS Image Collection and National Geographic for images that appear in chapter 3. The editors of the Hispanic Academic Program Anthology for hand-drawn images that appear in chapter 3. Damu, Roxanne, and Branden for literary works that appear in chapter 10.

CHAPTER ONE

New Literacies in a New Century

Jabari Mahiri

he Mis-Education of Lauryn Hill, an extremely successful rap music CD, begins with a familiar classroom scene. A teacher is calling role, and one by one students answer by saying "here." When Lauryn Hill's name is called, however, silence indicates that she is absent from school. Her refrain in the song that breaks this silence is: "You might win some but you just lost one." For Hill it is these "lost ones" for whom there is hope for more authentic lives and learning beyond the "mis-education" of school.

Contributors to this book have attempted to apprehend practices of literacy and learning in the lives of urban youth beyond schooling. The goal has not been to affirm or disaffirm Hill's lyrical premise, but to research and identify the specific nature and functions of an array of literacy practices that young people appropriate for learning and expression. These practices are not necessarily new, but their descriptions and assessments are anchored in perspectives from what has come to be called "New Literacy Studies."

Gee (1996), Street (1984, 1993), and others have discussed New Literacy Studies as a movement that challenges more traditional orientations that see literacy as relatively autonomous abilities to read and write in a given language. Gee (personal communication) defines New Literacy Studies as a field "which integrates a variety of disciplines (e.g., linguistics, social theory, anthropology, critical theory, cognitive science, and education) in order to take a view of cognition, language, and literacy as not just 'mental' phenomena, accessible to cognitive psychology, but as socially, culturally, historically, and politically situated practices through which people's identities are formed and transformed and through which institutions are produced and reproduced." The following chapters explore a number of urban scenes in order to engage, understand, and present multiple youth identities, attitudes, activities, representations, and stories connected to a range of situated, adaptive, and voluntary uses of literacy. Together, these studies contribute to a more comprehensive understanding of the pedagogies, politics, and possibilities of literacy and learning—in and out of school.

Soraya Sablo and I have promoted a conception of literacy that defines it as culturally connected "skills used in the production of meaning from texts in a context" (Mahiri and Sablo, 1996: 166). For us, the nature and function of skills, productions, meanings, and texts can vary significantly from context to context and can be based on different cultural models. We see these aspects of literacy as intricately interdependent, and argue for the importance of the delineation of each in relation to the others. The ten studies in this book extend the basic framework we established to explicate the various skills, the distinct methods of production or composition, the subjective and collective meanings, the mutable and variegated texts, and the dynamic contexts that urban youth utilize for expression and affirmation.

These situated ways of knowing, expressing, and being can be partially characterized by what Giroux and Simon (1989: 1) termed "a pedagogy of pleasure and meaning," or what Michael Dyson (1993: 64) referred to as "the pedagogy of desire" at work in what Willis (1990: 1) has called "the living common culture" of youth. Giroux and Simon (1989: 2) argued as long ago as the late 1980s that even radical educational theorists have often ignored "the notion of pedagogy as a cultural production and exchange that addresses how knowledge is produced, mediated, refused, and represented within relations of power both in and outside of schooling." They emphasized that "the production of meaning is tied to the production of pleasure and that both are mutually constitutive of who students are, the view they have of themselves, and how they construct a particular version of their future" (1989: 4).

With respect to popular culture, Michael Dyson (1993) argues that the desires of urban youth are learned and shaped by styles and products embodied in cultural icons that are seductively created and commodified for youth consumption. In certain instances these icons can operate as "public pedagogues" whose careers, according to Dyson, "educate us about productive and disenabling forms of knowledge, desire, interest, and culture" (1993: 65). In the realm of living common culture, Willis (1990: 1) noted: "Most young people's lives...are actually full of expressions, signs and symbols through which individuals and groups seek creatively to establish their presence, identity and meaning." In concert with these perspectives, contemporary youth in their everyday lives—often through powerful influences from electronically mediated popular culture—both construct and consume personal/cultural meanings, pleasures, and desires that prefigure and inform their engagements with school.

It is interesting to see how "new capitalism" (Gee, Hull, and Lankshear, 1996) commodifies messages and images from youth culture for global consumption while educators often disdain the use of popular cultural materials in schools. One clear example of the first point is in the decision of the Levi Strauss Corporation to use popular music to more fully exploit youth markets. According to reports from the company's brand manager, sales for Levi products had plunged 13 percent during 1998, so the corporation decided to up its marketing budget for music-related activities from 5 percent to as high as 50 percent (Emert, 1999: A1). A key entertainer they contracted to simply wear their clothes while she performed was Lauryn Hill. Having recently received the 30th Annual NAACP Image Award and having just appeared on the cover of *Time* magazine, she had clearly become a pervasive popular music icon.

One advertising executive discussed the efficacy of using artists like Hill to influence the thinking of youth. He noted that "[m]usic is very, very important to young people—far more important than almost any other part of their lives.... There are very few ways into young teens' heads and music is one of them. The trick, how do you make the association effective?" (Emert, 1999: A1).

Gee (2000) has identified a key feature of new capitalism that facilitates its making effective associations with highly specified markets. In synthesizing the views of several business experts, Gee noted that "[w]hat makes a product or service distinctive [and thus, effective] is the knowledge work that has gone into designing, producing, and marketing it on time and on demand for just the right niche market" (2000: 414). In this century, more knowledge work in schools will need to involve educators in understanding how students and communities use symbiotic resources for their own ends as well as for the dramatically changing literacy demands of sites beyond school. If schools are not able to meet this challenge, according to Willis (1990: 147), "they will become almost totally irrelevant to the real energies and interests of most young people and no part of their identity formation."

If we do not consider lit practices pop culture beyond school - we are non-adaptive, fail to meet students

Contemporary youth don't merely consume and blindly respond to messages and images of new capitalism or schooling, however. They also produce and propagate meanings and representations of their own which often challenge or work to counter the defining power of society and schools. Hill's CD, again, provided a provocative example of one way this process works. It began with the selection of its title in which Hill consciously alluded to historian Carter G. Woodson's 1933 classic text, *The Mis-Education of the Negro*. In one incisive quote, Woodson captured the key problem and contradiction of "the Negro's" mis-education.

> When you control a man's thinking you do not have to worry about his actions. You do not have to tell him not to stand here or go yonder. He will find his "proper place" and will stay in it. You do not need to send him to the back door, he will cut one for his special benefit. His education makes it necessary.

Beyond the correspondence between titles, the artist's rendition of Hill on the cover of the CD bears a close resemblance to the illustration of the young African American woman on the cover of the most recent 1990 edition of Woodson's work. The depiction on Hill's CD, however, is minus one dramatic symbol on the book's cover—a padlock on the mind of the young African American woman. The effected presence of the obvious similarities of these texts—the calculated attempts of Hill to use titles, themes, and images as oral and written, lyrical and visual texts to, in fact, *correspond* with Woodson's historical text—offers insightful considerations of "literacy" as "multiple literacies" situated in the cultural practices of (in this case) African American youth.

Essentially, Hill's text can be seen as a current version of a "signifying black text" that Gates described in *The Signifying Monkey: A Theory of African-American Literary Criticism*. Gates (1988: 171) noted that "[w]hat was at stake for the earliest black authors was nothing less than the implicit testimony to their humanity." Of most importance "was the negation of the image of the black as an absence" (1988: 171). Yet, there was always intense debate over what should be seen as an "authentic" black voice. Consequently, black authors continually read and revised images and themes they received from earlier traditions of black writing. Gates illustrated black texts signifying upon and revising other black texts through an example in the early paragraphs of Zora Neale Hurston's (1937) *Their Eyes Were Watching God* in which she utilized rhetorical techniques of repetition and reversal to signify upon and revise the trope of slave narration in an earlier writing by Frederick Douglass.

Like Hurston (and consistent with the multi-textual sampling of rap), Hill employed rhetorical features of repetition and reversal to signify upon and revise the trope of the mis-educated Negro. However, her absence from school was an affirmation rather than negation of the image of black as absence. Her body might be packaged in Levi's and other raiment of new capitalism, yet she simultaneously embodies a self-reflected pedagogy of desires and possibilities for urban youth. In *Black Noise*, Rose (1994: 22) noted that "hip hop transforms stray technological parts intended for cultural and industrial trash heaps into sources of pleasure and power. These transformations have become a basis for digital imagination all over the world." In the words of one youth, *The Mis-Education of Lauryn Hill* represents the soul of hip-hop, not just the commercial or entertainment side."[1] Contemporary youth clearly perceive and appropriate the complex meanings that Hill and other "public pedagogues" communicate through multimodal, multivoiced, cultural texts.

The studies presented in this book also reveal extensive practices and perspectives of learning and literacy in young people's everyday lives. The ten contributors whose studies are reflected in the nine chapters beyond the two I have written have several things in common. First, they were all doctoral candidates when they completed the research and writing of their chapters. Several have already gone on to tenure-track positions at major universities in the United States while the others have been in the final stages of completing their dissertations as this book was going to press. Over the past few years, each contributor had taken either one or both of two of classes I teach in the Graduate School of Education at the University of California, Berkeley: "Theoretical Perspectives in the Study of Literacy" and "Literacy Practices in Non-School Settings." They also have all had training in qualitative methods and discourse analysis.

Eight of these ten contributors began the research for their chapters as part of the required work for one of the yearly sections of the "Literacy Practices in Non-School Settings" course. Chapters for six of these contributors also represent the basic foci that they eventually developed into dissertation studies. In effect, the contributors became members of a research community that operated over time (and well beyond their coursework) to shape the separate projects as they developed. Except for chapter eight by Jane Stanley, these works also reflect the fluid considerations of doing qualitative research on language and literacy with informants in non-school settings. Hence, although the various research gazes have ranged far and wide into the cultural spaces and physical places inhabited by urban youth, they have for the most part been continually focused through core conceptual and methodological frames.

In earlier versions of the course on non-school literacy practices, there were not many book-length texts fitted for our specific purpose. Moss's (1994) edited work, *Literacy Across Communities*, became a good starting point. In concert with Chiseri-Strater's (1994) final chapter in that book, I encouraged the doctoral candidates to be "world travelers" to diverse cultural settings in order to learn about "literacies that would be inaccessible, even invisible, to outsiders to these nonmainstream communities" (1993: 179).

Pivotal studies that we used to establish conceptual and methodological frameworks for viewing language and literacy in conjunction with specific social functions and practices inside particular social contexts included Gee (1991, 1996), Heath (1980, 1982, 1983), Hymes (1996), Scribner and Cole (1981), and Street (1984, 1993). A key unit of analysis was Heath's (1982) notion of a literacy event in which a piece of writing is integral to the interactions and interpretive processes of participants in a situation. But we also utilized Street's (1993: 12) broader notion of literacy practices which "incorporate not only 'literacy events,' as empirical occasions to which literacy is integral, but also 'folk models' of those events and the ideological preconceptions that underpin them."

Building on Street's (1984) ideological model of literacy, Lankshear with Lawler (1987: 44) noted how "beliefs that literacy is unitary, neutral, and an independent variable, are readily seen to be mistaken." They summed up a key consideration from this line of research by noting that "literacies are social constructions forged in the process of humans pursuing values, goals and interests, under conditions where some groups have greater access to structural power than others" (1987: 79). Street (1993) also noted Grillo's (1989) extension of literacy to encompass types of "communicative practice" that include ways in which literacy activities are embedded in institutions and are implicated in wider social, economic, political, and cultural processes. At this broad level of conceptualization, there were direct connections to Gee's notions of "D/discourses"—their acquisition and learning, their delineation as primary and secondary, and his definition of literacy as "control of secondary uses of language (i.e., uses of language in secondary discourses)" (1991: 8).

These concepts provided generalized frameworks for all of the studies. We took up Gee's definition of literacy and assessed "uses of language" in terms of literacy events and literacy practices that revealed the multiple literacies through which many urban youth acquired and expressed certain values, beliefs, and identity associations, and in some cases learned to think and write critically about other secondary discourses—including dominant ones. Contributors also explored discourse practices with respect to tensions and connections between oral and written language and between language and other symbol systems and media. In this regard, a New Literacy Studies orientation to notions of *text* was central to the foci of all the research projects. An apt expression of this is found in the Interstate New Teacher Assessment and Support Consortium's Model Standards documents that provided the following definition.

> A (text) is any segment of language or symbol that creates a unit of meaning. Texts include print material like stories, poems, essays, books, newspaper and magazine articles; spoken representations of meaning like oral stories, discussions, or speeches; dramatizations, like live enactments, films, television; visual representations of meaning like paintings, cartoons, sculpture, graphics, and holography; tactile representations like Braille; and, even lived experiences like a day in the park, a conversation with a loved one, or an observation about some social situation.[2]

We additionally reviewed a number of studies that have operated within and contributed to these frameworks, such as: Camitta (1993), Dyson (1993), Farr (1994), Goodman and Wilde (1992), Heath and McLaughlin (1991, 1993), Lee (1991, 1993), Mahiri (1991, 1994a, 1994b), Schaafsma (1993), Shuman (1986), and Taylor and Dorsey-Gaines (1988). More recently, we looked at a number of other significant works that have been published more recently, such as Guerra (1998), Cushman (1998), Knobel (1999), and Kalman (1999) which provide in-depth treatments of specific discourse communities: Mexicanos and Chicanos, African Americans, Australians, and scribes in Mexico City, respectively. One thing that all these studies have in common is the use of qualitative methods for conducting research.

Qualitative research assembles and interprets evidence based on data from an array of sources, especially from informants who have "emic" or insider perspectives on the area of focus or study. Key issues regarding qualitative research have continually played out through various tensions, movements, reconceptualizations, and paradigmatic shifts that argue the limits and possibilities of writing and representing cultures. Sipe and Constable (1996), for example, mapped out four contemporary paradigms currently operating in qualitative research: positivist, interpretivist, critical theory, and deconstructivist. The last three can be seen as postpositivist in contrast to the positivist paradigm. Sipe and Constable explicated the range of "places to stand" that these paradigms allowed educational researchers, noting that "different paradigms are employed for different purposes" (1996: 153). These places to stand, however, also reflect particular views of the world and of reality. According to Guba (1990: 22), "in the positivist version it is contended that there is a reality out there to be studied, captured, and understood, whereas postpositivists argue that reality can never be fully apprehended, only approximated." Thus, postpositivists believe that positivist methods are but one way of telling a story about society or the social world.

In conjunction with a New Literacy Studies orientation, contributors to this book have taken a postpositivist stance in the use of qualitative methods to tell the stories of their informants. They have worked to include the actual voices of many of their informants in order to achieve more narrative equality. They have also attempted to tell these stories in accessible styles. Without sacrificing the complexity of what was being studied, they endeavored to reflect something of the excitement and energy of these non-static sites of literacy and cultural production. Essentially, in keeping with formulations like those of Denzin and Lincoln (1994), they were positioned as bricoleurs creating a bricolage by using strategies, methods, and empirical materials that were shaped to and by the contexts as well as their varying degrees of access to them. Authors of each chapter have delineated methods of data collection and analysis that they used. But because of length constraints, the comprehensiveness of individual studies is not addressed in full in favor of providing something of the breadth and variety of youth practices of literacy revealed in the array of studies included in this volume.

Taken together, these studies address literacy practices of African American, Latino/a American, Asian American, Iranian American, and European American youth and young adults. Work is presented on the voluntary writing of poetry and screen plays; the written and oral compositions of raps and their public and private performances along with other literacy activities associated with hip-hop culture; independent and school related video productions; and, involvements with gangs and gang literacies of African American youth. Work is presented on Latino/a American youth involvements with lowrider car culture and its associated literacies; graffiti writing and other visual literacies; as well as involvements with gangs and gang literacies. For Asian American youth, work is presented on the reading of Japanese, Chinese, and American comic books and their roles in the border discourses and identity constructions of Chinese immigrant youth as well as involvements with youth clubs and their associated literacies. For Cambodian and Iranian American youth, work is presented on the complex ways they practice gender out of school and in school and how these experiences also permeate academic literacy practices. For European American youth and young adults, work is presented on the reading of teen romance novels, internet involvement and cyber-literacies, and the literacy activities of working and middle-class white youth in service industry jobs.

A dynamic feature of this book is the way it brings major scholars in the fields of language, literacy, and cultural studies into dialogue with the authors of each of the studies. In this way key issues are extended in discussion and critique by respondents whose work and interests are highly relevant to each chapter's focus.

In the following chapter, I examine five African American urban youth attempting to come to terms with the violence and crime in their lives through acts of voluntary writing. I call the varied texts of this voluntary writing "street scripts" and analyze how youth use these scripts to reveal both their understandings of and their anxieties about the traumatic conditions they face. These youth already know that they are prime candidates for the juvenile justice system. They see how their lives are permeated with violence and crime. Yet, many of their texts reveal insightful personal perspectives that counterpose ways in which these youth are often portrayed in the media, in politics, and in public schooling. In creative and complex ways these young people question and speculate on how these inscriptions of violence and crime can be changed.

This second chapter argues that the texts that these youth compose and enact are unique "writings" that reflect significant literacy practices, and it explicates these works as one would other literacy texts using tools of critical literary analysis and interpretation. The discussant of this work is Pedro Noguera. In commentary following the chapter, Noguera contextualizes and critiques the analysis and findings of this work from the vantage point of his extensive research and writing on these critical issues facing urban youth.

In chapter three, Peter Cowan explores literacy events and practices in Latino social worlds in which customized cars known as *lowriders* are perceived as cultural objects of aesthetic and symbolic value. Through his research, Cowan argues that the definition of literacy needs to be expanded to include visual literacy to explain how people read lowrider cars and other visual texts. He also argues that participants in this Latino visual discourse community participate in a dialogical relationship with dominant discourses concerning the ways in which lowriders and Latino youth are represented. He concludes that teachers and education researchers need to continually examine their assumptions and be aware of students' literate behaviors lest they fall victim to "mainstream" representations and the ways these representations textually and visually create and perpetuate forms of ethnic and racial stratification. José D. Saldívar discusses this chapter and points out a number of richly creative "resistances" that can be read in the drawing and lowrider work of the Latino/a youth presented in Cowan's chapter.

In chapter four, Wan Shun Eva Lam examines the relationships between discourse, literacy practices and identity formation among Chinese immigrant teenagers whose social networks and cultural identifications are spread over multiple geographic territories. A key focus in this chapter is on their reading of Japanese, Chinese, and American comic books. She describes and analyzes how these teenagers create transnational social and cultural ties, and engage in voluntary discourse and literacy practices that serve to construct flexible cross-cultural identifications that represent a "third" positional space distinct from the first space of colonialism and imperialism, and the second space created by original inhabitants living within this first space. In this third space, these immigrant youth actively participate in border discourses and identity constructions that allow them to resist subordination and other constraints of the dominant social influences that surround them. The discussant for this chapter is Claire Kramsch, who analyzes the tactical resistances of the young men Lam studied by way of their literacy practices, set within the context of globalization.

"I used to go to school; now I learn" was one of the provocative statements from the young women who were informants in Beth Lewis Samuelson's study of unschoolers and homeschoolers presented in chapter five. Homeschoolers, and especially the unschoolers who are the focus of Samuelson's study, believe they learn in ways that are radically different from school learning. Their experiences, attitudes, and beliefs illuminate something of the character and possibilities for learning outside of formal schooling that have partially been made available to them by means of various technological developments. Through online journals and other communicative connections, this discourse community reveals and revels in the benefits they feel they experience by being unschooled while simultaneously engaging in an ongoing critique of the limits of compulsory schooling. Evidence is mounting that this growing movement is no longer confined to political or religious fringes and that it is achieving results that often surpass public education. Samuelson's analysis provides a compelling view of their unique discourse and learning activities. Carol D. Lee is the respondent to this chapter and brings to her discussion of this chapter keen insights into "unschooling" from both an historical perspective on Africans' enslavement and their literacy education in the U.S., and from her own extensive involvement in Independent Black Institutions.

After these initial chapters have examined aspects of the literacy practices in each of four racial/ethnic groups, the final six chapters constitute a series of duets. Chapters six and seven, respectively, look at literacy practices in cyberspace and in the work place. In chapter six, Jennifer Seibel Trainor focuses on electronic literacy practices of people who would identify more with Generation X than with urban youth. Nonetheless, the issues she addresses fall squarely within the book's overall focus on voluntary productions of literacy texts outside of school. She describes and assesses literacy practices of an online fan club—*The Gossamer Project*—that is centered on the popular television series, *The X-Files*. *The Gossamer Project* specializes in fan fiction—stories and novellas written by fans about the characters and situations depicted on the show. Trainor's study raises interesting questions about internet practices in general and about changes the internet promises in terms of our understanding of the social meanings of literacy. She argues that the internet fundamentally alters several categories of meaning relevant to most discussions of both literacy practices and popular culture. For example, issues of ownership, authorship, and access are all reconstituted by new technology. She concludes that traditional ways of thinking about popular culture and popular literacies—about the pleasure, play, and power involved in these literacies—become inadequate, even anachronistic, when seen in relationship to *The Gossamer Project*. Andrea Abernethy Lunsford discusses this chapter in relation to the very real tensions and paradoxes associated with and generated by copyright issues, changing conceptions of "the author," and the ownership of ideas and other commodities set within postmodern times.

In chapter seven, Tony Mirabelli looks at the literacy and discourse practices of waiters and waitresses in diner-styled restaurants. The number of "in-person" service workers (i.e., retail workers, hotel workers, flight attendants, taxi drivers, waiters, and waitresses, etc.) has increased dramatically over the past ten years in the United States, and under current economic conditions, will most likely continue to rise. The ranks of these service workers include high numbers of working class young people who are struggling to survive in an economy that provides far greater privileges and rewards to knowledge workers. Much of the research done on the kinds of literacy skills needed to be service workers is conducted from a management perspective and intended to serve management needs. Very little research has been done that considers the perspective of the service workers themselves—particularly in relation to how they perceive the language and literacy practices needed to do their work effectively. Tony Mirabelli examines the literacy and discourse practices of waitresses and reveals the variety of roles that literacy plays in how this work is organized and how it gets done. He also reveals the imbalances of power among service workers and management as well as between service workers and the public. Stuart Tannock responds to the arguments raised in Mirabelli's chapter by way of problematizing the relationship between academic research and claims of "empowerment" made on behalf of others, and underscores the importance of counteracting social and work-based prejudices against young people.

The two chapters that follow address practices of literacy and gender and how these are continuously at play in and out of school. Chapter eight, by Jane Stanley, synthesizes and analyzes the findings of a number of qualitative studies made of young romance readers and their responses to these texts. Stanley critiques the role of the publishing industry in nurturing the young romance reader market. At the same time, she offers alternative "readings" of young romance readers, and draws in particular on resistance theory as she explores and problematizes the question of why romance reading is such an ineluctable literacy practice for many adolescent girls. Gesa E. Kirsch locates her commentary on this chapter within the context of growing numbers of corporate-school partnerships and the ethical dilemmas such partnerships entail for educators. Kirsch closes her discussion with a list of thought-provoking research questions that opens up a range of education issues concerning adolescents—male and female—and their literacies.

In chapter nine, Amanda Godley explores how gendered practices are concomitantly expressed through practices of literacy in and out of school. Her study focuses on how high school students navigate and negotiate male/female gender borders, and pays particular attention to the kinds of knowledge they draw on in English classroom literacy experiences, as well as the knowledge they bring to these experiences from their lives outside of school. It is in high school that most youth start to position themselves as gendered subjects, such as girlfriend/boyfriend and later as mother/father. In many studies of gender and literacy, gender is viewed as a static, historic categorization of males and females. These studies often focus on the ways in which male and female students read and write differently, rather than on sociocultural factors that influence gender and literacy. Godley, however, uses a theoretical framework that recognizes both gender and literacy as contextualized social practices. She uses this framework to explore the ways in which students construct, reflect, and resist notions of gender through the practices of reading, writing, speaking, listening, and acting in and beyond structured classroom settings. Barrie Thorne is the discussant for this chapter and focuses on the "discourses of possibility" literacy offers young people in terms of talking within, across, and beyond culture and race, class, and gender differences.

The last two chapters return to literacy practices in African American communities. In chapter ten, Soraya Sablo Sutton examines performances of "spoken word." Though spoken word may initially be created as written text, this performance poetry is first and foremost experienced orally and extends from the intricate history of African American oral traditions. Sutton analyzes performance poetry as a distinct literacy event, as well as in terms of its functions and sociocultural meanings as a dynamic discourse inside the black community. She found this particular practice of literacy to be consistent with formulations from Freire and others who have argued that more than a set of skills, literacy involves an attitude of creation and re-creation that becomes self-transforming to the extent of motivating intervention in one's context. Sutton utilizes a number of poet/informants and their work to help us understand specific functions and meanings for a kind of poetry that should "not be so educated that it don't stop in/every now n then to sit on the porch/and talk about the comins and goins of the world" (Forman, 1993: xvii). June Jordan is the respondent to this chapter and emphasizes the importance of challenging taken-for-granted assumptions in education that literacy always only ever concerns something "written down."

In the final chapter, Ernest Morrell and Jeff Duncan-Andrade present their research on ways in which contemporary youth culture generally and hip-hop music specifically can be used as vehicles for urban youth to develop and express critical literacy skills. As teachers and researchers, they explored how students who were often labeled "non-academic" or "semi-literate" could critically analyze richly metaphoric and symbolic hip-hop music that they listened to in their everyday lives. At the same time, many of these same students were failing to exhibit similar analytical skills in class when relating to canonical texts. Eventually, they designed and evaluated a curricular intervention that embedded teaching hip-hop music as a literary genre within a scaffolding process involved in developing critical literacy skills in relation to canonical texts that students need to study in order to be successful in school. The findings from this study argue for a broader definition of school-based literacy that builds effectively on urban students' lived experiences and encompasses their cultural understandings and values, their self-awareness, and the development of critical consciousness. Jeannie Oakes is the discussant for this final chapter, and closes the volume with a keen-edged critique of dominant ideologies of intelligence and the cultural construction of "academic capital."

This collection comes at a time when youth generally and youth of color particularly have often been represented in society as dangerous Others. In developing this idea, Conquergood (1992) noted that increasingly urban youth are inscribed by stigmatizing images of social pathology in the official discourse of the media and the legal system as well as in social welfare and public policy institutions. By turning urban youth into scapegoats, these inscriptions actually work to hide another reality of U.S. society: the reality of rising crime and social pathology among adults. In *Framing Youth: Ten Myths About the Next Generation*, Males (1999) used extensive Department of Justice and U.S. Census Bureau data and statistics to convincingly argue that it is really white adults in contemporary U.S. society who are the "superpredators." According to Males, the "truth, abundantly obvious from official crime reports over the last one to two decades, is that it is not minority teenagers, but adults over the age of 30—white adults, most specifically—who consistently display the largest increases in serious (felony) violent, property, and drug-related crime rates" (1999: 5). The fact of rising adult crime, particularly white-adult crime, is the real irony of the politics surrounding the public debate and depiction of crime in connection with urban youth.

The chapters in this book allow for a more comprehensive view of urban youth and young adults than is usually presented in the media, in politics, and in schooling. Implications from these studies suggest that there do not have to be inherent discontinuities between young people's authentic life experiences and their experience of life in schools. Yet, some of the very perspectives and technologies that facilitate the sourcing of multitextual, multimodal, multicultural resources for learning are the ones least used or developed, especially in urban schools. As these studies show, however, many of these perspectives and technologies are being appropriated by youth themselves to circumvent limits on learning that often seem imposed by schools—to circumvent, as Hymes (1996: 14) has noted, "division of society into those who know and those who are known." The(question)that remains is: Can societal structures and school curricula accommodate and incorporate youth desires for knowledge and the new kinds of knowledge they need for negotiating the literacy demands and possibilities of a new century? Or, has the mis-education of the Negro become the mis-education of urban youth?

Notes

1. This quote is from an informant in an unpublished paper on the literacy practices in hip-hop culture titled "Break It Down" by Sanjiv Rao.
2. The Interstate New Teacher Assessment and Support Consortium (INTASC) of the Council of Chief State School Officers uses this definition of text in their Model Standards documents developed for use by member states.

Works Cited

Camitta, M. (1993). Vernacular writing: Varieties of literacy among high school students. In B. Street (Ed.), *Cross cultural approaches to literacy* (pp. 228–246). Cambridge: Cambridge University Press.

Chiseri-Strater, E. (1994). World travelling: Enlarging our understanding of nonmainstream literacies. In B. Moss (Ed.), *Literacy across communities* (pp. 179–186). Cresskill, NJ: Hampton.

Conquergood, D. (1992). On rappin' and rhetoric: Gang Representations. Paper presented at the Philosophy and Rhetoric of Inquiry Seminar, University of Iowa, (April 8).

Cushman, E. (1998). *The struggle and the tools: Oral and literate strategies in an inner city community*. Albany, NY: State University of New York Press.

Denzin, N. and Lincoln, Y. (1993). *Handbook of qualitative research*. Thousand Oaks, CA: Sage.

Dyson, A. (1993). *Social worlds of children learning to write in an urban primary school*. New York: Teachers College Press.

Dyson, M. (1993). *Reflecting black: African-American cultural criticism*. Minneapolis, MN: University of Minnesota Press.

Emert, C. (1999, March 8). Levi's uses music to woo youth market. *San Francisco Chronicle*.

Farr, M. (1994). En los dos idiomas: Literacy practices among Chicano Mexicanos. In B. Moss (Ed.), *Literacy across communities* (pp. 9–47). Cresskill, NJ: Hampton Press.

Forman, R. (1993). *We are the young magicians*. Boston, MA: Beacon Press.

Gates, H. (1988). *The signifying monkey: A theory of African-American literary criticism*. New York: Oxford University Press.

Gee, J. (1991). *Rewriting literacy: Culture and the discourse of the other*. New York: Bergin and Garvey.

———. (1996). *Social linguistics and literacies: Ideology in discourses*. Bristol, PA: Taylor & Francis.

———. (2000). Teenagers in new times: A new literacy studies perspective. *Journal of Adolescent and Adult Literacy*, 43 (5), 412–420.

———. Hull, G., and Lankshear, C. (1996). *The new work order: Behind the language of the new capitalism.* Sydney: Allen and Unwin.

Giroux, H. A. and Simon, R. I. (1989). *Popular culture, schooling, and everyday life.* New York: Bergin & Garvey.

Goodman, Y. and Wilde, S. (1992). *Literacy events in a community of young writers.* New York: Teachers College Press.

Grillo, R. (1989). *Dominant languages.* Cambridge: Cambridge University Press.

Guba, E. G. (1990). The alternative paradigm dialog. In E. G. Guba (Ed.), *The paradigm dialog* (pp. 17–30). Newbury Park, CA: Sage.

Guerra, J. (1998). *Close to home: Oral and literate practices in a transnational Mexicano community.* New York: Teachers College Press.

Heath, S. B. (1980). The functions and uses of literacy. *Journal of Communication,* 30, 123–133.

———. (1982). Protean shapes in literacy events: Ever-shifting oral and literate traditions. In D. Tannen (Ed.), *Spoken and written language: Exploring orality and literacy* (pp. 91–117). Norwood, NJ: Ablex.

———. (1983). *Ways with words: Language, life and work in communities and classrooms.* Cambridge: Cambridge University Press.

———. and McLaughlin, M. (1991). Community organizations as family. *Phi Delta Kappan,* 72, 623–627.

Heath, S. and McLaughlin, M. (Eds.). (1993). *Identity and inner-city youth: Beyond ethnicity and gender.* New York: Teachers College Press.

Hill, L. (1998). *The mis-education of Lauryn Hill.* Nashville, TN: Sony/ATV Music Publishing.

Hurston, Z. N. (1937). *Their eyes were watching God.* New York: J. P. Lippincott Company.

Hymes, D. (1996). *Ethnography, linguistics, narrative inequality: Toward an understanding of voice.* London: Taylor & Francis.

Kalman, J. (1999). *Writing on the plaza: Mediated literacy practices among scribes and clients in Mexico City.* Cresskill, NJ: Hampton.

Knobel, M. (1999). *Everyday literacies: Students, discourse, and social practice.* New York: Peter Lang.

Lankshear, C. with M. Lawler (1987). *Literacy, schooling and revolution.* New York: Falmer.

Lee, C. (1991). Big picture talkers/words walking without masters: The instructional implication of ethnic voices for an expanded literacy. *Journal of Negro Education,* 60 (3), 291–304.

———. (1993). *Signifying as a scaffold for literary interpretation: The pedagogical implications of an African American discourse genre.* Urbana, IL: National Council of Teachers of English.

Mahiri, J. (1991). Discourse in sports: Language and literacy features of preadolescent African males in a youth basketball program. *Journal of Negro Education,* 60 (3), 305–313.

———. (1994a). African American males and learning: What discourse in sports offers schools. *Anthropology and Education Quarterly,* 25 (3), 1–13.

———. (1994b). Reading rites and sports: Motivation for adaptive literacy of young African American males. In B. Moss (Ed.), *Literacy across communities* (pp. 121–146). Cresskill, NJ: Hampton.

————. and Sablo, S. (1996). Writing for their lives: The non-school literacy of California's urban African American youth. *Journal of Negro Education*, 65 (2), 164–180.

Males, M. A. (1999). *Framing youth: Ten myths about the next generation*. Monroe, ME: Common Courage Press.

Moss, B. (Ed.). (1994). *Literacy across communities*. Cresskill, NJ: Hampton.

Rose, T. (1994). *Black noise: Rap music and black culture in contemporary America*. London: University of New England Press.

Schaafsma, D. (1993). *Eating on the street*. Pittsburgh: Univ. of Pittsburgh Press.

Scribner, S. and Cole, M. (1981). *The psychology of literacy*. Cambridge, MA: Harvard University Press.

Shuman, A. (1986). *Storytelling rights: The uses of oral and written texts by urban adolescents*. Cambridge: Cambridge University Press.

Sipe, L. and Constable, S. (1996). A chart for four contemporary research paradigms: Metaphors for the modes of inquiry. *Taboo: The Journal of Culture and Education*, 1 (1), 153–163.

Street, B. (1984). *Literacy in theory and practice*. Cambridge: Cambridge University Press.

————. (Ed.). (1993). *Cross-cultural approaches to literacy*. Cambridge: Cambridge University Press.

Taylor, D. and Dorsey-Gaines, C. (1988). *Growing up literate: Learning from inner-city families*. Portsmouth, NH: Heinemann-Boynton/Cook.

Willis, P. (1990). *Common culture: Symbolic work at play in the everyday cultures of the young*. Buckingham, UK: Open University Press

Woodson, C. (1933/1990). *The mis-education of the Negro*. Trenton, NJ: African World Press.

CHAPTER TWO

Street Scripts:
African American Youth Writing
About Crime and Violence

Jabari Mahiri

While doing research in two San Francisco Bay Area high schools on ways to use African American youth culture as a bridge to writing development, I also encountered provocative writings of African American youth created for their own purposes.[1] Many of their texts revealed insightful, personal perspectives on crime and violence that counterpose the way these youth are portrayed in politics and the media. I call these writings "street scripts" for two reasons. First, although in most cases they were not actually created on the streets, their themes and images resound with authentic youth perceptions and experiences of being young, urban, and black. The authors already know they are prime(d) candidates for the juvenile justice system. They see that the texts of their lives have already been inscribed with violence and crime. The abiding question is: How can these scripts be changed? In our concern over prospects of "losing a generation," we need to know more about the generation we are losing. We need to know how their particular voices and choices reflect their own apprehension—both their anxiety and their understanding—of their conditions. We can glimpse this knowledge in the array of scripts that these youth compose and enact.

The second reason for calling these writings "scripts" is to create conceptual space for a critique of the various texts that these youth produce, perform, and publish. To really hear their voices, we have to tune into the actual mediums and contexts that they appropriate for expression. Camitta suggests that these kinds of written expressions, which are within the framework of adolescent culture and social organization, can be called "vernacular writing" because they are "traditional and indigenous to the diverse cultural processes of communities as distinguished from the uniform, inflexible standards of institutions" (Camitta 1993: 229). She sees vernacular writing as literate behavior through which adolescents look for meaning and truth. In her study of African American youth in Philadelphia, Camitta shows how these adolescents attempted to "act on experience by writing it," to "control, shape, and manipulate its properties—time, space, and inhabitants—through texts and their use" (1993: 240). Camitta argues that the youth she studied perceived that writing for their own purposes and in their own mediums could be a powerful and meaningful way to capture and even to alter their experiences.

I appreciate Camitta's designation and description of vernacular writing, but I use the term "voluntary writing"—writing created for their own purposes beyond school—instead for describing the work of the youth I present in this chapter because some of this work is not written in black vernacular. Moreover, some of this work is not usually considered to be *writing* at all in a traditional sense of inscribing words on paper. Yet, I argue that the texts or scripts that these youth compose are in fact "writings" of their perceptions and experiences that reflect significant practices of literacy. Thus, the concept of "voluntary writing of street scripts" is used to capture and frame the forms and functions of the work of these youth.

I am cautious not to overemphasize the ultimate power or transformative possibilities of this writing (or any writing) outside considerations of other sociocultural forces. As Stuckey cogently argues in *The Violence of Literacy* (1991: viii), literacy itself is not the solution; it lies rather in economic enfranchisement. She shows how practices and conceptions of literacy in the United States specifically, and in Western culture generally, essentially perpetuate social injustices by deflecting focus from the real issues of economic and social opportunity, while simultaneously being used as a key mechanism for the maintenance of economic and social advantage. According to Stuckey,

> literacy is a function of culture, social experience, and sanction. Literacy education begins in the ideas of the socially and economically dominant class and it takes the forms of socially acceptable subjects, stylistically permissible forms, ranges of difference or deviance, baselines of gratification. (1991: 19)

One of her conclusions is that literacy teaching is a regulation of access.

I do not want to overemphasize the ultimate power of street scripts, although I *do* want to acknowledge ways in which their production and propagation resist, and in some cases, replace the "socially acceptable sub-jects, stylistically permissible forms, ranges of difference or deviance, baselines of gratification," and so on, that have been imposed by the dom-inant culture. The question of their real power, of course, is tied to whether their creation and uses can actually change the regulation of access to societal resources in any viable and sustainable ways. In this chapter, I address these issues by presenting and discussing the street scripts of five African American youth—Reggie, Geoff, Troy, Keisha, and Jay. Reggie and Geoff attended one of the urban high schools that I had focused on in my research mentioned earlier. Troy and Keisha attended the other focal high school participating in that research, and some of their work has been presented in an earlier article (Mahiri and Sablo, 1996). Jay, however, was in the San Francisco Bay Area in order to attend the University of California, Berkeley. Geoff is the only one of these young people whose real name is being used because his work is already in the public domain in his name.

Hopeful Adolescents

With the possible exception of Troy, all of the youth whose work I discuss in this chapter fit McLaughlin and her colleagues' (1994) notion of being "hopeful adolescents." These youth have effective support systems in at least one institution; such as family, church, a community organization, specific youth-focused organizations, sports, or, in some cases, schools. McLaughlin and her associates contrast these youth with the "frightening number of inner-city youth [who] share...[a] hopeless view of their future" (1994: 1), and exemplified by one young woman who explains,

> You don't plan your future; you just take it as it comes. Life's a constant struggle 'cus you can't count on anything. You don't know for sure what's even gonna happen the next day. You could get shot walkin' down the street. (McLaughlin et al., 1994: 1)

McLaughlin and her colleagues call attention to the fact that 40 percent of the waking hours of these "hopeless" youth are discretionary, and when they get out of school (if they go to school at all) they are claimed by the streets (1994: 7). As we are aware from so many official indices, their lives in the streets are often filled with incidents of violence and crime—homi-cide is the number one cause of death among African American males in the 15 to 30-year-old age group, and this group is more likely to enter prison than college (Brown, 1988).

West (1993a) suggests that this devastating situation is partially the result of a nihilistic threat that comes from a complete loss of hope and absence of meaning. This, in turn, gives rise to a numbing detachment and destructive disposition toward self and others. However, hooks (1992) cautions that though our intentions are good, we often end up reinforcing negative images of African American males by projecting them animalistically as an endangered species. An example of this is the huge billboards posted near urban high schools that read in bold print, "Not Another Dead Child." Although designed to be part of a campaign for the prevention of violence, these messages also serve to emphasize above all the violence within the environments in which these youth live.

McLaughlin and colleagues (1994: 3, 5) note that even hopeful adolescents have to move in this "same hellish vortex," where "messages of rejection are everywhere." Close analysis of these hell-like depictions and messages of rejection reveal the subtle and not-so-subtle ways in which certain agents and forces within the dominant culture work to characterize, stigmatize, and finally marginalize these youth as "dangerous Others": gang members, drug dealers, juvenile delinquents, and criminals. One example of this subtlety can be found in an article in the *San Francisco Examiner Magazine*, written by a Stanford University professor on the connection between testosterone and male violence. Ostensibly, he is arguing for an understanding of the limits of biology; that is, not to make the simple equation that more testosterone automatically equals more violence. However, of particular note are the images he selects to exemplify this point:

> Testosterone is never going to tell us much about the suburban teenager who, in his after-school chess club, has developed a particularly aggressive style with his bishops. And it certainly isn't going to tell us much about the teenager in some inner-city hell-hole who has taken to mugging. (Sapolsky, 1997: 35)

We need a better analysis to successfully navigate the distance and differences between characterizations of an "after-school chess club" and an "inner-city hell-hole."

Some of this analysis is provided in the street scripts presented in this chapter. These scripts reveal how aware these youth are of the ways in which various messages of rejection are racially motivated and patently false. They expose contradictions in the ways they are depicted by politics, the media, and other societal institutions, and consequently, by individual members of the dominant culture. They expose what a student in one of the focal high schools termed "that everyday slave mentality" on the part of many members of the dominant culture.

Insights from street scripts echo and amplify the analyses of scholars seeking to understand and transform everyday slave mentalities and the ways in which these mentalities operate as obstacles to social justice. The concept of "dangerous Others"—named and explicated by Conquergood (1992: 3)—is key to the illogic of modern day slave mentalities. Focusing specifically on youth gangs, he notes that they are "constructed in public discourse as the cause, effect, and aberrant response to urban decay." Thus, other social forces and institutions are absolved from any responsibility. Chomsky (1995: 134) connects the ways in which people who are perceived as dangerous Others are ultimately turned into scapegoats in this society:

> The building up of scapegoats and fear is standard. If you're stomping on people's faces, you don't want them to notice that: you want them to be afraid of somebody else.... People are scared, they're upset, the world isn't working and they don't like the way things are. You don't want people to look at the actual source of power, that's much too dangerous, so, therefore, you need to have them blame or be frightened of someone else.

Fine and Mechling (1993: 123) put this process of scapegoating into perspective in recent U.S. history with respect to a concept of symbolic demography which they define as "the tendency of people to act in the present according to images and ideas acquired earlier in a particular social, demographic location." They argue that in the 1950s the new white middle-class—and later their baby-boomer children—through the help of new media narratives modeling their way of life, came to believe that "they were the normal American family, and it is that 1950s family that became the benchmark for judging 'threat' to the family over the next four decades" (Fine and Mechling, 1993: 123). They further argue that these new middle-class parents worried about their children being "infected" by lower-class values and behavior. Consequently, in conjunction with psychologists, teachers, and other experts, these middle-class parents constructed an ideology of the "normal child," and simultaneously created an image of its threatening alternative—the juvenile delinquent whose characteristics they connected with the lower classes (Fine and Mechling, 1993: 124–125). Fine and Mechling conclude their analysis by noting that "the 'discovery of poverty' in the 1960s helped solidify the professional middle class' identity by clarifying what it was not—namely, poor, black, or brown, and uneducated" (1993: 126).

Reggie, Geoff, Troy, Keisha, and Jay know that their lives, desires, and dreams are quite different from how they have been constructed in the public spaces of politics and the media. So, their street scripts are not mere mirrors that reflect back the violence and crime that surround them. Instead, Reggie's hip-hop documentary, Geoff's video essay, Troy's rap, Keisha's screen play, and Jay's poems are powerful lenses through which these youth view and reflect on life in the streets.

Reggie's Hip-Hop Documentary

Reggie was a student at one of the focal high schools; however, I didn't learn about him until a woman in one of my graduate classes, Sharon Wachs, brought up his work with film in connection with one of our discussions on theories of literacy. I asked Sharon to see if Reggie would come to one of our graduate classes to talk about his work, and he agreed. Reggie was a "C" student in high school, and at the time when he scripted and produced his 17-minute film on rap music and hip-hop culture, he was a 15-year-old. A slightly older Reggie came to our class and anchored an hour of discussion of his work after we viewed his film. He titled his film, *Hiphopumentary*, and the sophistication of his work as well as his presentation were impressive. We learned that he had also written a screenplay based on newspaper and magazine accounts of an 11-year-old boy in a Chicago gang who had murdered a young girl. He wanted to make this story into a film too.

Reggie's work incorporates media and thematic issues from each of the other young writers discussed in this article. It is a video narrative, as is Geoff's work; it features performative raps and poems like the works of Troy and Jay; in addition, in the way it is scripted, it also relates to the kind of screenplay that Keisha produced. Thus, my discussion of Reggie's work provides an introduction to issues, images, and textual mediums that will also be encountered in works of the other authors.

Hiphopumentary starts with a completely black screen. Then, coming out of the blackness, rappers' voices are soon heard, dialogically setting the tone and agenda of the film: "Hip-hop is rappin' and rhyming. This is hip-hop music. This is all we got. A way of life. To hold the mike in your hand, and crush everything in front of you. That's hip-hop." As the rappers say these words, images of someone break dancing take shape in the blackness, as do images of a graffiti artist doing his work on a wall in the dark. The shapes drawn by the graffiti artist seem to replicate the shapes created from the body in dance. All these shapes fade into an image of a young person smoking a blunt, and that smoke itself clouds to become a blank gray screen on which the word Hiphopumentary appears as if it, too, is a graffiti script.

The next scene features a rapper giving his definition of the most basic elements of hip-hop—"all that is essentially needed is a voice, a beat, and a lot of creativity—taking what you got and making the best of it." There is a shift to a street scene of several young rappers doing an improvisation that demonstrates these fundamental elements of rap. Yet the viewer soon sees that it is more complicated than that. Next, Hodari Davis—a teacher at Reggie's high school and the coordinator of the Live Lyricists Society, a Friday, lunch-time rap workshop where young rappers co-produce opportunities for performance and critique—is shown giving a more explicit definition of what it means to be a rap Master of Ceremony. His discussion is backgrounded by scenes from a Live Lyricists Society workshop in progress. Hodari makes the following statement:

> Presently in LLS [Live Lyricists Society] we have some really good word-users. Presently in LLS we have some people who aspire to be MCs. There is a myth about being an MC. That all it is is getting on stage and saying what you've written, saying what comes to your mind. But part of being an MC is being a Master of Ceremony. And a Master of Ceremony is somebody who has mastered the rituals that are part of that ceremony. And so, to be an MC, you almost have to be a priest or a prophet of hip-hop. So, I wouldn't say that there are any MCs in LLS, yet.

Hodari acknowledges on the video, however, that there are many talented young rappers who are on the path to eventually becoming MCs. The scene then shifts back to the earlier rapper who defined the most basic elements of rap, but this time he is talking at length about the economics of rap music and hip-hop culture, as well as the politics of who gets paid. Almost unbelievably, Reggie augments this discussion with an actual scene he was able to film of a young rapper getting arrested while selling his self-made rap tapes on the streets. "They trying to just shut us down," we learn in a cut back to the earlier rapper. "The reason that hip-hop is out like it is, is that somebody is getting their pay cut." There are several other imaginative scenes of rappers defining through dialogue or demonstration the dynamics and complexities of rap music and hip-hop culture before *Hiphopumentary* ends with a DJ showing the differences between East Coast and West Coast rap.

Reggie's work powerfully captures the politics and economics of rap music and hip-hop culture, as well as their aesthetics. That it does so much so well with so little in such a short time is all the more amazing, and not least because it was produced by a 15-year-old. His scripted, narrative video text simultaneously incorporates modes of definition, description, comparison and contrast, process analysis, and argument and persuasion in a sophisticated synthesis of images, voices, music, and written signs. His work clearly merits a closer analysis than I will provide here, but using the description given so far, I will explicate some of what Reggie projected politically, economically, and aesthetically about his subject.

Politically, Reggie is aware of how perceptions of rap music are negatively constructed and how its legitimacy is continually challenged by dominant cultural institutions, especially within and through the mass media. He is not aware of the work of scholars like Tricia Rose and Julia Eklund Koza, but his intuitions and experiences have led him to similar conclusions. Koza (1994), for example, analyzed all the articles about rap that appeared in the three most widely circulated news magazines in the United States and Canada (*Newsweek*, *Time*, and *U.S. News*) during the decade from 1983 to 1992. From this analysis she made a compelling case that the vast majority of these articles "reinforced a link between rap and specific negative themes" (1994: 184). She further noted that the significance of these negative representations of rap should be seen in the light of theories "that negativity is a strategy of containment that tends to reinforce dominant ideologies" (1994: 184). Tricia Rose (1991, 1994) has further argued that strategies of containment associated with rap music and culture extend even into physical spaces. Along with other issues raised in her article, she illustrates how policies of containment are reflected in stringent permit procedures and other obstacles of access to the venues in which rap concerts and associated events take place.

By means of the scene of the young rapper being arrested for selling his tapes on the streets and in other scenes, Reggie portrays some of the containment strategies in place on the streets and deftly links them to particular economic interests. The voice-over commentary makes it clear that Reggie and his informants on the video are well aware of the implications of these strategies—"They trying to just shut us down"—and the economic interests that these strategies are designed to serve. As the rapper mentioned earlier noted, "The reason that hip-hop is out like it is, is that somebody is getting their pay cut." He went on to detail ways that major music industry labels do not want independent entrepreneurs producing and selling their own creations because that siphons off their profit potential. He uses an example of a tape he had purchased on the street for five dollars and notes that "all money that they git goes to they pockets so they can re-cop [take possession of it], you know what I'm sayin'." This kind of critique is akin to what West (1993b: 65) had in mind when he noted that some rap artists "attempt to do what I attempt to do, as a public intellectual. And that is, to tell the truth.... There's no doubt that there's a very, very powerful critique of white supremacy in the work." Through the "public intellectuals" that Reggie brings into his script, he exposes the paradox of capitalist motives to both contain and exploit the cultural material of hip-hop and rap.

Perhaps Reggie's most convincing argument against the negative positioning of rap music and its continued association with problems of violence and crime is found in what he reveals about the aesthetic qualities and authentic functions of this art form on its own terms, when it is not forced to serve outside commercial interests. These interests intentionally link hip-hop and rap with images of gang violence, drug use, and misogyny, and they consciously select and project rappers with these styles and messages for mass consumption. These "studio gangster" messages and styles are in sharp contrast to the more authentic functions of forms of rap that Reggie portrays. First, he clarifies the nature of a rap aesthetic through a number of his informants and especially through Hodari, who defines the escalating levels of rap mastery. "A Master of Ceremony is somebody who has mastered the rituals that are part of that ceremony. And so, to be an MC, you almost have to be a priest or a prophet of hip-hop." Reggie also extends the nature of the rap aesthetic to its functional connections with black culture and other features of hip-hop culture, such as break dancing, graffiti art, youth language use, and clothing styles.

In the first scenes of his video, Reggie weaves all of these elements together using the same sophisticated composing strategies of patchwork, pastiche, and mosaic that characterize contemporary raps. His visual technique of having these elements gradually take shape on a screen that is initially and completely black is pure brilliance. It is reminiscent of Henry Louis Gates Jr.'s meditations on "the blackness of blackness" in his definitive book, *The Signifying Monkey* (1988). Gates felt that the traditional classic text on the blackness of blackness was to be found in the prologue of Ralph Ellison's *Invisible Man*. At one point in the prologue, the narrator, in a hallucination induced by reefer while he listened to Louis Armstrong sing "What Did I Do to Be So Black and Blue," slips between the notes of the song and descends deeper and deeper into blackness. He sees an old woman singing a spiritual on one level, a naked slave girl on an auction block on another, and finally a black preacher on a lower level still, who attempts through his sermon to bring the text of blackness to light. In *Hiphopumentary*, Reggie takes us on a descent into blackness, and as various levels of images and actions take shape, original connections between rap music and black culture are also brought to light.

sum

Geoff's Video Essay

Geoff would consider himself to be a rap artist; but, like Reggie he was also extremely interested in film. Geoff notes, "I'm really into like writing things, stories. I like to write screenplays. I like every aspect of movie making, the camera work, the gaffer, the best boy. Directing is my specialty." When I was conducting research in his high school, there was also a film project going on in which about 40 seniors had been recruited by a film team that was funded to give them a year-long class on video journalism. The project resulted in a two-and-a-half-hour documentary film that played as a Public Broadcasting Station (PBS) special titled, *School Colors* (1994).

Geoff was one of the seniors who was selected for the video journalism class, and he and his work were featured more prominently in the PBS special than any other student in the school. One reason was his was personal and intimate involvement in some of the school's most pressing controversies surrounding violence and crime on the high school campus. Another reason was that his four-minute video essay on crime and violence at the school was a dazzling, thought-provoking statement that explored perceptions and perspectives from the vantage point of students of color. Geoff wrote, casted, directed, and filmed his video essay in conjunction with the film project at his school, but I also consider it to be an excellent example of an illuminating street script.

Perhaps Geoff focused his video essay the way he did because he often found himself caught up in the school's traditional responses to violence and crime on the campus. These responses are merely school-based versions of other institutional responses that characterize and stigmatize African American youth as juvenile delinquents who are more likely than not in gangs and/or on drugs—the dangerous Others, the scapegoats.

The PBS documentary actually shows Geoff ensnared in the net of contradictions that are revealed in the practices of the school's discipline policies. The scene—a suspension hearing—begins in the discipline office where Geoff, dressed in a hip-hop style white, hooded sweatshirt, is at one end of a long table, with two white men, a teacher and the discipline officer, at the opposite end. This image alone dramatically depicts the distance between the two parties at the table even before the substance of their discussion is heard. This is a discipline hearing concerning Geoff's involvement in a fight at school. The white teacher, in trying to break up the fight, grabbed Geoff, who was also actually trying to break up the fight. But the fight itself is not the issue. The teacher feels that Geoff threatened him when he grabbed Geoff. Geoff argues that he merely issued a warning. He didn't feel another man had the right to grab him in that way (especially since he was not fighting), and he says he warned the teacher not to put his hands on him again.

At this point a pivotal dialogue occurs. The discipline officer tells Geoff,

> The rules are laid out there. We'll talk about it, and I'm not gonna do anything arbitrary. But I am letting you know that, that you will receive a suspension if it comes to a point in some place where it looks like that you have stepped over and threatened somebody...when there was a situation that could have been avoided. We can learn from this.

As the discipline officer is saying this, a look of utter resignation comes over Geoff's face. Geoff responds to this comment with as much a question as a statement: "It's your opinion that it was a threat; it's my opinion that it was a warning. But your opinion outweighs my opinion." Here, the teacher intervenes and says, "And that I agree with, yes. You're right. Unfortunately, the administration makes that decision." Geoff does not say another word. Instead, he gathers his belongings and leaves the room. As he is leaving the teacher and the discipline officer stand up and face each other, and when the door swings shut the two men shake hands.

In a critical analysis of responses to school violence, Pedro Noguera (1995: 198) points out that "the exercise of discipline in schools takes on great importance because it serves as the primary means through which symbols of power and authority are perpetuated." Part of Geoff's frustration in the above scenario is that he feels his perception and explanation of what happened was never really taken into account. He senses that the conclusion to the event in question is already foregone, based on the interpretations and perceptions of it by the two men in authority, and he clearly understands the futility of attempting to argue the validity of his point of view. A discourse analysis of this scenario might show that based on the separate cultural perspectives represented, the teacher could have actually perceived that he was threatened while Geoff could have really perceived that he was issuing a warning. But there is something more fundamental at stake here than just getting at the truth. In the following quote, Noguera (1995: 198) continues his analysis of school discipline:

> The disciplining event, whether it occurs in public or private, serves as one of the primary means through which school officials "send a message" to perpetrators of violence, and to the community generally, that the authority vested in them by the state is still secure.... From a symbolic standpoint, within the context of the school, the student expulsion hearing is perhaps the most important spectacle at which the meting out of punishment upon those accused of violence can be used for larger political purposes. As a quasi-judicial ceremony, the formality of an expulsion hearing often contains all of the drama and suspense associated with a courtroom trial. Though the event itself is closed to the public, news of the decision rendered by the school board or hearing officers often travels quickly, particularly when the student is charged with committing an act of violence.

At a crucial point in his suspension hearing, Geoff reveals that he is fully aware of the limits of trying to logically plead his case. His resignation comes from understanding that within the boundaries and sanctioned practices of this institutional setting, he does not have power or privilege in support of his point of view. Interestingly, however, he does find power and privilege for his views through his video projects, and that may be why he decided to focus his video essay on perceptions of violence and crime. Geoff introduced his work in the PBS documentary by saying, "You know, we worked well together. Did a little fear. I put all the ideas together; put it on edit. We 'bout to show it."

The very structure of Geoff's video essay addresses the question and potential contradictions of opposing perceptions of similar events—the same issue that was brought out in his suspension hearing. The structural legs on which his video text stands are two filmings of the same event. He sets up the event with a montage of various members of the school community talking about fear in general, as well as the fear they carry based on the threat of violence in and around the school. By isolating fear, Geoff probes beneath the instances of violence and crime to an emotion that everyone in the school community can relate to—a white male teacher admitting that there are times when he has been afraid; a black male teacher noting philosophically that the fear present in the school is a microcosm of the fear in the larger society; a number of students talking about their fears of being in the halls of a particularly isolated building on campus.

These samples are augmented by Geoff's narration throughout the video. Early on he connects the abstract feeling of fear to the concrete place on campus where many people fear going at certain times of the day. As narrator Geoff explains, "Fear. It enters the minds of nearly every person on this earth. These very halls have been said to cause fear. Why?" The film cuts to the dark halls of this building, and utilizing the camera's angle as if it were the view of a person standing at a locker, the first version of an incident is recorded. The incident involves a hood-wearing character coming down the hall, who then forcefully tells the "person" standing at the locker to open it up, ostensibly for the character to take what he wants.

Here the screen fades to black, and Geoff narrates, "Is that what's really going on in people's mind? Total darkness? Is it because if they fear if they open up their eyes, it will be to a reality that looks something like this?" Before showing an alternative rendering of the hallway scene, the video surveys several other scenes of people in the school community trying to deal with the issue of violence. Notable among these scenes is one in which the principal of the school is arguing in a PTA meeting that the school needs to put a fence up around the entire campus. One teacher responds "that [what] we may find is that the fence has now made the lunatics stuck in the asylum." When the hallway scene does run again, the same hooded figure approaches only to ask the time. With the screen fading again to black, Geoff provides a final narration:

> Why is there so much darkness in people's minds? When will they ever take the time to shake off their frustrations, and slowly but surely get up and tackle their truest fear? But what is their truest fear? And then again, what is yours?

Geoff's own commentary on his project gives additional insight into what he was trying to do:

> I wanted people to look at the fact that a lot of things in the school based on fear are being overlooked. Fear is not looked at as the problem, but...just another thing that happens as a physical reaction to what happens. When actually, fear is one of the main roots of the problem.

One wonders how much the problem of divergent perceptions described in the suspension hearing actually turned on an axis of fear.

A hooded sweatshirt or a skull cap and dark glasses on an African American male often invoke fear. These items are part of the streetgear of many urban adolescents. Geoff could easily be one of the faces behind dark glasses, under a hood. The content of his life, his desires, and dreams are quite different from how he is most often construed. For example,

Geoff wants to produce movies and own a recording and distribution company. "I want to do the music shottie," he says. "It's just a matter of what drops first. But it all will be accomplished." He already seems to know what Stuckey's (1991) work argues; that the real violence is in not being enfranchised economically, especially from the products of one's own experiences.

Geoff is out of high school now and attending a major black college. I believe that he has a message for teachers and students alike based on his own experiences from streets to schools. According to Geoff:

> As far as school is concerned, I have always had problems.... Academically, I have always been able to achieve, but you come into contact with teachers who just don't care.... I feel that they should be going for imagination and creativity. That's the only way that things get invented. I mean if you can imagine it, then there's a possibility that you can do it and that you can make it. But if you don't take time to imagine it, it can never come forth.

Troy's Rap

Troy and Keisha both attended the other focal high school in my research project. Their writings reveal that they were intimately aware of the violence, crime, and drugs in their neighborhood. Through working on an ongoing curriculum intervention in their classes, I had gotten to know many of the students at this high school, and it was possible for me to inquire about the writing students were doing on their own. Troy and Keisha were each engaged in literacy practices in part to help them make sense of their lives.

Troy was in the eleventh grade. He had been composing rap verses and songs since sixth grade, but felt that the only real file of his work was "in his head." Currently he composes and performs rap songs both individually and as a member of a group called Realism. He hoped that his talent would help him become a professional rapper some day. When asked approximately how many songs he had written, he replied, "too many to count." Troy shared some of his compositions orally, and when requested, he also brought in transcribed lyrics for a few of his favorites. Despite this oral/written mix, Troy definitely considered himself to be a writer, and he signed his work "writer/lyricist, TROY."

In the case of Troy's compositions, though, the notion of writing itself needed to be revised. Sometimes he did actually write out his raps, but as he had noted, Troy also stored many of his songs in his head. He was able to recall and recite an amazing number of raps instantly—his own as well as others by professional rappers. That these texts stored in Troy's mind could be transformed easily and consistently into oral and/or written texts led me to define their creation and performance as street scripts. Just as a writer could compose and store a text in a computer, for example, and afterwards select among several options and formats for printing or reproducing it in another material form, Troy composed and stored his texts in the microprocessors of his mind and selected among several options—oral text, audiotape text, or written text for their material reproduction. In the process of producing meaning in these texts, Troy evidenced significant knowledge and literacy skills, and he also revealed how his street scripts actually functioned in the context of his day-to-day life.

One of Troy's favorite compositions was a rap titled "Family Fam." The complete text is below, and Troy also provided an audiotaped version.

FAMILY FAM
Writer/lyricist TROY

> Can't nothing take me from my ken folk my blood,
> even when I sold drug I still got love.
> never was there any discrimination,
> when I had the homelessness, at my lowest,
> just reality conversation.
> they pushed into my brain that crime is slavery, Troy,
> but, ain't no freedom in having no money, just hate.
> I be gettin' all emotional when I be broke,
> you don't feel me doe.
>
> It may look like I'm havin a good day,
> but that's a cover-up for my quick-to-flash skanless way.
> they took their time wit me and said that I needed peace,
> but that's impossible when we ain't even got a piece,
> of bread to split-n-half and be happy,
> a brother ain't even go no pappy,
> hurt from bein' nappy.
> never been spooked on the streets so,
> I got two families that love me doe.
>
> But the house where my momma stayed at is the spot 4 real,
> eat fat, still have skrill, automobile,
> and better chances on not gettin' killed.
> I will, lay my head for any one of my family members,
> even get my leg chopped off by white boys yellin' timber.
> I love each and every best friend of mine,
> that other family that I have on my flowamatic grind.

> kan't nothing take me from my ken folk my blood,
> cus, even when I sold drug I still got love.

Although this discussion focuses on the written text version, I recognize that it is based in part on limitations of the medium of this book to adequately portray aspects of other forms of its production. "Family Fam" exemplified a central theme that ran through the majority of Troy's lyrics—the tensions in his life and his survival strategies for dealing with them. The tensions in this particular rap were between the pull of his biological "Family" toward more traditional life choices and the push of his other "Fam" (his peers) toward a "skanless" (scandalous) life on the streets.

Troy began this rap by describing the unconditional love that he received from his family. Yet he also uses these lyrics to take a hard look and perhaps come to terms with his "skanless" lifestyle. Although Troy heard the advice of his family and knew that they were right ("they pushed into my mind that crime is slavery, Troy"), his "reality conversation" (with his peers) was just as pervasive an influence on him to sell drugs in order to survive—"but ain't no freedom in being broke, just hate." These early lines of the rap convey something of the tensions inherent in Troy's situation by illuminating the contradiction of him freeing himself from the slavery of crime only to become equally enslaved in poverty.

Later in the rap Troy revisits the contradiction of his family's "sound" advice with a skillful play on the homonyms "peace" and "piece."

> they took their time wit me and said that I needed peace,
> but that's impossible when we ain't even got a piece,
> of bread to split n half and feel happy...

Though Troy tried not to show it, below the surface he was seething:

> It may look like I'm having a good day,
> but that's just a cover-up for my quick-to-flash skanless ways.

Yet, Troy did show many facets of himself and his situation in his rap texts, and one of the most telling lines came toward the end when he spoke about his mother's house. It was considered a safe haven because he knew that he could always get a hot meal without spending any money; he had access to a car; and it was much safer than his life on the streets.

> the house where my momma stayed at is the spot 4 real,
> eat fat, still have skrill, automobile,
> and better chances of not getting killed.

Key to keeping Troy going was this knowledge that no matter what else was happening, he could always go home.

The structure of this rap does not follow the AB AB rhyme scheme found in many raps. In fact, some lines do not rhyme at all. Troy was also prolific in his use of highly figurative African American language styles. Throughout his rap songs he used words such as "skrill" (cash), which was a combination of the terms "scratch" and "mill." "Scratch" was an earlier African American term that meant money, and "mill" was short for "million," or it could also refer to a "meal ticket." Within African American language styles, new words and phrases are often created in this fashion as users of the language constantly experiment with ways to better express themselves. Troy used other rhetorical devices reflective of certain African American language styles. For example, when he used the line "you don't feel me doe" (though), he did so to emphasize his point in a way that was similar to black preaching.

Troy also provided rhetorically sophisticated treatments of complex, provocative themes. For example, "Family Fam" employed a number of intricate comparison and contrast strategies that revealed complexly interwoven thematic considerations. However, in school the explication of these strategies and themes would often be arrested at the level of the style of language in which they were encased. Mike Rose spoke to the ways that writing instruction in schools often teaches students "that the most important thing about writing—the very essence of writing—is grammatical correctness, not the communication of something meaningful" (Rose, 1989: 211). He had observed considerable appreciation for linguistic complexity in a student of his who was an avid listener to rap music, but noted that the instruction of language use confronting him in class "strips away the vibrancy and purpose, the power and style, the meaning of the language that swirls around him" (Rose, 1989: 212).

With Troy the focus was above all on the creation of oral texts, which were the ultimate end product—a product intended and designed for aural rather than visual consumption. When he did write down his raps, they were still formed as writing to be said rather than read. Yet, these were viable and valued literacy practices that showed Troy's mastery over some of the processes through which culturally significant meanings were coded. They revealed Troy as a producer—not just a consumer—of culturally relevant street scripts that were appropriate for his audiences in informal conversations and formal performances. In effect, Troy himself became a living text, displaying his compositions through the software of sound, in real time on the variegated screens of urban streets.

Keisha's Screen Play

Like Troy, Keisha lived under incredibly difficult conditions and engaged in the construction of texts as both an expression of and a response to them. An African American female in the tenth grade, Keisha was perhaps one of the most prolific and versatile writers I encountered during my research project.

I was surprised to find that Keisha carried much of her work with her wherever she went. For example, after agreeing to share her work, she reached into her backpack and pulled out three thick notebooks full of poems, songs, and rap lyrics. Then she said, "Oh, yeah, and here's my play." Beyond the numerous lyrics which Keisha had composed, she had also written a four-act screenplay titled, *Jus' Living*. Like Troy, Keisha also has been writing since the sixth grade; in her estimation she has written more than 40 songs, poems, and plays. She felt that writing came rather easily for her and noted that it took only a few minutes for her to get ideas for her pieces.

Besides being prolific, Keisha is a very thoughtful and careful writer, and her work offers one way to illuminate and come to terms with things she encounters on the streets of her neighborhood. Her inspiration derives from her friends and other people with whom she comes into contact. Themes in her writing, she said, were "mostly about love and society, things around me." However, I found a different pattern in Keisha's topics and themes: they mostly focused on the harsh realities of her everyday life. For example, the first stanza of one of Keisha's songs (also titled, *Jus' Living*) tells the story of the chaotic circumstances she lives with every day.

Jus' livin' on the eastside taking a chill,
watchin' young brothas being shot and killed.
Coming up fast, clocking Kash,
niggaz be having dreams, getting shot, but it can't last.

But at the same time they doing the crime,
sitting behind bars without a nickel or a dime,
can't come out and kick it,
but I'mma wicked old fe-mac and that's how I'm living.

Keisha's play echoes similar themes. It begins with the narrator setting the scene and tone. "It starts as an early morning in Oakland, California. A mother and her two sons, Robert, 16, and Rocheed, 15, struggle to survive in the heart of the ghetto." It is soon learned that this family is living in the midst of gang violence and drugs. The mother, Ms. G, wants to move her family to a better neighborhood, but is unable to do so for financial reasons. Robert, being the man of the house, attempts to get a job in order to help his mother out. When Robert, who has no work experience, is not successful in finding employment, he turns to what appears to be a more viable option: selling drugs and gang-banging. As one of his friends advises, "A job?!... You betta get yo' grind on fool!"

The play reveals the intense peer pressure placed on Robert as he grapples with his decision to join the gang. This conflict is similar to the one Troy faced in "Family Fam," but Keisha adds another insight. "Grinding" and "banging" are presented not only as ways to make some quick cash, but in Robert's world they are also associated with manhood. When Robert begins to have second thoughts about this lifestyle, his friends press, "I thought you was a real old school gangsta." Robert makes this choice, but must live with the consequences. To be initiated into the gang, he must participate in a drive-by shooting of Dino, a rival gang member. In retaliation for Dino's murder, the rival gang comes back to kill Robert. However, in an effort to protect her son, Robert's mother gets caught in the crossfire and is killed instead.

Keisha's play offers an intricate plot, rounded characters, and complex thematic considerations. For each scene, she also includes directorial notes and specifications for appropriate background music. Keisha allows her intended audience to clearly picture Ms. G as she "gets an attitude" and "puts her hand on her hip." Keisha thought out every movement and emotion that she wanted her characters to feel and her readers/audiences to see. As in her poems and songs, the screenplay reveals sophisticated rhetorical devices, such as her use of foreshadowing to provide subtle clues to the surprising end. For example, at one point Ms. G said to Robert, "You and Rocheed always act like ya' handicapped and always looking for me to do everything. Well, one day I ain't gon' be here, then who you gon' be danging and telling it ain't no milk?" Later, when Robert informed his friends of his decision to start banging, his brother's girl-friend, Shyra, responded by saying, "Why you gon' do yo' momma like this?" While Shyra was reacting to the fact that Robert was starting to hang out with the gang which was a disgrace to his mother, her comment also prefigured the ending. *Jus' Living* was a remarkable dramatic piece, but the real drama was the extent to which its scenes may have been collateral to scenes in Keisha's life.

Both Keisha and Troy used street scripts to help them make sense of their social worlds. Their works probed for meaning and order in the mercurial flow of their experiences. Like so many adolescents living in their community, they had seen more violence and pain in their 15 or 17 years than many adults will ever see. When this is combined with other difficulties that every teenager faces growing up, it becomes a wonder how they handle it all. In part, they tried to get a handle on it through writing—in actively conceiving and critiquing the nature of their experiences by naming and explicating the paradoxes that clouded their lives.

Jay's Poems

Jay differs from Reggie, Geoff, Troy, and Keisha in that he was not a high school student. Instead, after completing college at 21 with degrees in physics and Spanish, he came to the San Francisco Bay Area and matriculated to graduate school at the University of California, Berkeley, with GRE scores in the 98th percentile. While he was an undergraduate he wrote poetry. When he shared some of his poems with me, I was amazed at how consistent many of his images and themes were with the street scripts of the youth I have already discussed. Consequently, I believe his work gives an additional sense of how pervasive the perceptions of violence and crime really are for all African American youth regardless of their placement or accomplishments within the society.

Jay's poems are voluminous, but I will use two examples to illustrate these points. The first one, entitled "Magic Number 25," was written when he was 19.

I can't wait 'til I'm 25
Then maybe I won't have to pray.
Cause that's when I'll be safe
At least that's what the stats say.
Between 18 and 25 years of age
is the most dangerous time for Black males
(in America)
That's what I've been told
since I was about 10 years old
and I see my mom hoping she won't have to hold
my dead body laying cold...
in her arms,
While I pray that I won't fold
under all the pressure
    The pressure to succeed
    The pressure to achieve

    The pressure to be good
    The pressure to survive
that's right
I always worry about staying alive.
Well,
at least I won't have to worry
when I reach twenty-five....

In discussing this poem with Jay, I commented on how it gave a different sense to the community practice of "playing the numbers." He responded, however, that "Magic Number 25...takes the randomness out of playing the numbers. It is as if when we hit 25 we are safe." He continued, "It's almost like car insurance. As soon as you hit 25, your insurance drops. Like that one day changes everything... But we are never safe... [despite] what the stats say." As a teenager, Jay would have been considered one of the hopeful adolescents that McLaughlin et al. (1994) have identified as having effective support systems. Yet, like Troy and the other youth discussed in this chapter, Jay is intensely aware of the ever-present possibility of his own mortality. His support systems, his college degrees, his SATs and GREs still do not guarantee a "spot 4 real," where he can "eat fat...have skrill...and [have] better chances of not getting killed."

In a poem titled, "The Cells of My Mind," Jay reveals other ways in which youth may feel imprisoned mentally and spiritually, even when they have not been jailed physically.

I wonder how many others
think of jail cells—prisons —
the way i do.

how many people
worry about going to jail,
for no particular reason
other than someone wanting them
there

seeing bars all around:
on windows
of houses,
schools,
stores

metal detectors everywhere:
in schools,
stores,

airports—trying to escape
prisons
in an airtight box

going far
far
    far away
to no where
    somewhere else

It sucks growing up
    with prisons—cells—
        built
into your mind.

Perhaps Jay's perceptions of the mental constraints—the subtle and overt messages and images that attempt to delineate rigid boundaries of thought and action for African American youth—are cause for our greatest concerns. His skillful movement from ever-present symbols of violence and crime like iron bars on houses and stores and metal detectors in schools to a potential consequence of "[jail] cells—built into your mind" reveals critical insights into the nature and contradictions of growing up black in the United States.

Conclusion

Ultimately, Jay is much more like Reggie, Geoff, Troy, and Keisha than different from them. His record of achievements may eventually be matched or surpassed by any one of the others. At the same time, his potential for being engaged in incidents of violence and crime, or for becoming entangled in the criminal justice system, may not be that different from theirs. Even if they don't actually share the same social space, to a great extent they do share and have the same position in the physical space of the streets. Yet, their words and works demonstrate that their lives differ greatly from how they have been socially constructed.

Their works go beyond the socially acceptable subjects and stylistically permissible forms of writing most often valued in schools, and in so doing challenge some of the socially constructed obstacles to cultural difference that use literacy as well as other institutionalized mechanisms to regulate access to societal resources. When we take the time to explicate their works and to hear their voices as we would with other literacy and literature scripts, we find that their writings are not just mirrors, but lenses through which they view and reflect on their lives. They also reveal the personal views of these youth in critique of their social worlds. These views are comforting and disturbing—comforting in what we learn about them as youth, disturbing in what we see about ourselves as adults responsible for shaping the world that they will inherit and inhabit. Their street scripts teach us that the struggle to save this generation of youth is synonymous with the struggle to save ourselves.

POWERFUL

We need to change

Note

1. This chapter originally appeared as an article in *Social Justice*, (24) 4: 56–76 (1997).

Works Cited

Brown, L. (1988). *The state of black America*. Chicago: The National Urban League.

Camitta, M. (1993). Vernacular writing: Varieties of literacy among Philadelphia high school students. In B. Street (Ed.), *Cross-cultural approaches to literacy* (pp. 228–246). Cambridge: Cambridge University Press.

Center for Investigative Reporting. (1994). *School colors*. Boston, MA: WGBH Educational Foundation.

Chomsky, N. (1995). A dialogue with Noam Chomsky. *Harvard Educational Review*, 65 (2).

Conquergood, D. (1992). On rappin' and rhetoric: Gang Representations. Paper presented at the Philosophy and Rhetoric of Inquiry Seminar, University of Iowa (April 8).

Fine, G., and Mechling, J. (1993). Child saving and children's cultures at century's end. In S. B. Heath and M. McLaughlin (Eds.), *Identity and inner-city youth: Beyond ethnicity and gender* (pp. 120–146). New York: Teachers College Press:.

Gates, H. L. Jr. (1998). *The signifying monkey: A theory of African-American literary criticism*. New York: Oxford University Press.

hooks, b. (1992). *Black looks: Race and representation*. Boston, MA: South End Press.

Koza, J. E. (1994). Rap music: The cultural politics of official representation. *Review of Education/Pedagogy/Cultural Studies*, 16, 1.

Mahiri, J., and Sablo, S. (1996). Writing for their lives: The non-school literacy of California's urban African American youth. *Journal of Negro Education*, 65 (2), 164–180.

McLaughlin, M., Irby M. A., and Langman, J. (1994). *Urban sanctuaries: Neighborhood organizations in the lives and futures of inner-city youth*. San Francisco, CA: Jossey-Bass.

Noguera, P. A. (1995). Preventing and producing violence: A critical analysis of responses to school violence. *Harvard Educational Review*, 65 (2).

Rose, M. (1989). *Lives on the boundary*. New York: Penguin Books.

Rose, T. (1991). Fear of a black planet: Rap music and black cultural politics in the 1990s. *Journal of Negro education*, 60 (3), 277–291

Rose, T. (1994). *Black noise: Rap music and black culture in contemporary America*. Lebanon, NH: University Press of New England.

Sapolsky, R. M. (1997). Male call. *San Francisco Examiner Magazine* (June 8), 14–15, 30–35.
Stuckey, J. E. (1991). *The violence of literacy*. Portsmouth, NH: Boynton/Cook.
West, C. (1993a). *Race matters*. Boston, MA: Beacon Press.
———. (1993b, September). Interview by James Ledbetter. *Vibe Magazine*, pp. 63–67/

"Street Scripts"

Pedro A. Noguera

Through his analysis of the five "street scripts" presented above, Jabari Mahiri makes a compelling argument that these texts produced voluntarily by the youth in his study constitute a potent form of resistance to the ways in which black youth are marginalized and maligned in American society. Though he is careful not to overstate the ability of such expression to concretely transform the social and economic conditions that constrain the life chances of these youth, he does suggest that these scripts reveal how young people attempt to challenge the larger societal script which positions them as "at-risk," troubled and dangerous.

At the core of Mahiri's study is an effort to explore the ways in which those without power, wealth, and status in American society exercise agency to counter their structured powerlessness. This is an important and highly significant issue, for—more often than not—social science has conceived of the poor and powerless in one of two dominant theoretical frames. The conservative frame places the emphasis on individual choice and responsibility, and within this scenario the poor have no one but themselves to blame for their plight. In contrast, the progressive frame treats the poor as passive victims of circumstance whose life chances are determined by larger social, economic, and political forces, which render individuals helpless since they are beyond their control (Pivan and Cloward, 1979; Massey and Denton, 1992). Through the voices of the young people in his study, Mahiri attempts to chart out a third way; one which acknowledges the power of social structure without eliminating the possibility of individual agency.

None of the young people he presents—Reggie, Geoff, Troy, Keisha, or Jay—express the kind of unfettered faith in the American Dream identified by other researchers (McLeod, 1988), or an abstract optimism about their personal futures. Rather, each of their narratives contains a powerful critique of the forces which constrain their lives, rooted in a realism born out of deep introspection and a critical reading of the society in which they live. It is perhaps even more significant that their pragmatic reading of social reality—which is based on a recognition of the statistical likelihood of their becoming victims of violence, being unjustly punished at school, or incarcerated for reasons beyond their control—does not yield to nihilistic resignation. Instead, their street scripts reveal a glimmer of hope derived from their ability to articulate the character of the injustice that engulfs their lives but fails to crush their spirits.

How do we make sense of such resilience? How could it be that young people who might typically be written off as failures, or in the case of Jay, as an individual over-achiever who's managed to escape the odds, would still find within themselves a means to challenge what might seem to be overwhelming obstacles? More often than not, such youth would be characterized as exceptions whose very existence proves that individual responsibility rather than structured inequality ultimately determines patterns of mobility in society (Jencks, 1992). But we must keep in mind that Mahiri discovered these youth and their texts serendipitously. With the exception of Jay, none of these youth were of the sort whose names appear on honor roles or who are distinguished from their peers through acts of individual achievement. No, these were fledgling organic intellectuals (e.g., Gramsci), writers and artists who use literacy for self-expression rather than for grades or scholastic rewards. The fact that they exist and could be discovered accidentally, should cause all who are prepared to write off as hopeless a generation of poor, black, urban youth to think twice, and hopefully even more.

The good news is that intergenerational poverty, social isolation, environmental degradation, crime and all of the other hardships which beset urban youth, are still not able to extinguish the sense of hope and possibility that countless numbers cling to. Even though many succumb to these circumstances and become victims or victimizers as a result, it does not mean that hope is lost or that young people have given up en masse. Rather, these invisible writers and artists demonstrate in a powerful way that even the most oppressed and powerless people have the capacity to question the source of their oppression, and when possible, to act against it. For educators who teach such youth, for service providers and advocates who try to assist them, and for those distant allies who may never encounter them in any meaningful way but who feel a sense of solidarity and empathy with their plight, the presence of these invisible producers of culture should compel us to rethink how we perceive them. Rather than missionary compassion or bleeding heart paternalism, young people such as these are searching for allies to assist them in finding ways to beat the odds and overcome the obstacles that stand in the way of fully realizing their individual potential and the well-being of their families and communities. Their voices must not be interpreted as weak cries for help, but as powerful indications that even those who are most likely to be written off as failures have refused to accept the scripts which render them helpless. In so doing, their writing not only affirms their humanity but also reminds us of their capacity to be much more than victims of circumstance.

Works Cited

Jencks, C. (1992). *Rethinking social policy*. Cambridge, MA: Harvard University Press.

Massey, D. and N. Denton. (1992). *American apartheid: Segregation and the making of the underclass*. Cambridge, MA: Harvard University Press.

McLeod, J. (1988). *Ain't no makin' it*. Boulder, CO: Westview Press.

Murray, C. (1984). *Losing ground: American social policy 1950–1980*. New York: Basic Books.

Pivan, C. and Cloward, M. (1979). *Poor people's movements: Why they succeed, how they fail*. New York: Pantheon Books.

CHAPTER THREE

Devils or Angels: Literacy and Discourse in Lowrider Culture

Peter Cowan

One day in June just after school let out, I spent the afternoon paddling my canoe on a local lake, and on the way home stopped at a convenience store to buy a cold drink. Tired of reading my high school students' essays, I longed to read something different. I saw *Lowrider* magazine, and it called to mind drawings of lowrider cars and cholos that my summer school students in the Hispanic Academic Program drew. The Hispanic Academic Program was a summer school program designed to encourage Latino junior high school students from schools in the Latino district of Bayside, a working class city in northern California, to aim and prepare for college.

A lowrider is a genre of customized car associated principally with the Mexican American community. Classic lowriders are Chevrolet Impalas from the 1950s and 1960s, lowered to the ground (often using hydraulics), riding on skinny tires (usually mounted on spoked wheels) with elaborate paint schemes (mostly featuring icons found in the Mexican American/ Chicano community).[1] Stone (1990: 120) notes that the term cholo, "refers generally to any Mexican American working class youth. Cholos often organize themselves into clubs or barrio-centered gangs. The cholo dress style is frequently associated with lowriding." The term *Latino*, on the other hand, identifies a category within the social and racial stratification of the population of the United States. *Latino* identifies people who came from the territory in the Americas colonized by Latin Nations, and includes people who speak or whose ancestors spoke Spanish (Oquendo, 1998: 60).

The close association of lowriders and cholos with gangs means that the terms "lowriders" (used, depending on the context, to denote the customized car, or one who builds such cars) and "cholos" are often considered derogatory.[2] That I canoe for recreation and shared these negative associations of lowriding, reflect how the context and circumstances of my adolescence—spent in white, upper middle-class suburbs—was very different from the context and circumstances of adolescence for the Latino students I was teaching in a working class city in Northern California. For my purposes here, I call this community, "Bayside." Reading *Lowrider* was an astonishing experience for me because it challenged the negative associations I acquired growing up, and it began an important part of my education about Latino adolescents. Although *Lowrider* features pictures of customized cars with bikini-clad women and advertisements for parts and accessories, it had regular features unlike any I had seen in other car magazines. These include, for example: "La Raza Report," which comprised a few pages reporting political happenings in Latino communities across the U.S.; "Arte," a section dedicated to drawings that featured lowrider cars, like the ones my students drew, and sent in by readers; pictures of Aztec and Native American warriors and maidens; portraits of loved ones; and letters from readers on diverse subjects such as asking for and offering advice on relationships. But what really piqued my curiosity was an essay—"Chicano 'History'"—a polemic in which the writer criticized his teachers for failing to teach him his Chicano history.

The question that occurred to me on first reading *Lowrider*—and that inspired my initial exploration of lowriding as a distinct discourse community—was in what ways would such an essay influence people who read *Lowrider*? To answer that question I sought out people who interacted in various ways with what I will call *lowrider culture*. Consequently, this chapter explores the literacy events and practices of car customizers who build and show lowrider cars, and the literacy practices of Latino adolescents who use icons from lowriding in an active visual culture. The findings in this chapter are based on two qualitative studies I conducted within Latino social worlds that perceive lowriders as objects of aesthetic and symbolic value. In the first study, I collected data by attending *Lowrider's* 1997 "Lowrider History Tour" in Bayside. I approached and audiotaped five interviews with male, lowrider owners who were showing their cars. My informants were skilled practitioners of lowriding—men who had devoted considerable time, money, and effort to building lowriders, and who derived satisfaction from competing in shows. In particular, I use the comments of one informant, David, attending with his godson, Sonny, who was particularly helpful and whose insights were representative of what I heard from others.

The findings from this initial exploration made me feel like I could see intentionally constructed meanings in drawings my Latino students created during summer school. Thus, in my second study, I chose six drawings produced by Hispanic Academic Program students, and conducted a number of semi-structured interviews with young Latino adults who had grown up in Bayside. I wanted to hear their retrospective accounts of when and where they saw these kinds of drawings, who drew them, what they meant, and how they interacted with them. Contrary to my original assumptions, my findings from both studies suggest that in these youthful Latino social worlds, lowriding—both the practices of designing and customizing cars, and of creating visual representations of them in distinctive artwork—does not reflect actual or prospective gang involvement. Rather it reveals a form of visual literacy that is clear and comprehensible to members of a particular discourse community who have been socialized into it.

Drawn Into Lowriding

I was hired straight out of my teaching credential program to teach about forty Latino students in the Hispanic Academic Program. Students in this program met in donated classrooms at a Catholic high school in the heart of Bayside's Latino community. The ceilings were high, the floors were polished, and the classrooms were light and airy. To my initial surprise, students gathered early in the mornings on the front steps to talk, and greeted us, the teachers, with enthusiasm.

Trained as a writing teacher, I used the computer lab each summer to motivate students to write, revise, and publish an anthology of their writing. As an afterthought and in the second year of my involvement in the program, my colleague asked students to submit artwork to include in the anthology. What struck me was that many of these students used distinctive iconography—such as lowriders, cholo images—in the drawings they contributed to each of the six anthologies we published. Given my limited knowledge, these images made me wonder about the students' involvement with neighborhood gangs.

Other educators shared this suspicion. For example, early in the school year following my first summer teaching in the Hispanic Academic Program, I taught middle school classes in an historically Mexican neighborhood. A district administrator who had grown up in this neighborhood paid a visit to my class. In very strong terms, he said that gang-related activity—which he identified as wearing certain brands or labeled clothing or hats, or writing gang-related graffiti on one's body or books or school property—would not be tolerated. Adding additional force to his message, and shortly after his visit, a special assembly was held for the gang-officer from the Police Department to talk to faculty and students about local gangs, their histories and recruitment activities, and how to recognize gang signs. Although I knew nothing about gangs, I began using the signs I'd been warned about to identify students who might be members of the local gang. In addition to distinctive clothing, these students spent much of their time in my class practicing their graffiti-style script and sometimes drawing cholos, or cartoon characters dressed as cholos, or lowrider cars, either singly or in combinations.

When I bought that first issue of *Lowrider*, I recognized it as a resource for learning about my students' interests. When I conducted my first study of lowriding, I assumed my focus would be the magazine; that I would be analyzing literacy events as "occasions in which written language is integral to the nature of the participants' interactions and their interpretative passages and strategies" (Heath, 1982: 50). What I found was surprising and far more interesting: The written text in *Lowrider* was secondary to the visual images of the cars and details of their customization. Thus, the primary text was the lowrider car itself—either a physical car or a visual representation of one—and members of this discourse community were "reading" lowrider cars and pictures of them as (visual) texts. Reading written text was a way of obtaining additional information about what was being observed.

Heath (1982: 74) additionally noted that "[l]iteracy events must also be interpreted in relation to the *larger sociocultural patterns* which they may exemplify or reflect" (emphasis added). Working with the concept of literacy event creates the opportunity to expand the definition of literacy beyond a narrow conception of it only having to do with reading and writing. As Mahiri and Sablo (1996: 166) have suggested, literacy can be seen as "skills applied to the production of meaning in or from texts in a context." They emphasize that the nature and function of skills, productions, meanings and texts could vary significantly in diverse contexts. Thus, in terms of lowrider culture, literacy skills, processes of production, texts, and literate behaviors can all be seen to be distinctly *visual*. But before discussing the visual literacy events in lowrider culture—the visual texts, the skills necessary to produce and interpret them, and the cultural meanings they encode—it is important to sketch a little of the sociohistorical context in which lowriding evolved.

Lowriding in the United States

Lowriding developed out of the convergence of historical, economic, and cultural factors before, during, and after World War II. During the 1930s and 1940s, many Mexican families, joined by "Oakie" families—a Diaspora of farmers and farm workers from the U.S. Midwest fleeing the Depression and long-term consequences of soil erosion—eked out their livings as migrant farm workers in California. One necessity for their economic survival was a good, reliable, used car; another was the resourcefulness and mechanical skills to fix, or find and replace parts that wore out.

World War II also produced a generation of young men with well-honed mechanical skills developed as a result of being in the military. Indeed, this war created conditions that encouraged the acquisition of mechanical skills and resourcefulness in the general population by halting civilian production of new automobiles from 1942 until the end of the war. At the same time, consumer demand for new cars increased so much that, when released with the resumption of automobile production after the war, the used car market became flooded with cheap cars as people upgraded to new ones. This meant that young people were suddenly able to afford a car that would have been unavailable to them only a year or so previously. Out of these circumstances grew the youth-oriented, male-dominated, car customizing culture of the 1950s.

Lowering a car to within a few inches of the ground grew out of the low-slung custom look developed for new, American-made cars in the 1950s. Although lowriding has always been diverse and multiethnic, as a genre of car customizing it became most closely associated with a distinctively Mexican American oppositional style: *Pachucismo*. Pachucos came to prominence in the 1940s and tended to be located geographically in cities of the southwestern United States. They "dressed distinctively, and they rebelled against assimilation into the mainstream culture" (Polkinhorn et al., 1986: 46).

César Chavez makes explicit connections between the importance of the car to migrant families as well as between pachucismo and lowriding as representations of an oppositional identity in an interview published in an issue of the early *Low Rider Magazine*.[3]

> We were traveling around and we were pretty obvious because we were *pachucos de verdad* [authentic pachucos]...you always wanted to go to the dance [looking] right...and we would come in good cars—we were migrants and the cars meant quite a bit....They were family cars but we used to [fix them up].... *In those days you went the opposite*—low on the back. We lowered the springs on the back. Had fender skirts. Two side pipes. It was mostly cosmetic stuff. (in an interview with Gutierrez, 1980: 43)

When a lowrider car (lowered to within inches of the ground, riding on skinny tires, decorated with accessories, and promenading slowly down the boulevard for maximum exposure) is compared to a hot rod (a small sedan, the rear end of the car raised to accommodate fat tires, powered by an engine modified for speed), and a high-rider (a four-wheel-drive pickup truck or jeep, with the front and back raised by heavy-duty suspension springs to accommodate oversized, knobby tires, and powered by big engines), the lowrider creates a visually, aesthetically, and performatively provocative contrast. The hot rod and high-rider are two cars customized according to the aesthetics of white male, working-class dominated genres. When asked "Why are your cars low?" a member of Chicano's Pride, a San Jose car club, responded, "Whose cars are high?" (Trillin & Koren, 1978: 73).

Acquiring Literacy Skills and Literate Behaviors in Lowrider Culture

My exploration of lowriding suggests that to understand the visual discourse and literate behaviors of members of these Latino social worlds, one must see the lowrider car as a socially constructed and culturally valued form of expression, and as a symbol of an oppositional stance to the pressure to assimilate into the American mainstream. The primary text is visual; it is the lowrider car itself, or a drawing comprising distinctive artwork featuring, among other icons, lowriders and cholos. These icons are invested with particular and symbolic meaning, and written text necessarily becomes of secondary importance within these literacy events. Within lowrider culture, individuals become "literate" by means of engaging in a variety of activities that are quite different from the kinds of behaviors associated with acquiring reading and writing skills in school settings.

In lowriding reading is a matter of knowing what is salient, what particulars make a customized car a lowrider—that in addition to being low-slung and riding on spoked wire wheels, the car shows off its unblemished body with a nice paint job running the gamut from original solid colors through to a welter of custom graphics or murals. Writing thus becomes a matter of implementing the skills needed to build a lowrider. Literate actions—which many scholars have defined in terms of thinking critically and analytically, but as not necessarily tied to a written text (Farr, 1994)—become critical or analytical thinking about lowriders. For example, the lowriders I talked to learned the aesthetics of lowriders by seeing and admiring these cars in their neighborhoods, and often they were given their start in lowriding by older, male family members or friends. David explains how he became involved in lowriding:

> When I was a kid I liked the lowrider cars.... A friend of mine, his dad gave him his truck when he turned fifteen. It was a 1950 Ford. And his dad gave it to him all painted up and done up already. So I worked in the summer with my father, who's a chain link fence contractor, and a couple of months after I turned sixteen I bought this 1953 Chevy truck for $800.... Driving around, seeing all the older guys. I was pretty young with this old car, just kind of got me excited.

Acquiring the aesthetic sense to recognize and admire lowriders comes from seeing them in one's community and from appreciating the work and taste involved in putting them together. Becoming a lowrider, however, entails more than acquiring a vehicle—it also means finding and apprenticing to a practitioner in the lowrider community. David describes this process as follows:

> [The] friend, whose father gave him the 1950 Ford, his father...helped me. He tried to show me how to do it, and he said, like I told my (god)son, you know, I'll show him the first time, but after that I expect him to be able to pick it up.

David's comments reflect how learning to be a lowrider is organized around social relationships: He began learning from his friend's father, that he learned by doing, and that he has taken on Sonny, his godson, as his own apprentice.

Sonny started working on David's cars at eleven, learning first to clean and detail them. In 1997 Sonny was seventeen and a senior in high school. He had developed so much expertise by that stage that he was responsible for preparing David's cars for shows, and even some of David's friends asked Sonny for advice on detailing their own cars. Over the years Sonny helped David build a lowrider bicycle and trailer to display along with David's original truck, and David had shown Sonny how to change a vehicle's oil, spark plugs, and the starter motor, how to do brake jobs, and the like. Given that Sonny had demonstrated his interest and mastered the tasks of maintaining a lowrider, his father and David agreed that he was ready for more responsibility and a bigger challenge. David explains:

He's graduating this year, so he's getting a truck like this. His dad…got the truck because he knows that Sonny loves my truck since he was a little kid. So when he found it he called me and asked if it's a good deal and this and that and I told him, "Yeah."

Thus, the pattern for learning the skills necessary for being a literate member of the lowrider discourse community begins with seeing and admiring lowriders and learning their aesthetics, to learning to build and maintain them. This also includes entering into the male-dominated, social network of lowriding and finding a skilled practitioner to apprentice to.

At the "*Lowrider* History Tour" David told me that it was his first show in some time and he hoped to win a trophy. I phoned him a week later and he described how he had won first place for "Best Bomb Truck," and had received a trophy. *Bomb trucks* are pickup trucks from the 1940s and 1950s—mostly Chevy and General Motors makes—so-called for their distinctive rounded styling. However, it had been David's understanding that along with the first place trophy came one thousand dollars in "sweepstakes money," yet he hadn't received any money. Frustrated, David had called the show's production company in Southern California and asked that his judging sheet be faxed to him. He was disgusted to learn that his truck had earned only 90 out of a possible 260 points. When he looked at the details, he couldn't believe what he read: for example, he had not received any points at all for his hydraulics system. Searching for an explanation, he speculated that the judge had not noticed his hydraulics because David was clever and skillful about concealing the pumps and batteries. Ironically, David had hidden them to earn more points at shows. In the end, all David could do was question this judge's competence, and implied that he lacked the literacy skills and behaviors to be able to read lowriders accurately in shows, and lacked the ability to think analytically and evaluate how David was able to achieve the distinctive lowrider effects on his truck.

Talking to David about his experiences both in terms of becoming a lowrider and in relation to mentoring Sonny, I was struck by the emphasis on traditional, North American values. For example, in talking about all that went into creating a lowrider, David emphasized the importance of having and keeping a job, of saving money, of learning the skills to do most of the work on the car oneself, of delaying gratification. That a lowrider is an object of aesthetic and cultural value has already been established, that it is also an object of economic value was confirmed when David mentioned that his truck had been appraised recently for insurance purposes to the tune of $32,000.

If becoming a lowrider means acquiring skills that also instill traditional values like hard work, thrift, and resourcefulness, then the question remains as to why lowriders, and everything associated with lowriding (such as wearing distinctive clothing or drawing pictures of lowriders and cholos) often are associated with gangs and their violent and criminal associations. The answer may well lie in understanding that what is being contested is the ideological meaning of *lowrider*. In some contexts, such as at the "*Lowrider* History Tour" it is associated with traditional values. In other contexts, it is associated by "outsiders" with gangs, violence, and crime. Bakhtin usefully conceptualizes this ideological conflict as *dialogic*. Bakhtin perceived that words are rarely—if ever—abstract and neutral, and showed how we learn our words within social contexts saturated with ideological meanings. According to Bakhtin, words with contested ideological meanings are signs, and, as signs, their ideological meaning depends directly on the context in which they are used. Bakhtin uses two dynamic functions in describing the contestation of the meaning of signs: the *centripetal* function seeks to unify and fix meaning, whereas the *centrifical* function resists the fixing of meaning by creating alternative possible meanings. Bakhtin refers to the centripetal function as being *monologic* in nature, and to the centrifical function as being *dialogic* in nature. Thus, for example, the word *lowrider* is a sign. Some mainstream magazines act as monological texts that try to fix in place a single meaning for this term. Lowrider magazines, of which *Lowrider* is one, are dialogical texts and resist a fixed, single meaning for the word, *lowrider*, by posing alternative meanings by means of photographic, computer-generated, and hand-rendered drawings and images, through texts and by hosting car shows, among other things. In this case then, the dialogic function operates both visually and textually.

To illustrate one way in which lowriding can be depicted as a negative practice, it is worthwhile analyzing the textual and visual content of a page from an article published in the June 1980 issue of *National Geographic*. Embedded in the article, "The Mexican Americans: A People on the Move," are two photographs and an accompanying caption (see Figures 1 and 2). The caption refers to both photographs and reads:

SHADOW OF A BOXER plays against the wall at Cleland House, a gang rehabilitation center in East Los Angeles. Along East L.A.'s Whittier Boulevard, youths in the garb of the *vatos locos* (crazy guys) watch a nightly ritual: the promenade of "lowriders," low-slung cars popular among young Mexican Americans.

The phrase in the first sentence of the caption, "at Cleland House, a gang rehabilitation center," immediately stands out and begs the question as to whether the meaning of the image changes significantly if the caption read: "Shadow of a boxer against a wall in East Los Angeles?" The long-term wall poster advertising a forthcoming boxing match, makes it unlikely that omitting the mention of the gang rehabilitation center would indeed change the meaning of the image significantly.

Nevertheless, there must be a reason for including reference to the gang rehabilitation center within the context of these two photographs. I propose the purpose of this information is to alert the reader to the presence of gangs in East Los Angeles. The second sentence in the caption identifies the young men in the picture by means of the label gang members use to describe themselves—*vatos locos*—confirms the presence of gangs. The caption overtly links apparent gang members and lowriding—and, I would argue, links gang members and all "young Mexican Americans"—by means of the reference to lowriders and lowriding: "the *vatos locos* watch a nightly ritual: the promenade of 'lowriders,' low slung cars popular among young Mexican Americans." In Bakhtin's terms, the coupling of the images and caption serves a monological function.

In Figure 3 that follows, I cropped the second picture from *National Geographic* shown in Figure 2, and placed it above a dialogical response from *Lowrider* (Figure 4). I am not suggesting that *Lowrider* was responding directly to *National Geographic*, but I do want to suggest that the *Lowrider* logo resists how lowriders are marked and defined as gang members by the ways in which they are represented in popular media. In the first of the two images presented in Figure 4, what began as a creative symbol for the $1.00 price of the original *Low Rider* evolved into the "Lowrider Man" that *Lowrider* trademarked in 1980; and which in the second image in Figure 4 had been modified and used to help promote the *Lowrider* Magazine Scholarship Fund. There is a coincidental visual correspondence between the young man in the fedora with his eyes hidden by the brim in the cropped photograph in Figure 3, and the fedora-wearing, "Lowrider Man" logo below. In the former, the young man is marked as a gang member; the latter, particularly the Lowrider Man wearing the mortarboard, resists that association by positing an alternative: That young Latinos go to college. These Lowrider Man images serve a dialogical function.

My research finding that people within the social contexts organized around lowriding read lowrider cars as visual statements of aesthetic and cultural value made me reconsider the drawings published in the Hispanic Academic Program student writing anthologies. When I looked closely at

Figure 1: Shadow Boxer, *National Geographic.* June, 1980 (p. 801). (Credit: Stephanie MAZE/NGS Image Collection)

Figure 2: Mexican American Youth, *National Geographic.* June, 1980 (p. 801). (Credit: Stephanie MAZE/NGS Image Collection)

Figure 3: Mexican American Youth (detail) A cropped photograph of youths watching a parade of lowriders along Los Angeles' Whittier boulevard.

Figure 4: Lowrider Men, (Left) *Lowrider* magazine's "Lowrider Man" logo, circa 1980 (*Lowrider*. January, 1997: 82), and (Right)"Lowrider Man" promoting *Lowrider* magazine's annual Scholarship Fund (*Lowrider*, May 1997: 66).

these drawings certain—possibly intentionally—constructed meanings became apparent. Some of these drawings appeared to be resisting stereotypes of Latino adolescents, or at least to be reflecting the conflict Latino adolescents must be feeling about how they are portrayed in mainstream texts in comparison with how they may feel about themselves.

For example, in 1993, Javier submitted his drawing, "Puro Latino" (Pure Latino), to the Hispanic Academic Program anthology (see Figure 5). "Puro Latino" is not a gang name he is claiming, but it is the name his group in Hispanic Academic Program gave themselves. However the form in which he has chosen to write "Puro Latino" demonstrates his familiarity with graffiti-style script. The cartoon in the upper right corner, "Devils or Angels," foregrounds a cholo dressed in a style popular among urban youth: baggy pants, t-shirt, knit cap, and a tattoo of a cross on his right forearm. Behind this character is a lowrider. The text, "Devils or Angels," acts as a rhetorical question concerning the "nature" of this character, and Javier has drawn him so he can be read as an angel and/or devil. The character has a shiny halo over his cap, and another halo dots the "i" in Devil; he also sports a pair of wings on his back. However, he is also holding a baseball bat behind his back, his eyebrows are arched, and he has a devilish grin—all suggesting a potential for mayhem, if not violence.

The written text, "Puro Latino" works in tandem with "Devils or Angels" to pose an implicit tension in relation to being pure Latino. It suggests on the one hand that being pure Latino means being literate in graffiti script as well as being a cholo and lowrider. On the other hand, it plays on an ambivalence concerning the nature of these cultural expressions: whether being Latino, a cholo, and a lowrider means being a devil or an angel, or both; whether it means being peaceful and proud of cultural markers of Latino identity such as tattoos, cholo-style clothes, a lowrider car; or whether it means being potentially violent and dangerous, and living "la vida loca:" the *crazy life*, the gang life (Rodriguez, 1995: 254). As such, this ambivalence may have posed a quandary for the Hispanic Academic Program students, the majority of whom were immigrants—or the first American generation born of immigrant parents—who, at twelve, thirteen, or fourteen years of age, were beginning to sort out for themselves what it means to be *Latino*. To determine whether these drawing intentionally communicated these kinds of meanings, or whether I was simply projecting my curiosity about Latino adolescents' cultural identities onto these images, I turned to the literature on visual literacy and conducted the second of my two studies, this time focussing explicitly on images and icons.

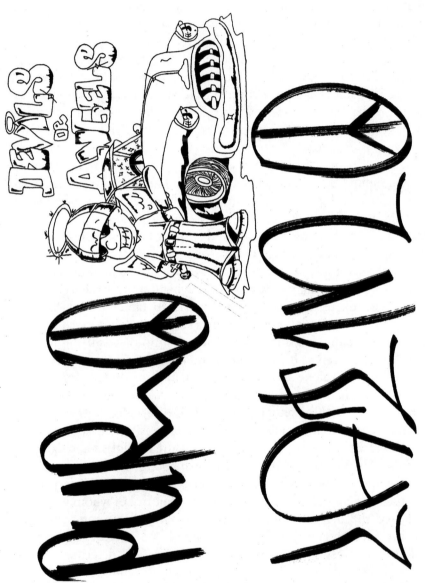

Figure 5: *Puro Latino* (Javier, 1993).

Visual Literacy

The contemporary study of visual literacy assumes that images must be understood as a kind of language—that "instead of providing a transparent window on the world, images are now regarded as the sort of sign that presents a deceptive appearance of naturalness and transparence concealing an opaque, distorting, arbitrary mechanism of representation, a process of ideological mystification" (Mitchell, 1986: 8).

In a new theory of visual literacy, Kress and van Leeuwen argue that images have pictorial structures, and that these structures function like grammar in language to encode experience visually. In short, images can be read for consistent—although contextually dependent—meanings just as written texts. In *Reading Images: The Grammar of Visual Design* (1996), they argue that visual literacy is analogous to language and meets three communicational and representational functions. Drawing on linguist Michael Halliday's theory of language, they label and define these functions as follows: the *ideational metafunction* concerns the ways in which a semiotic system represents things in the world; the *interpersonal metafunction* describes how an image constitutes interactions between and among the things depicted, the image-maker, and the viewers; and the *textual function* refers to the way in which images create texts that cohere both internally and with the context and purpose for which they were produced.

Employing their theory of visual grammar in my second study, I developed interview questions that corresponded to each of these three metafunctions. If my interview subjects' answers were consistent, then it suggested that the drawings I showed them were being read for particular, analyzable meanings. I analyzed my interview data in relation to the ways in which the drawings represented ideological views of the artists' worlds and values; the kinds of interactions that the drawings made available to a viewer and interactions organized around the drawings; and how the drawings as texts belonged to the context and purpose for which they were made. In what follows I discuss each visual literacy metafunction using comments three people made about one of the drawings I showed them (see Figure 7).

The Ideational Metafunction

Using the ideational metafunction, it is possible to analyze the pictorial structure of Karina's drawing for the underlying visual grammar and the meaning it makes available to a viewer (see Figure 7). Karina's picture is a revision of the traditional depiction of *La Virgen de Guadalupe* (cf. Figures

Figure 6: *La Virgen de Guadalupe,* (ACS Alma S.A., c.1994)

6 and 7). According to Kress and van Leeuwen's theory, one way in which visual grammar produces ideological depictions of reality involves examining how participants (subjects and objects) are represented as embodying a particular "essence" or semantic role:

> Symbolic processes are about what a participant [i.e., an object or element in a pictorial structure] *means* or is...there are two participants—the participants whose meaning or identity is established in the relation, the *Carrier*, and the par-

ticipant which represents the meaning or identity itself, the *Symbolic Attribute*.
(Kress and van Leeuwen, 1996: 108)

In Karina's drawing, the *Carrier* is the chola whose essence is established
pictorially in relation to the visual elements that represent the *Symbolic
Attributes*. These *Symbolic Attributes* are (a) the mantel, halo, pose, and
facial expression of *La Virgen de Guadalupe*, (b) the cholo figure under-
neath the chola in the place occupied by an angel in the traditional depictions of the Virgin, and (c) the folded bandana between the two figures.
As such, in Karina's pictorial structure, the chola in a reverential pose, and
the cholo with his arms outstretched, are set in relation to each other; and
both are positioned in relation to the political and cultural power and religious grace of *La Virgen de Guadalupe*. The ideological meaning could be
a challenge to the commonly held view that the chola and cholo are
threatening or contemptible figures; it could well be an assertion that they
have their own political, cultural, and religious power.

Juana was in her early twenties, had grown up in Bayside, and was a
community college student. I recruited Juana by asking a colleague at the
community college where I taught if I could make a short presentation to
her students in her Puente Project class.[4] I presented myself as someone
interested in other cultures, as a former community college student, and
as a fellow student doing research for a class project: in this case for a
graduate class in my doctoral program. I briefly described the Hispanic
Academic Program in which I taught, held up some of the drawings I had
selected so that the Puente students could see them, and explained how I
was interested in talking to them about these pictures. Juana was one of
the volunteers from that class who signed up to be interviewed. Although
Juana regarded *La Virgen de Guadalupe* as an image traditionally associated with the Mexican community—she herself had been born in the U.S.
of Guatemalan parents—she nonetheless closely identified with Karina's
drawing.

> I do remember seeing all this vivid stuff in junior high…I have a whole bunch of
> different drawings that my friends drew for me, and I just kind of collect it all. I
> have it all in my room. Some of them are so old that they're falling apart. But it's
> just something that we identified ourselves with. I felt like I identified with, like
> this is us, looking at us the real way…. There were a lot of different images like
> the one, this one of the Virgin Mary. This one tripped me out though. I remem-
> ber when I saw it for the first time, because you always, we always identified the
> *Virgen de Guadalupe* as the leader of Mexico. I'm not Mexican right, but it was a
> trip when I saw it for the first time [referring to Karina's drawing]. I was like, oh

Figure 7: Karina's Image

how cool. Because I mean it gives us an image of a girl who we are, of the way we dress you know and the kind of lifestyle we live.

Even though Juana distinguishes herself as "not Mexican," she reveals her close identification with the chola as representing the kind of girls she and her friends are, and with *La Virgen de Guadalupe* as a significant icon for Mexicans. This suggests that the chola and the Virgin, in the context of Juana's adolescent social world, represent markers of membership in a U.S. Latina ethnic category/community. Having lived this "lifestyle" and spent her adolescence within this cultural milieu, Juana also read an ideological challenge to negative assumptions of being chola that the drawing presents.

> When they put the rag here [pointing to the bandana between the chola and cholo, and referring to it—*rag*—using the name for bandanas that gang members use to claim their affiliations] it was identified more as a gang-like situation, right. Not in a bad way 'cause there were girls that hung out with gang girls and stuff, but they weren't bad at all.

This reflects Juana's awareness that cholas and cholos are commonly associated with gang activity, and her experience that one could be a chola or cholo and not be in a gang, not be "bad at all." To Juana, Karina's drawing and the other drawings I showed her, reflected the way in which she saw herself and her friends in junior high school. They were the expression of her truth as she saw it: that her friends were artistically gifted; that, although they were cholas and cholos, they were not necessarily in gangs and they were not bad, as they were often assumed to be; that this truth often went unrecognized.

> I just loved all the drawings. I liked them a lot because they were so tied to me. They had this gift for art like, I mean, we're talking about people that are like, some of them were teenagers who were, a lot of people were in jail, or they were just part of like supposedly the gang life they would say. And they would have this art and nobody really recognized that it was something that they could devote themselves to, some profession.

For Juana these drawings reflected a truth that differed from what others assumed about her and her friends—that obvious artistic talent was overlooked because of the preoccupation that these drawings were always indicators of gang involvement. In Juana's comments it is clear that she is reading Karina's drawing as an expression of the artists' world and values, and as an ideological challenge to dominant stereotypes of cholas and cholos as "bad" gang members.

The Interpersonal Metafunction

The interpersonal metafunction constitutes the interaction between the producer and the viewer of an image. It is clear that Juana read Karina's drawing as a statement about the nature of being a chola. It is also clear that this representation resonated with her own experiences and that she identified with Karina's challenge to conventional ways of reading cholas and cholos. The interpersonal metafunction accounts for these interactions between the participants in the picture and between the picture and the viewer. There is a third kind of interaction, however; the relation between producers and viewers of images—the things they do to or for each other. I found that not just the content of these drawings is associated with Latino adolescent cultural identity, but the uses to which they are put are also related to cultural identity.

Marisa was a U.S. born, Mexican-descent undergraduate at a prestigious public university. Her father is Mexican American and her mother is European American. At the time of my study, Marisa was in her early twenties, had grown up in a mixed commercial and residential neighborhood in Bayside, and had been a student of mine when I had taught at a Catholic high school in Bayside. I ran into her a few years after leaving my position as a high school teacher, and, remembering that she came from a family of artists, asked if she would look at some drawings I had and tell me about them. When I met Marisa for coffee, I showed her the drawings I had selected, including the one by Karina (see Figure 5 above). Not wanting to reveal my own ideas about them, I explained only that I had become interested in them and asked her what she could tell me about them. This is part of what she said:

> A lot of these images remind me of the t-shirts the kids wear, especially in middle school. It's really popular to wear that if you're Mexican. They have the picture, like of the chola with her hair and maybe the lowrider car and the guy, the *pachuco* with like a bandana or it will have the Aztec picture—it's the famous story of the mountain top where it looks like a woman and a man. I forget what the name of the story is. When you wear a t-shirt like that you're showing *Raza* [race] pride. And so since it was so important in middle school to have an identity, to be part of something, because it's such an insecure time, anyways, wearing that was like (pause) you know. And so a lot of people draw images like that, which were the lowrider cars, the cholos, and a lot of people did the writing, the tagging, the graffiti and stuff like that, and dressed like this so already the dress

was like another way of showing who you were and who you were identifying with. All these images were really prevalent.

Marisa is making connections between being in junior high school, feeling insecure and needing to claim an identity, asserting a Mexican identity by wearing t-shirts with particular images that show "*Raza* pride," and students drawing their own variations of those images. It is clear that the icons in these drawings evoke Latino cultural identity, a feeling of "*Raza* pride." In Marisa's comments, it also becomes clear that how these drawings are used is also associated with Latino adolescent cultural identity.

When I asked Marisa about what people did with the drawings they made, this is what she said:

> People would just sit there and draw, like you'd be bored in class and you'd just sit there drawing stuff like this. You know, hey da da da, look at this, oh that's cool. You'd give them to somebody and they would like put them in their binder, you know the binder that opens? They have a little (clear pocket on the cover) and you can stick them in there. Or you'd have like this particular guy or girl in class that's really good at drawing, okay can you draw me a picture with this and this and this on it? Like a lowrider car with a girl or something like that, and they'll go, oh okay, and they'll draw it for you. Put it in your locker, put it on the wall in your room. It shows again who you're affiliated with, who you are. I mean right there, blam, your locker, that's who you are right there, right there. And to have (a drawing) in your binder you're always identified with that, you know, your *Raza*. You go into class and you go sit with other Latino students, you go to lunch and you sit with them, and you all identify with these symbols, you know, of the cars and the Aztecs and stuff like that.

Although students identified with the icons in the drawings, it wasn't just the icons themselves that had the power of articulating a Latino identity, it was how the drawings were used and displayed. Marisa's comments also suggest that there were a few good artists, but that there were more students who wanted the drawings to collect and display to assert their own cultural identity. So good artists were often commissioned to draw particular icons or particular compositions, and other students acted as collectors.

Juana described herself as a collector who commissioned drawings her friends made for her.

> I would ask them to draw this for me, or do this for me…I had two folders of a lot of artwork. I would keep them all over the place everywhere with me. If we ever moved somewhere, I would get my little two folders and throw them in there and just leave them there. And it was a trip though, because as I got older a lot of my husband's cousins, they're just growing up, you know they're eleven

> or twelve, thirteen, another is fourteen years old. They would see sometimes that I would have that and they would pull it out. Even, I have a brother, he was like, oh, you've got stuff, you should give some to me so I could see how they look and how they drew it. And they would just look at it, and then they would start drawing to see if they could do something like that. I said here, I was like, oh, here take it. I don't need it no more now. I started giving them my stuff, and I had a book and I gave it to one of them…. But I did keep some stuff that I liked the most, and I was not going to give that away.

In this Latino, adolescent social world, drawings have value both in themselves as statements of cultural identity, and as objects to be collected and displayed to claim that identity for oneself. Juana discussed how people in this visual discourse community acquire their literacy skills by studying drawings. They get ideas, learn the icons, and often what the icons mean and how they are related to Latino history. Artists often first acquire their skills by studying and copying drawings to reproduce those they admire, before creating their own.

What is interesting in Juana's discussion of her collection and how she came to give it away, is not that the drawings no longer had value to her. It's obvious from her keeping them for so long, taking them with her whenever she moved, and keeping her favorite ones, that they are still important and valued objects. But she perhaps felt that as she grew older she did not need them anymore, but that the younger generation did. She assumes that if her brother and husband's cousins are like her when she was their age—that is, in the midst of constructing their own cultural identities—then entering into this visual discourse community offers answers to them as it offered answers to her. These drawings then may have an important function to initiate some individuals into the icons of Latino cultural identity and history.

The Textual Metafunction

The textual metafunction offers a theory of how, in a visual semiotic system, complexes of signs cohere with the context for which they were produced. I employed this explanatory concept as I explored the presence of other visual texts in the larger context of Latino social worlds; I asked where else one could see the kinds of cultural images my Hispanic Academic Program students had produced and what these other images meant in larger contexts.

Armando teaches at the Bayside middle school that he himself attended. When I met and interviewed Armando at a café in our neighborhood,

I asked him where students saw these kinds of images. He answered by referring to the presence of religious imagery important to Catholicism.

They see it in a couple of places. The ones that go to church see the Virgin everyday and some even wear medallions. It's kind of funny that here these kids that get into fights and they're wearing their medallions and all these religious symbols. So they'll see them in the neighborhood.

Given the ubiquity of images of *La Virgen de Guadalupe*, it is no surprise that she is a frequent feature in students' drawings. But it did come as a surprise to me when Juana told me she had seen the image of a chola drawn in the aspect of the Virgin of Guadalupe before.

Juana: It was a trip when I saw it for the first time. I was like, oh how cool... It tripped me out [referring to when I showed Karina's drawing to her Puente class]. That's why I was like, oh I remember this. I remember when Leo did this, because he used one of my friends as a model and he drew her. He put her hands there like that. So it was a trip.

Peter So you're saying when you saw this picture, it reminded you of another picture that you had seen?

Juana: Yeah. It was just the background of the Virgin Mary, but with what we call "cholias;" that's cholas. Everybody grabbed a copy because once they saw the drawing everybody made [photo]copies of it. They took it home and they would frame it or they would carry it inside their binder. They would tape it inside so every time you opened it you saw it there.

This substitution of a chola for the Virgin creates a provocative image that resonates instantly with some Latinas and creates a strong identification. Juana's story raises the question of whether Karina and Leo coincidentally drew similar images or whether they had seen this image before. It may well exist in this visual discourse community as an image invested with a particular kind of power and reverence that makes people want to have and keep it. Having heard from Juana that she had seen that image before, when I showed it to Armando, I asked him if he had seen it before. He replied,

I don't recall having seen it before...I have seen this where, you know, where different images will be put in it. It's used in pictures where people go take their pictures at quinceaneras [a Mexican girl's formal 15th birthday ceremony, part of which takes place in a church]. She's part of the ceremony where...the young lady gets and presents flowers to the Virgin of Guadalupe. She goes and kneels, puts flowers and pictures are taken. Sometimes, if for some reason she can't do that, they will do a double, they'll have her kneeling, take a picture and they will superimpose (the Virgin).

This may explain some of the resonance of Karina's drawing. A quinceanera is an important event in an adolescent, Mexican girl's life, (it's part birthday party, part coming of age party), and since *La Virgen de Guadalupe* plays an important role in the religious part of the ceremony, then the Virgin may be an important coming-of-age symbol in their imaginations.

Armando frequently made similar connections between the Catholic upbringing many Latino students received at home, religious icons, and the presence of these icons in artwork that was used in other, particularly adolescent, contexts.

> Armando: Kids would make "Rest in Peace" drawings. They'll put someone's face and a religious symbol. Unfortunately we've had some instances in the last couple of years, not there [meaning, at school], but you know someone's friend passes away.... Sometimes like if a teacher knows the family, the teacher would get all these basically hand made sympathy cards and take them and give them to the family, to the mother. We had one incident, I think it was a little bit over a year ago. One of our students was shot to death. It was a major thing and we had to do counseling and therapy the whole day....
>
> Peter: Were students encouraged to draw pictures?
>
> Armando: Yeah. Like someone said, they'll sit there for hours and just practice their tag. They'll just practice calligraphy. In class they'll scribble scrabble you can't even tell the numbers and letters apart. But when they're doing something like this, they really take some pride in it. They're really meticulous about it.

When I began the interview, I asked Armando to tell me about these drawings from a duel perspective: what he remembered about them from when he had been an adolescent, and how he sees them now as a teacher at a predominantly Latino middle school. He explained that he came from a large family that spoke Spanish at home, and attended Catholic mass regularly. In junior high school, Armando identified himself as a "Mexican" kid, rather than as a more Americanized "Chicano" kid.

> There's two mentalities to the Latino thing that we have going on now. When I was in school you were either Chicano or you were a Mexican. If you were a Chicano you were more outspoken, you associated yourself with certain things. You probably had like the Impala [car] stickers on your books, or things like that, the hairnets were popular at that time. Then there were the more traditional Latinos, they didn't really stand out. We, I associated myself with the latter, we don't really want to stand out. I guess maybe we weren't at that stage yet where we had to feel that sense of, okay, where do I belong. You know, what's my identity? Maybe it's because we weren't right at that identity crisis yet, that we all kind of go through. Like who am I?

In making distinctions between Chicano and Mexican identities within the ethnic category *Latino*, Armando links being "more outspoken" and icons associated with lowriding with being Chicano, and not wanting "to stand out" with being Mexican. However, the criterion for affiliating with one or the other identity is not country of birth, but rather how one answers the questions, who am I? what's my identity?

> I've seen it go both ways ... As a matter of fact, it was funny, because again, our sense of identity sometimes clicks in later on. This one friend of mine, who hung around with the traditional kids in high school then started to hang around with the traditional Chicano kids. He got a lowrider and he got into that. He and his friend they went and bought Impalas. With their money over the summer they painted them. One started his own detail shop for a while. And of course you'd see the cars with the Virgin on the side and really doped up or souped up [slang for modifying the engine for greater speed].

What is interesting about this recount is the mixing of symbols. Here Armando associated the Virgin with particular contexts and activities, like on the side of his friend's lowrider Impala, or in Karina's drawing, with Chicano identity. Indeed, Armando read Karina's picture as drawn by a person with and expressing Chicano cultural knowledge:

> This is probably someone [referring to Karina through her drawing] who is starting to get into the quote unquote Latino Chicano movement and the Virgin of Guadalupe is important because they see it, that's the only Virgin of brown skin so she's one of our people. That's why, you know it's important, it's not another fair skinned person to dominate. And that's taught a lot at home. Especially the fact that this is our Virgin, you know, she's like us. She, the Virgin, came down to address us because we are the chosen people. Everyone wants to be the chosen right? So that's why the Virgin of Guadalupe is used quite frequently.

Yet, Armando also associated the Virgin with a traditional Mexican upbringing. He described her as an important icon for immigrant families like his; families who seem to have brought that understanding with them from Mexico.

> I remember going back to Mexico. My cousin says, you know, it's nice that we have our own Virgin. Someone that's like us. So here they'll hear it from their parents, and then they're starting to hear it in school, you know, yeah, you need to be proud, you know you're Chicanos. Okay. It's an easy mesh.

Here in the U.S. the Virgin of Guadalupe gets transformed into an icon that resonates with and is used in this new cultural context to represent the Chicano identity; here it gets used to represent very different kinds of experiences.

> I've seen this [Karina's drawing] used sometimes when a loved one is lost to incidents like drive-bys, things like that. They'll use the combination of religious symbols with the gang-related thing. Not everybody that dresses like that is affiliated with a gang. But you know it's definitely, they want to be different at that stage, and this definitely sets them apart from everyone else.

Armando says three important things. First, he's describing how the image of the Virgin is used to communicate particular kinds of inner-city, Chicano experiences such as experiencing the sudden, violent deaths of family, friends, or acquaintances who may be involved in gangs, or are innocently caught in contemporary urban gunfire. Second, he is saying that even though cholas and cholos are associated with gangs and gang activities, "not everybody that dresses like that is affiliated with a gang." Third, he notes that the desire to dress like that is a product of the adolescent desire to affiliate with a particular group.

The religious images that children become familiar with in their families and the Catholic church are used in response to the realities of inner-city violence often associated with gangs, and as challenges to the dominant denotation of cholas and cholos as always associated with gangs. In this way, Karina's drawing represents a challenge to hegemonic thinking that links Latino youth with gangs. This is why Armando characterizes Karina, the artist, as a young woman "who is starting to get into the quote unquote Latino Chicano movement." Even though he didn't self-identify as a Chicano himself when he was Karina's age, from his adult vantage Armando understands Karina's use of the Virgin to challenge conventional ways of reading cholas and cholos as a developing critical and political awareness.

When one thinks about the ubiquity of images—religious symbols in church, wearing religious medallions, photographs that use these religious icons, images of lowrider cars, cholas, cholos, pachucos with bandanas, Aztec warriors and maidens on the t-shirts kids wear to school, hand done drawings produced in class and used to decorate binders and lockers, and collected at home in folders or hanging framed and unframed on walls, or drawings made and collected at school as expressions of sympathy for a grieving family—it is clear that there are multiple sites for creation and interactions with visual texts that mark something uniquely Latino.

Conclusion

The data I collected show that Kress and van Leeuwen's theoretical frame is useful in explaining how Marisa, Juana, and Armando read Karina's drawing in consistent ways, with some variation given their different experiences. The data also show that the content, the icons in Karina's drawing, was an articulation of Latino adolescent cultural identity. Finally, the interview data suggest that the power these drawings have to assert cultural identity derives from their use—including the ways in which they were commissioned, collected, passed on, and displayed in public and private spaces—and by the social interactions that took place within these different sociocultural contexts. For example, it wasn't just taking the image of the Virgin of Guadalupe out of the church, it was seeing her on the side of a lowrider car, or replaced by a chola and taped inside someone's binder that affirmed being a Latina or Latino adolescent.

These drawings cannot be understood in isolation from the context for which they were made (Kress and van Leeuwen, 1996). My analysis supports the finding that they also cannot be understood in isolation from their use in the contexts for which they were made. Part of this context is how both their content and their use is interpreted by those outside of this visual discourse community. For example, how I, as an agent of the school, initially assumed that these drawings were gang-related. Of course, some drawings are gang-related. Some of them, like Karina's, clearly are not. When lowriding and Latino adolescent artwork are seen as products of social processes of taking and making meaning valued in one's community, they can be seen to exist in opposition to and as challenges to pejorative assumptions. They can be read as counterdiscourses to dominant discourses about young Latinos.

As a teacher and education researcher who does not share the same cultural background as my students, it is incumbent upon me to continue to challenge my own assumptions about what it means to "be Latino." Not being aware, not paying attention to what students are doing, and not being inquisitive about it, leaves me vulnerable to mainstream representations and the ways in which they textually and visually create and perpetuate forms of ethnic and racial stratification.

Notes

1. The Mexican American community in the United States is heterogeneous, and includes foreign born residents and U.S. born residents, some of whose families were absorbed into the U.S. following its imperial expansion during the Mexican American

War. I use *Chicano* to designate, in a narrow sense, Americans of Mexican descent who share cultural pride, an awareness of their history of oppression in the United States, and political activism (cf. Polkinhorn, Valasco, and Lambert, 1986).

2. For example, the term *lowrider* has been "appropriated by Chicano barrio youth to describe the style and people linked to local gang structures" (Rodrigeuz, 1993: 254); or, "*Cholo/a* (standard meaning) Half-breed; *mestizo*; an Indian who has adopted Mexican civilization. (Non-standard meaning) A lowrider; a Chicano street-gang member" (Polkinhorn, Valasco, and Lambert, 1986: 21).

3. The original *Low Rider Magazine* was published 1977–1985. In June of 1988, a resurrected *Lowrider* was published by original staff members; it has been published monthly since then.

4. The Puente Project is an Innovations in American Government award-winning program (1998), designed to increase the number of Mexican American/Latino community college students transferring to four-year colleges and universities.

Works Cited

Farr, M. (1994). *En los dos idiomas*: Literacy practices among Chicago Mexicanos. In B. Moss (Ed.), *Literacy across communities* (pp. 9–47). Cresskill, NJ: Hampton.

Gutiérrez, J. (1980). Interview: César Chávez. *Low Rider*, 3 (12), 42–53.

Heath, S. B. (1982). What no bedtime story means: Narrative skills at home and school. *Language and society*, 11 (1), 49–76.

Kress, G. and van Leeuwen, T. (1996). *Reading images: The grammar of visual design*. London: Routledge.

Mahiri, J. and Sablo, S. (1996). Writing for their lives: The non-school literacy of California's urban African American youth. *Journal of Negro Education*, 65 (2), 164–180.

Mitchell, W. J. T. (1986). *Iconology: Image, text, ideology*. Chicago: University of Chicago Press.

Oquendo, A. R. (1998). Re-imagining the Latino/a race. In R. Delgado and J. Stefancic (Eds.), *The latino/a condition: A critical reader* (pp. 60-71). New York: New York University Press.

Polkinhorn, H. Velasco, A., and Lambert, M. (1986). *El libro de calo*: The dictionary of Chicano slang (revised edition). Los Angeles, CA: Floricanto Press.

Rodriguez, L. J. (1995). *Always running. La vida loca: Gang days in L.A*. New York: Touchstone.

Stone, M. C. (1990). *Bajito y suavecito* [Low and slow]: Lowriding and the "class" of class. *Studies in Latin American Popular Culture* 9, 85–126.

Trillin C. and Koren, E. (1978). Our far-flung correspondents: Low and slow, mean and clean. *New Yorker*, 10 July, 70–74.

"Devils or Angels"

José David Saldívar

eter Cowan provides in his wondrous essay a lucid, informed account of the literacy events and ideological practices of U.S. Latino/a car customizers—lowriders—who build, transculturate (Ortiz, 1995), and display their cars in Bayside, a multicultural, northern California community. Making pointed use of the lowrider as a sign and dialogic "form of expression," Cowan charts the related processes of how Latino/a youth overturn the dominant culture's view of them as either incorrigible or as violent gang members. "Devils or Angels" is a thought-provoking essay that is important for those of us interested in the new literacy studies and in U.S. cultural studies more generally. Cowan's essay, thus envisaged, seeks better knowledge of the shifting and shifty configurations of dominance, and negotiation and resistance in order to respond to and transform it.

On another level, I found Cowan's argument that Latino/a adolescents in their lowrider-making and in their visual drawings of religious icons such as *La Virgen de Guadalupe* are involved in constructing alternative literacy and knowledges to be satisfyingly far-reaching and illuminating. As Cowan suggests, "the lowrider-maker creates a visually, aesthetically, and performatively provocative contrast" to middle-class hotrodders and high-riders. Through the voices of his informants such as David, Sonny, Javier, Karina, Armando, and Juana in North America, Cowan maps out how the border migrations of many Latinos also imply the migrations of the languages, icons, and memories from the South upon which human and discourse communities are built. For instance, one of his Latina students reminds him how "people in the artistic and visual discourse community acquire their literacy skills by studying drawings" of their peers. They get ideas, learn the icons, and often what the icons mean and how they are related to Latino history. If Javier, Karina and Juana's drawings and collections of drawings of "cholos," lowriders, and *La Virgen de Guadalupe*—as Peter Cowan rightly argues—contribute, directly or indirectly, to a broader understanding of contemporary Latino literacy practices and history, their drawings can also be related to the larger histories of writing as well as to the history of conflicting literacies in the Americas since at least the Renaissance. Allow me to explain briefly.

When the Europeans first came to the Americas, their literacy practices and alphabetic writing practices "tamed" the voices of the Mexicas— the name the Aztecs used to refer to themselves—and Mayans, among other subalterns (Mignolo, 1995). Writing, for the European Spaniards, was for controlling the Amerindians and not for representing their voices and their codices (which were writings without written words).

To be sure, the dominance of alphabetic writing over Amerindian writing systems was not an entirely smooth victory. Mignolo argues, for example, that during the early modern colonial period, Amerindian writing systems challenged the European distinction between the Holy Book and the secular book. While the Europeans believed that Amerindians did not have a language sufficient to explain the paradoxes of the Catholic faith, the Europeans were incapable of imagining that their own languages and literacy practices were "insufficient to account for Amerindian matters" (Mignolo, 1994: 275). Briefly stated, the Mexicas throughout the Renaissance not only adopted the literacy practices of alphabetic writing but also hybridized and braided it with their own alternative writing practices. Writing in the Americas was therefore not "evolutionary" but "co-evolutionary," a writing that acknowledged both alphabetic forms of writing and alternatives to it. Writing was not only philosophical in the Americas, it was also political.

The U.S. Latino/a youth drawings Peter Cowan explores can therefore be situated within the long history of modern, colonial semiosis (Mignolo, 2000), geocultural identity and territory, and cultural studies theory. This is the history Juana alludes to when she suggests that Latino/a youth "acquire their literacy skills by studying drawings." Their drawings thus, as Cowan puts it, reflect "the conflict Latino adolescents must be feeling about how they are portrayed in mainstream texts in comparison with how they may feel about themselves."

Let me end my comments by focusing on the simple fact that the lowrider car is not only a "sign," but also a hybrid commodity form. What does it really mean that many male U.S. Latino youths are daily involved in customizing and chopping a U.S. object (the car) that has already been "Taylorized"—through the assembly line, the interchangeability of car parts and workers, and the standardization of tools? What is Cowan suggesting when he writes that in "becoming a lowrider" and acquiring the things "associated with lowriding (such as ... drawing pictures of lowriders and cholos) what "is being contested is the ideological meaning of *lowrider*"? My sense is that if Latino youths are responding to the highrider cultures of white suburban SUV (Sports Utility Vehicle) cultures, they are also responding at a more basic and material level to the ubiquity and banality of the commodity car object itself. Driving low and slow down the mean streets of Bayside, California, perhaps has the effect of slowing down the clock of the assembly line at work and at school and of commodity modern time itself. Modernization—the car as commodity—is surely, too, what the lowriders are customizing, negotiating, braiding, and attempting to resist. As it stands, Cowan rightly places a heavy accent in his essay on the materiality of U.S. Latino/a youth cultures and on the youths' own braided self-descriptions.

Works Cited

Mignolo, W. (1994). Afterword: Writing and recorded knowledge in colonial and post-colonial situations. In E. Boone and W. Mignolo (Eds.), *Writing without words: Alternative literacies in Mesoamerica and the Andes* (pp. 292–312). Durham, NC: Duke University Press.

———. (1995). *The darker side of the Renaissance: Literacy, territoriality and colonization.* Ann Arbor, MI: University of Michigan Press.

———. (2000). *Local histories/global designs: Coloniality, subaltern knowledges, and border thinking.* Princeton, NJ: Princeton University Press.

Ortiz, F. (1995). *Cuban counterpoint: Tobacco and sugar.* Durham, NC: Duke University Press.

CHAPTER FOUR

Border Discourses and Identities in Transnational Youth Culture

Wan Shun Eva Lam

An authentically migrant perspective would, perhaps, be based on an intuition that the opposition between here and there is itself a cultural construction, a consequence of thinking in terms of fixed entities and defining them oppositionally. It might begin by regarding movement, not as an awkward interval between fixed points of departure and arrival, but as a mode of being in the world. The question would be, then, not how to arrive, but how to move, how to identify convergent and divergent movements; and the challenge would be how to notate such events, how to give them a historical and social value. (Carter, 1992: 101)

[There is a] need to construct a notion of border identity that challenges any essentialized notion of subjectivity while simultaneously demonstrating that the self as a historical and cultural formation is shaped in complex, related, and multiple ways through its interaction with numerous and diverse communities. (Giroux, 1994: 38)

This chapter explores the relationship between discourse and identity for Chinese immigrant youth whose cultural identifications are spread over multiple geographical territories. For these immigrant youth, school is often the setting where they are socialized into the dominant discourses of U.S. society, or excluded from it by various means (Cook-Gumperz, 1986; Gee, 1996; Lankshear with Lawler, 1987). The latter can be seen in different forms of tracking, and the marginalized status of English as a Second Language and bilingual programs in schools, as shown by Olsen (1997), among others, in her ethnographic research of an American high school.

The first set of mechanisms and ideology that surround immigrant students' "incorporation" into U.S. society can be seen as an assimilationist process, whereby these newcomers are to adopt the values and social practices of "mainstream North America." In the educational arena, this process is found in cultural literacy propaganda that aims at dealing with difference by eradicating it: All Americans should read from the same largely white, Western literary and factual canon and adopt a common set of values and linguistic conventions (Macedo, 1995, provides a critical review) A similar ideology and process is also found in the second language acquisition research and teaching profession, where the model of the "native speaker" and the norm of standardized language use are hailed as the target and epitome of second language learning (see, for example, Kramsch, 1997, for a critique of the "myth of the native speaker"). In the educational discourse of bilingualism, Rampton (1995: 338) notes that "a fictional norm of perfect monolingual competence against which the abilities of bilinguals are measured" has become institutionalized. The creative potentials and strategic deployment of linguistic abilities of bilingual speakers as historically situated persons are overlooked in favor of how "balanced" they are, or how fully they attain the linguistic profile of each of their monolingual halves.

The fear and stigmatization of "un-Americanness" that is part and parcel of this assimilationist discourse also find their expression in the process of subordination of immigrant students in American schools. This second set of mechanisms for "incorporating" immigrant students can be seen in how they are disproportionately labeled and tracked in remedial and special education classes (Nieto, 2000; Skutnabb-Kangas and Cummins, 1988). It can also be seen in the movement from nationality to "race" in the U.S. school system—immigrants gradually move from a strong identification with their national origins to becoming absorbed into particular racial categories within the U.S. (Olsen, 1997). Through this segregationist and classificatory process, immigrant students are "safely incorporated" into certain social classes and racial groups, and, hence, pose no danger to the status quo of "mainstream America."

Although both of these two containment processes aim to place immigrant students into existing social categories within the national borders of U.S. society, there is reason to believe—based on recent studies in post-colonial theory and transnationalism—that many immigrant students may also be, to a greater or lesser extent, mobilizing various social, cultural, and linguistic resources to forge new grounds for defining themselves and relating to the sociopolitical structures around them. In this chapter, I explore alternative sources of cross-cultural identity formation for immigrant youth in the border zones of cultures. The experiences of one young Hong Kong immigrant and his reading of translated Japanese comic-books, which he juxtaposes with varieties of U.S. and Hong Kong comic-books, are examined in order to build a better understanding of some of the ways in which immigrant youth actively participate in the construction of border discourses and identities that they use to resist subordination and the constraints of the social systems around them.

Theorizing Border Discourses and Identities

The term (discourse) is used here to refer to the ways in which spoken and written language is used by specific groups of people to construct realities for themselves, based on their shared values, beliefs and historical experiences (i.e., their shared culture). As Gee explains, "Discourses are ways of behaving, interacting, valuing, thinking, believing, speaking, and often reading and writing that are accepted as instantiations of particular roles of specific *groups of people*...They are always and everywhere *social*" (original emphases; 1996: xix). Integrating methods of analysis from language studies and social and political thought, Fairclough (1992) promotes the study of discourse as a *social practice*, and points out both the socially determined and socially transformative properties of discourse. With respect to this view of discourse, he writes: "Firstly, it implies that discourse is a mode of action, one form in which people may act upon the world and especially upon each other, as well as a mode of representation.... Secondly, it implies that there is a dialectical relationship between discourse and social structure" (Fairclough: 63–64). Hence, if discourses are viewed as forms of social practice which are intimately tied to the cultural affiliations of groups of people, a person's adoption and use of particular discourses would signify his or her alignment with or membership in particular cultural groups (see also Gee, 1996).

In a multiethnic society, a person's identity may be seen as the behaviors, beliefs, values, and norms that define that person as a member of a particular ethnic group. However, social categories—such as ethnicity, race, and gender—are not innate characteristics of people, but are socially constructed attributes and boundaries that are often used to differentiate people from one another for economic and political purposes in ways that often ensure some groups obtain more social and material privileges than others (Omi and Winant, 1994; Roediger, 1991). Thus, the construction of such social categories, and the concepts an practices of geographically bounded citizenship and nationhood itself, are accomplished to a great extent through discursive means (for example, see Anderson, 1991, for an illuminating discussion of the discursive construction of nations). In short, discourses are group-specific and, in a society where the distribution of privileges is exercised through group differentiation and social hierarchy, the discourse practices of diverse cultural groups often stand in conflict with one another. Thus, as mentioned above, a person's alignment with or opposition to a certain cultural group can be seen in how he or she adopts or resists the discourses of different groups.

One danger to be avoided when engaging with this approach to discourses is understanding group relations simply in terms of binary oppositions (the dominant versus the dominated; the oppressor versus the oppressed). Many—if not most—people belong to more than one social category or cultural group that may be more or less in conflict with one another (Gee, 1996), which requires careful negotiation between various discourse practices. Immigrants, in particular, are constantly negotiating the dominant discourses of their adopted country and the discourses that signify their ties to their native country and to various other communities. The complexities this entails means that increasing numbers of social scientists are examining immigrants' "transnational connections" rather than their "nation-bound" identity. In other words, the ways in which immigrants' social networks and identities transcend the totalizing concept of nationhood are becoming important research foci within social science research.

In the field of anthropology, for example, Basch, Schiller, and Blanc (1994) examine the ways in which immigrant populations from St. Vincent, Grenada, Haiti, and the Philippines construct transnational social fields to counteract the hegemonic forms of political and economic oppression in both their host and home countries. For instance, through channeling economic resources back home and participating in the nation-building projects of their countries overseas, Vincentian and Grenadian immigrants in New York are able to secure for themselves and their families a higher social standing in their home countries than they had before coming to the U.S. With this elevation in social position back home, and the forging of ties with other West Indian minority groups in the U.S., the Vincentian and Grenadian transmigrants are redefining their social and political locations within U.S. society.

Similarly, Ong (1993) argues for an understanding of the identity formation of overseas Chinese in a confluence of family and economic interests that transcend traditional conceptions of *nation* and *citizenship*. For many overseas Chinese, a Confucianist practice of capitalism anchors the family in the center of expanding capitalist interests. Hence, even though the family often is settled in a place of greater political stability and educational opportunities, financial and economic resources may be dispersed over several riskier territories than would be the case if they had remained in China. In many cases, these transmigrants use their multiple subject positions—situated in various cultural and sociopolitical arenas—to subvert the social categories imposed on them by any one system.

In exploring the cultural aspects of transnational connections, Hannerz (1996) proposes for contemporary cultural analysis the adaptation of Bauman's notion of *habitat*—in which agency operates. In his opinion, a flexible sense of habitat where the subject/agent utilizes different forms of cultural connections to serve specific needs or purposes may become a new unit of analysis in cultural studies. This sense of a shifting, interstitial and intersecting place or space has been theorized to a certain extent in the developing body of works in cultural geography and post-colonial studies.

In studying the history of colonial enterprise in Africa and the Caribbean, Pratt (1992) proposes the concept of *contact zone* for capturing the creative aspects of colonial cultural encounters. Besides domination and subjugation, the contact zone describes the complexity of new ways of life and cultural categories arising from the colonial process: an intermingling of lifestyles among settlers and natives; transracial love stories and sexual alliances; and in the U.S. in particular, the emergence of the autobiographical writings of exslaves who inserted themselves into the European print culture with the help of the abolitionist movement in the last decades of the eighteenth century. These early slave autobiographies marked the beginning of African American literature; instead of constituting an authentic native voice they were characterized by a transcultural and dialogic mode of expression. As Pratt argues, "[i]n very elaborate ways, these early texts undertook not to reproduce but to *engage* western discourses of identity, community selfhood, and otherness. Their dynamics are transcultural, and presuppose relations of subordination and resistance" (1992: 102).

The movement of people on a massive scale across territorial boundaries—set in motion by the colonial disruption of relatively closed communal living in various parts of the world—has served to problematize the definition of *native* and *authenticity*. For instance, Chambers (1994) points out that uprooted "native" cultures and the transient nature of the electronic age have transformed the notion of authenticity into "an authentically migrant perspective," which is open to multiple possibilities and transmutation. Similarly, Said (1979) has long argued that the transmutation and hybridization of cultural identity, and the syncretic perspective that arises from it, can constitute a new space for the study of culture. Colonial subjects, having their precolonial nature unsettled by imperialism, developed a "second nature" in the midst of cultural contact and having to live under domination. However, neither of these identities fully describes the legacy of colonialism; it is necessary "to seek out, to map, to invent, or to discover a third nature" wherein resides the potential for better understanding the experiences of the postcolonial subjects (original emphasis; Said, 1993: 226). In the same vein, Bhabha (1994) reacts against the polarization and simplification of culture that recent critical theories dwell on in the binary opposition of self and other, center and periphery, oppressor and oppressed. He uses the metaphor of "a third space" to signify a new frame of reference and process of signification that occurs *in between* cultures as a result of contact and the clash of difference. For Bhabha, there is no simple definition of *nation* in a world where the movement of people and cultures has been occurring on a massive scale. Many of us are forever dwelling in the "in-between space" on the margins of nations. For Bhabha, hybridity is never an admixture of established cultures or identities, but the elusive conditions where signs and meanings can be "appropriated, translated, rehistoricized, and read anew" (1994: 37).

Bhabha uses the notion of hybridity to examine the space of resistance and re-definition in colonial encounters. As a problematic of colonial representation, hybridity engages with but also displaces colonial authority by introducing other "denied" knowledges into the dominant discourse and estranges the basis of its authority. An example is the English Bible that was translated into a local language in India in the early nineteenth century and appropriated by the local group to break down the distinctions of the caste system and the authority of the Brahmins, and to form their own beliefs in the Biblical God in ways that deliberately diverged from Christianity. Objects of knowledge such as the translated book resignify colonial authority in a way that is "less than one and double" (Bhabba, 1994: 102–122). While on the one hand, some symbol or meaning of authority is maintained (but not completely—less than one), on the other hand, it is re-defined through an alienating strategy of doubling or repetition. Doubling instantiates but also diminishes the presence of authority by articulating it in conjunction with other knowledges and positionalities that both subvert the dominant discourse and produce new forms of knowledge. In this space of dynamic engagement, the identity of the postcolonial subject is situated less in the polarity of the native, minority discourse or the dominant, colonial discourse, but in the "cutting edge of translation and negotiation," (Bhabba, 1994: 38) where new subject positions may be formed.

While Bhabha theorizes this interstitial or border zone of enunciation with a focus on texts, Lavie and Swedenburg (1996) call for its exploration in the practices of everyday life. For them, it is important to "stake out terrain old in experience and memory but new in theory, a third timespace, and [they] call for its ethnographic examination. This is a terrain where opposition is not only responsive, but creative. It is a guerrilla warfare of the interstices, where minorities rupture categories of race, gender, sexuality, class, nation, and empire in the center as well as on the margins" (Lavie and Swedenburg, 1996: 165–166). The study of this third timespace is an attempt to displace the notion of the autonomy or boundedness of culture, and to map out some of the everyday practices that create historically grounded, multiple subject positions. It is in this border culture that the minorities may resist subordination and the terms of their incorporation into the dominant structure; here is also where they may create new alignments and solidarities with one another.

In creating transnational social ties and cultural identifications, immigrants may engage in discourses that serve to construct an in-between space or trajectory for speaking and that they use to subvert the dominant discourses of both their native and adopted countries. It is also in this border zone that they may mobilize their subject positions in different social systems and cultural fields to forge new grounds for defining themselves in relation to both their host and home societies.

Context and Methods

The case study presented here forms part of an ongoing ethnographic research project that explores the cross-cultural literacy practices of adolescent immigrants in a metropolitan city on the west coast of the U.S. In the fall of 1996, I began meeting students as a classroom observer in an urban high school where I taught English as a Second Language and Chinese bilingual classes a few years prior to the initiation of the study. Using the classroom and the school as my starting point, I interviewed the students about what they read and write, and spent time as an observer in some out-of-school settings where they practiced forms of literacy in both their native and non-native languages.

This research takes an ethnographic approach to theory construction that is grounded in the everyday life of the people we study, their social activities in specific contexts, and what these activities mean to them (Glaser and Strauss, 1967; Erickson, 1986; Watson-Gegeo, 1988; Ramanathan and Atkinson, 1999). As a case study that emerged out of the larger ethnographic project, the investigation reported in this chapter aims not at generalizing from its findings, but at expanding upon and providing alternative visions of literacy practices (see, for example, Dyson, 1995). The in-depth study of cases helps to illuminate the situated nature of reading and writing, the complexity of individual persons, and the practices of literacy. It holds the potential to destablize conceptual boundaries and contribute new understandings of the concepts under study (Stake, 1995).

My research with Willis,[1] the focal student in this case study, was centered around his reading different national and transnational varieties of comic-books. Willis introduced me to his collection of comic-books during my first visit to his home, where I was able to look at the variety of his entire collection and later borrow some for closer reading. I conducted in-depth interviews with Willis, as well as a number of group discussions and conversations with Willis and his friends regarding their comic-book reading practices and other aspects of their daily lives—particularly in relation to their immigration experiences.

In the following, Willis's activities are situated within the larger context of his immigrant experiences and the social practice of comic-book reading as a form of popular culture. My analysis then focuses on how Willis constructed alternative subject positionings via his reading. Most of the interactions reported below were conducted entirely in Cantonese, and subsequently translated into English. In order to preserve the code-switching in Willis's talk in quotes presented below, italicized words were said in English by Willis, while capitalized words indicate emphatic stress.

The Transnational Discourse of Comic-Books

Willis, a 16-year-old high school junior, emigrated from Hong Kong to California with his parents and his older sister before Hong Kong was reverted to Mainland China.[2] After the family had settled down and the father had found work as a Chinese restaurant chef, Willis's mother returned to Hong Kong to continue working in horticulture for the Hong Kong government, which, according to Willis, secured a better income for the family. The family maintained close ties with one another through

Pull between pros/cons
of "non-nativeness"
better opp BUT marginalized
Border Discourses / 87

regular long-distance phone calls and written correspondence. When asked about his immigration experience, Willis said that "his family's identity had fallen" after immigration because of their lack of fluency in English: "We don't know how to talk." However, it also seems that coming to live in the U.S. could provide more political security for his family and educational opportunities for himself. He predicted that Hong Kong would become more like the People's Republic of China (PRC) after the reversion of the British colony to the PRC: "Hong Kong will get worse after the takeover. They [PRC government] say Hong Kong won't change for 50 years, it can change overnight! You really can't trust the Chinese government." In regard to his educational prospects, he thought that the educational diplomas here are widely recognized around the world, and could afford him a more competitive edge even if he was to go back to work in Hong Kong. He had heard from his mother that a son of her friend, who was educated in a lower-track college in the U.S. and who had returned to Hong Kong to find work, was able to compete with graduates of the local prestigious universities and obtained a well-paying job.

Willis traveled in the summer of 1996 to visit his mother and relatives in Hong Kong and in the Guangdong Province of China, during which time he also bought and read a large number of comic-books. In a conversation with some friends from Hong Kong during a social gathering where I was present, Willis commented on what he saw during his visit home last summer. He made some criticisms about the crowded, fast-paced life, the snobbishness of some people in Hong Kong, and the rush to modernize China. Willis recounted how he had witnessed corruption firsthand: The police had unjustly accused and fined his uncle for a misdemeanor, but had pocketed the money themselves.

Willis's schooling experiences were not without obstacles. Like many other immigrant students in the U.S., he felt marginalized both academically and socially in school. When he entered middle school, he was placed in a "low-level" class after being tested on English and Chinese. Although he did well on the Chinese part of the exam, his poor English assessment results led him into a very elementary class with other immigrant students, where, he said, he learned nothing at all for an entire year. After four years of English as a Second Language and bilingual programs, Willis transferred to regular classes within the school. He mentioned that he once "fought" with the school counselor to be placed in the regular and honors classes; the counselor had originally placed him in some English as a Second Language sheltered classes because these classes fitted best with Willis's weekly lesson schedule. Willis recounted how he was afraid that having too many sheltered classes on his transcript would affect future college admission opportunities. He was also taking a number of literature classes because, he said, he had been taunted for being an English as a Second Language student by his peers for too long, and he had to "catch up."

On several occasions, he expressed anger over how some students laughed at him and other Chinese immigrants for their heavy accents and lack of fluency in English, and tried to imitate their speech disparagingly. In an Ethnic Literature class that I visited, I noticed that Willis was unusually quiet and low in morale, and found out later that it was one of the classes where he and a number of Chinese students had been taunted by other students for speaking Chinese and for their accents in English. He described what had happened to one of his classmates:

> Like Feng Jin, he is in 12th grade. He always speaks Chinese, and he speaks English with a heavy accent. He doesn't read very well in English, but it's not really that bad. But then, those people always laugh at him, and imitate his voice, and they imitate in a really disgusting way. He is actually very angry with them, but he always tries hard to keep it down. He has told me, "When it gets to a point I can't stand it any more, I'm gonna knock them over real bad."

In a conversation with Willis and his friends, they told me how the "ABCs" (American Born Chinese) and other "Americanized" Chinese immigrant students looked down on people who spoke Chinese and regarded them as "foreigners" and "stupid." About these peers, Willis and one of his friends said, "They have forgotten their roots, they are also Chinese." They mentioned, as an example, a student from Hong Kong who had been in the U.S. for about 9 months and who claimed he had "forgotten" how to speak Chinese. They said he spoke English all the time, but they didn't think his English was good. "He tries to exaggerate the 'r' sound, but it doesn't really sound right," said Willis in a jocular tone.

Willis added that it was because of this discrimination that Chinese students didn't "mix well" with their English-speaking North American peers. He himself, even though he had made great leaps in his academic studies, did not participate much in the social life of the school. He was unable to make friends with students from "other races" in the classrooms or school clubs, and only sometimes with other Asians. The only reason he had joined two clubs during the past year was that he hoped it would be an advantage to him in applying for college admission. He had heard some teachers and school officials say that doing well academically was not enough to get into the more prestigious universities. At the same time, he was also trying not to let these social activities take time away from reading comic-books—especially Japanese ones—which was one of his favorite pastimes outside school, and which often occupied most of his evenings at home.

The Japanese comic-books—or *comics* for short—that Willis and some of his Chinese peers read were translated into Chinese and copyrighted in Hong Kong. The trading and circulation of comics among these teenagers is a frequent practice, although the number of comics in each personal collection varies from person to person. Willis had one of the largest collections of comics among his peers, and was often sought after for borrowing from. In his judgment, both the ideas and artistic quality of the Japanese comics were superior to those produced in the U.S. and Hong Kong. He had started taking some Japanese language classes offered in his high school in anticipation of reading these comics in their original versions.

As an immigrant student in the American school system—and an immigrant minority within the larger society—Willis's subordinate position was constructed in the school discourse associated with immigrant students, and which is connected to larger societal discourses concerning immigrants. At the same time, he was in a similarly powerless position in the discourse of Chinese Nationals, where the Chinese political system allows little dissension and has compelled his family and many others to emigrate. However, it is important to note that Willis was able in some instances to strategically maneuver himself around these discourses by, on the one hand, using his Chinese sociocultural ties to resist wholesale assimilation into the U.S. society, and, on the other hand, using his sociopolitical status as a legal resident of the U.S. to criticize the social situation and political system in China. Moreover, in participating in a transnational discourse of Japanese comics he is also associating himself with a third community associated with Japanese popular culture, and that does not necessitate any sociopolitical affiliations. Speaking from a position located within Japanese popular culture, Willis simultaneously connects himself to U.S. and Chinese counterparts, and engaging in critique of the two without having to affiliate with either one immediately. By creating a "third space" (Bhabha, 1994) for himself in a transnational discourse of popular youth culture, Willis was able to develop a sense of agency by means of making flexible cross-cultural identifications and in critiquing the sociocultural practices represented in and by different comics. In the following, I discuss this space of transnational critical discourse by analyzing some of the social, discursive and textual dimensions of Willis's comic-book reading practices.

Comic-Book Reading as a Social Practice

As a practice in popular culture, reading comics can be seen as a culture of the people. It is an active form of cultural production by common people that demarcates itself from the elite culture. For instance, Willis and a close friend of his, Randy, who read mostly American and Hong Kong comics, made the following remarks when I asked them how they thought people who were not into comics might regard comics:

Randy: Maybe the more snobbish ones will say, "They're so stupid."
Willis: Yeah, yeah.
Randy: They may show off their great big textbooks and say, "Look at my book!"
Willis: "Look at how sophisticated mine is, yours is so stupid." They're just ignorant.
Randy: They don't know how to appreciate the [comic] books.
Willis: Yeah, they don't know how to appreciate the books, those silly people. The reason they don't read is because they don't know, not because the books are low in quality.

Both the visual (perceptual) and verbal (conversational) aspects of comic-book texts possess the qualities of immediacy and face-to-face interactions which are close to everyday life. The distribution and circulation of these texts among readers (and, in this case, among teenagers reading and circulating them under their desks, in the hallways, during recess, and before and after school away from the surveillance of teachers and other school authorities) is also a practice of the people that produces solidarity and communal life. It is this embodiment of the textures of everyday life that makes comic-books a popular vehicle both for the dissemination of certain cultural values and for opposition to dominant values.

Although the production of comics is controlled to quite an extent by corporations that have a stake in perpetuating the existing norms of society, it is also a form of popular cultural production that needs to be tailored to the needs of the people and amenable to being appropriated by them (Fiske, 1989; Willis, 1993). Some manifestations of its oppositional nature can be found in the use of taboo and vernacular language (measured against standard linguistic norms and standards), the celebration of the wits and prowess of the ordinary person (as opposed to the educated elite), and especially among the teenagers I studied, the deconstruction of the image or essence of "academically poor" students, as I discovered from talking with Willis and reading some of his personal library of comic books. For instance, the teenage male protagonist in Willis's favorite comic-book series, who is branded as a poor student in school, is able to demonstrate his intelligence and passion for justice by solving many puzzling criminal cases.

As a form of transnational popular youth culture, the translation of national varieties of comics and their distribution across national boundaries have, on the one hand, generated a high degree of cross-cultural exchange and fusion, and, on the other hand, facilitated a process of sociocultural critique through the comparison and contrast of different national varieties. Willis's reading of Japanese comics and the critical discourse that emerged from it were situated within the larger social practice among his peers on both sides of the Pacific of reading comics from both the U.S. and Hong Kong. Hence, by carving out a discursive practice for himself in the midst of this transnational circulation of comics, he was able to engage in critique of the U.S. and Hong Kong (Chinese) societies. It is this discursive construction of Willis's reading practice that I turn to next.

Reading Translated Japanese Comics

An analysis of the translated Japanese comic books shows a cross-cultural mixture of signs and images. As a text that originates from Japanese society, Japanese comics undoubtedly encode many of the beliefs, values, behaviors, and material conditions of Japanese life. These appear, for example, in the titles of people (such as parts of Japanese honorifics), the terminology for different social institutions (such as schools and government offices), and the untranslated written artifacts within the stories themselves (such as receipts and bulletins written in Japanese script). However, in their Chinese translation, these inscriptions of Japanese culture are shadowed by the Chinese cultural resonances that signified in the Chinese linguistic code. Although much of the translation is in standard written Chinese, it is also interspersed with a considerable amount of Cantonese vernacular language, since the market for such comics is predominantly located in Hong Kong and other related cultural milieux. Moreover, in many of these books, different types of Westernized or Americanized images appear in parts of the texts—in the form of English words in the table of contents, in the sketches of the authors and characters (for example, one picture shows the author with a cup of coffee and a doughnut in hand), and in the subject matter of and settings for the stories (for example, one story depicts a group of teenagers performing a Western drama in a European-style mansion in Japan). Hence, these translated Japanese comics, as hybrid textual forms, facilitated Willis's participation in a transnational popular youth culture.

On several occasions, both during casual conversations and more focused interviews, Willis contrasted the different varieties of comics according to the professional attitude, creativity, artistry, and cultural character of the people who produced them. He mentioned how, compared with the artistic design of the Japanese comics, those in Hong Kong were lower in quality due to their pursuit of quick profits:

> The difference between the comics of the Hong Kong people and the Japanese people is in the BACKGROUND. Those [artists] who are well-known in Japan are never so lazy [sloppy]. But those in Hong Kong, because they want to turn things out really fast, they are more lazy. I just don't appreciate that type of thing.

As for the American comics, Willis criticized them for their extreme self-glorification and lack of creativity:

> I really don't appreciate those, because... their heroes seem like they will never, never be defeated, even if they are beaten up like CRAZY [original Cantonese idiomatic phrase has the meaning of "handicap"]... in the end they are bound to win again... Even if they have *tragedy ending*, they will still make themselves... very ARROGANT. Like *X-men*, *Swamps*, *Spiderman*, *Batman*, I almost can't bear to read them... What the Americans come up with are only... if it is not about the hero saving the pretty girl, then it is about victory and glory. And no matter what, they are fighting all over the place and beating up one another... And they make THEMSELVES, THEMSELVES... usually they themselves are the heroes. For example, the United States has also produced a version of the *Streetfighter* [comic and video game; the original version is from Japan]. The main character in the *Streetfighter* isn't *Gaile*—seems like it should be *Waile*, a Japanese fellow. They [Americans] make *Gaile* the main character, the strongest one in the whole *story*, and how he is *hero*, things like that. I mean, they sort of make themselves, themselves the greatest, the United States, long live the United States!

By contrast, in talking about Japanese comics, Willis mentioned a list of distinguishing characteristics, such as creativity, variety, educational quality, and poignancy, that he could identify with and quite strongly desired. In the the following quote, Kam Tin Yat is the teenage male protagonist in one of Willis's favorite Japanese comic series. Kam Tin Yat is branded as a poor student in school, but he is able to demonstrate his intelligence and passion for justice in solving many puzzling criminal cases in the community.

> After reading them, you want to follow them. You also want to have that sort of thing. For example, like when I saw *Ding Dong* [Japanese comic book]... if I had this Ding Dong (chuckles), I could even control the world. What I'm saying is you fantasize together with the book... there are things you can think about. And sometimes there are books which contain some lessons in them, some educational stuff. Those books sometimes teach you perhaps not to be greedy, or, uh, uh, to be more kind to others, not to be arrogant, stuff like that. Sometimes they would... like Kam Tin Yat... After reading it, you will feel that you can think more. Those books would sometimes talk about some FACTS. I mean, like those things you don't usually learn at school, you can sometimes learn from reading those books... Those that fantasize oneself as the hero, although I haven't really done so myself. But, but those can be, uh, pretty *attractive* too... And their stories are a lot more attractive. They have some that are really intriguing. And some are... as you read it, you feel a little sad, and things like that. How will you ever feel sad when you read *X-men*? One falls dead and another rushes up, one falls dead and another rushes up. That's the difference.

A closer look at Willis's discourse on comics shows us how each text positions Willis differently as a reader and offers him a different socio-cultural identity. His use of personal pronouns is one way in which he indexes his relationship to American and Hong Kong cultures. The use of third-person collective pronominal forms. For example, using "they" and "those people" to designate the people in Hong Kong, and "they" and "themselves" to designate the Americans, sets both up as distinct objects of criticism. The repeated and emphatic stress on the reflexive pronoun "themselves" serves to accentuate the self-centeredness and self-aggrandizement of the American psyche. While Willis is distancing himself from these two groups through third person pronouns, he identifies himself with other readers of Japanese comics through the use of first and second person pronouns. These pronouns express a distinct personal relationship to the Japanese experience in relation to Japanese comics.

The different social realities depicted in these comics are revealed through Willis's linguistic modalities. The hype of American rhetoric resonates through his use in Cantonese of emphatic modifiers such as "a lot," "very," "incredibly," "never," and the superlatives "strongest," "greatest." Such modifiers give a factual and categorical quality to his statements. Willis's interpretation of the automaticity, almost robot-like behavior of American characters is also signaled through the repetition of words and phrases such as "beaten up like crazy," and "one falls dead and another rushes up." In contrast to these, Willis's description of Japanese comics is much more nuanced. Here, modal auxiliaries and adverbs such as "could," "would," "sometimes," "perhaps," and the conditional "if" (as in, "If I had this Ding Dong"), serve to create a relativized world of possibility and human contingency. Indeed, the verb "want" (as in, "You want to follow them") expresses Willis's desire to make this possibility a reality.

By projecting himself into the textual community of Japanese comics, Willis, a non-native reader, has discovered a new self-aligned with what he perceives as the Japanese "hero"; one that is distanced from both U.S. and Hong Kong comic-book "heroes." Comparing the construction of heroes in these different societies, he said:

> The U.S. [hero] is the most... upright and courageous one. There are the good guys and the bad guys, and nothing else. The ones in Hong Kong, there is this group and that group, the good guys and bad guys, and some sort of in-between. Most of them just follow what's in the games and movies, usually they just follow what's trendy... As for the Japanese characters, they won't be drawn... all handsome and stuff. They have some who are ugly, silly, and tall, and short. The American ones are like: if you are not smart enough you are ruled out of the game, that's what is in the story.... The Japanese hero... like Kam Tin Yat, you can hardly call him a hero, but I guess you can still call him a hero. He sometimes *acts* like an *idiot*, and does some stupid things; like he would trip over while walking along the street (laughs)...I can't imagine the U.S. will produce a character like that—almost impossible.

It is clear that Willis found the Japanese notion of "hero" in the texts he read more appealing than in the comics produced in the U.S. or Hong Kong. He even had difficulty equating the Japanese male protagonist he described as a "hero" with the way in which the Americans or Hong Kong people view heroes. Here, where the nature of the Hong Kong "hero" is nondescript (possibly reflecting the lack of clear status and autonomy of Hong Kong society), and the American "hero" is the quintessential good guy with a standard form and character (suggesting perhaps the monolithic construction of a U.S. national culture that marginalizes what it views as "other"), Willis sees the Japanese "hero" as "the common folk," as the less than perfect people, who live through predicaments in life with thoughtfulness and a sense of humor. Willis's place is indeed an in-between place. Between the impossibility of identifying with the native Hong Kong person he used to be, and his refusal to identify with the standardized American person whose English he now speaks. Willis has appropriated a textual identity from the Japanese comics and uses it—within the context of this research study—as a third place from which to reflect on the cultural practices of U.S. and Hong Kong society.

Conclusion

The discourse of comics practiced by Willis can be seen as a localized space that is created out of a transnational flow of cultural and material production and his own migrant experiences and perspectives. The cross-cultural characteristics of the transaction of comics in today's world makes possible both the contact of different cultural forms and the creation of a transcultural world of readers. In creating his own (third space) in a transnational culture, Willis is drawing on the discourses from his home and host countries, as well as on the discourse derived from the textual world of Japanese comics. And it is within this (border culture) that he exercises agency in defining his subject positions and reflecting on the different social systems and ways of life around him.

This case study attempts to show that while many immigrant youth are subject to discrimination in the U.S. school system and society, there are still sources of potential empowerment for them through their engagement in practices that develop their intercultural voices and perspectives. Listening to and observing Willis talk about his experiences and participation in the popular culture of comics, I was able to witness how the special places of immigrant youth could be valued and promoted. This is a place where there are multiple linguistic and cultural affiliations, where the formation of identity reaches beyond the national borders, where people actively mobilize their diverse sources of identifications to resist subordination, and where new subject positions emerge out of cross-cultural exchange and the negotiation of difference.

The experiences of Willis help us to see the limitations of a certain popular formulation of "multiculturalism," which allows for only a certain degree of diversity by treating minority cultures as the inherent and discrete attributes of groups of people—often aestheticized as ethnic food, commodities and festivals—who continue to exist on the fringes of U.S. society. Instead, we need to understand multiculturalism as extending beyond national borders and constituting the experiences of more and more people in this age of increasing globalization (Appadurai, 1996; Hannerz, 1996; Grossberg, 2000). It is a form of multiculturalism that converges in the individual, and gets expressed in various ways as the individual enters into different social contexts and relationships (Johnston and Bean, 1997; Rampton, 1995). In this reconception of multiculturalism, the immigrant students are perceived not through the lens of a "national culture" and found lacking, but are valued for their unique cross-cultural perspectives, and their potential for bringing cultures together for mutual critique and enrichment.

Notes

1. The names of my study informant and other students are changed for confidentiality.
2. The data presented here also are discussed in Kramsch and Lam (1999).

Works Cited

Anderson, B. (1991). *Imagined communities: Reflections on the origins and spread of nationalism*. London: Verso.

Appadurai, A. (1996). *Modernity at large: Cultural dimensions of globalization*. Minneapolis, MN: University of Minnesota Press.

Basch, L., Schiller, N. G., and Blanc, C. S. (1994). *Nations unbound: Transnational projects, postcolonial predicaments, and deterritorialized nation-states*. Luxembourg: Gordon & Breach Publishers.

Bhabha, H. (1994). *The location of culture*. London: Routledge.

Carter, P. (1992). *Living in a new country: History, travelling and language*. London: Faber & Faber.

Chambers, I. (1994). *Migrancy, culture, identity*. New York: Routledge.

Cook-Gumperz, J. (1986). Literacy and schooling: An unchanging equation? In J. Cook-Gumperz (Ed.), *The social construction of literacy* (pp. 1–25). Cambridge: Cambridge University Press.

Dyson, A. (1995). *Children out of bounds: The power of case studies in expanding visions of literacy development*. Berkeley, CA: Center for the Study of Writing.

Erickson, F. (1986). Qualitative methods in research on teaching. In M. Wittrock (Ed.), *Handbook of research on teaching* (pp. 119–161). New York: Macmillan.

Fairclough, N. (1992). *Discourse and social change*. Oxford, UK: Blackwell Publishers.

Fiske, J. (1989). *Understanding popular culture*. Boston, MA: Unwin Hyman.

Gee, J. (1996). *Social linguistics and literacies: Ideology in discourses*. London: Falmer.

Giroux, H. (1994). Living dangerously: Identity politics and the new cultural racism. In H. Giroux and P. McLaren (Eds.), *Between borders: Pedagogy and the politics of cultural Studies* (pp. 29–56). New York: Routledge.

Glaser, B. and Strauss, A. (1967). *The discovery of grounded theory: Strategies for qualitative research*. Chicago: Aldine Publishing Co.

Grossberg, L. (2000). History, imagination, and the politics of belonging: Between the death and the fear of history. In P. Gilroy, L. Grossberg, and A. McRobbie (Eds.), *Without guarantees: In honor of Stuart Hall* (pp. 148–165). London: Verso.

Hannerz, U. (1996). *Transnational connections: Culture, people, places*. New York: Routledge.

Johnston, B. and Bean, J. M. (1997). Self-expression and linguistic variation. *Language in Society*, 26 (2), 221–246.

Kramsch, C. (1997). The privilege of the non-native speaker. *Publications of the modern language association of America*, 112 (3), 359–369.

——— and Lam, W. (1999). Textual identities: The importance of being non-native. In G. Braine (Ed.), *Non-native educators in English language teaching* (pp. 57–72). Mahwah, NJ: Lawrence Erlbaum.

Lankshear, C. with Lawler, M. (1987). *Literacy, schooling and revolution*. London: Falmer.

Lavie, S. and Swedenburg, T. (1996). Between and among the boundaries of culture: Bridging text and lived experience in the third timespace. *Cultural Studies*, 10 (1), 154–179.

Macedo, D. (1995). *Literacies of power: What Americans are not allowed to know*. Boulder, CO: Westview Press.

Nieto, S. (2000). *Affirming diversity: The sociopolitical context of multicultural education*. New York: Longman.

Olsen, L. M. (1997). *Made in America: Immigrant students in our public schools*. New York: New Press.

Omi, M. and Winant, H. (1994). *Racial formation in the United States from the 1960s to the 1990s*. New York: Routledge.

Ong, A. (1993). On the edge of empires: Flexible citizenship among Chinese in diaspora. *Positions*, 1 (3), 745–778.

Pratt, M. L. (1992). *Imperial eyes: Travel writing and transculturation*. New York: Routledge.

Ramanathan, V. and Atkinson, D. (1999). Ethnographic approaches and methods in L2 writing research: A critical guide and review. *Applied linguistics*, 20 (1): 44–70.

Rampton, B. (1995). *Crossing: language and ethnicity among adolescents*. London: Longman.

Roediger, D. R. (1991). *The wages of whiteness: Race and the making of the American working class*. London: Verso.

Said, E. (1993). *Culture and imperialism*. New York: Vintage Books.

———. (1979). *Orientalism*. New York: Vintage Books.

Skutnabb-Kangas, T. and Cummins, J. (1988). *Minority education: From shame to struggle*. Clevedon, UK: Multilingual Matters.

Stake, R. E. (1995). *The art of case study research*. Thousand Oaks, CA: Sage.

Watson-Gegeo, K. A. (1988). Ethnography in ESL: Defining the essentials. *TESOL Quarterly*, 22 (3): 575–592.

Willis, P. (1993). *Common culture*. Boulder, CO: Westview Press.

RESPONSE to

"Border Discourses"

Claire Kramsch

In her study of Willis, a 16-year-old high school immigrant from Hong Kong, Eva Lam shows how linguistic marginalization and cultural alienation can lead youngsters to seek alternative communities of practice—such as the community of consumers of Japanese comics—to regain their sense of dignity and self-worth. Not only does Willis develop an expertise in the aesthetic and moral evaluation of these comics, but he becomes a member of a transnational popular youth culture that is neither Chinese nor American, but a hybrid mix of Japanese culture, Chinese language, and American icons. This textual world of common folk Japanese characters, with human frailties that remind him of his own, leaves him "room for manoeuvering" (cf., Chambers, 1991). Not only do these characters exercise humor and irony towards themselves and each other, but readers are free to both enjoy and critique the design, the narrative, the language, and the social practices represented in these comic books. This aesthetic stance enables Willis to find a social identity for himself in the realm of the imagination and in the interstices of dominant cultures.

Through Lam's analysis, we discover that the problem Willis had with his English is not, in fact, a linguistic problem, but a problem of subject position. Resenting both the aesthetic sloppiness of the design of Hong Kong comics, and the patriotic arrogance of American plots, Willis finds a singular pleasure in entering the less-than-perfect world of Japanese heroes in their Chinese translation, where Japanese, Chinese, and Arabic typographical characters are counterpoised in a hybrid in-between space of global youth culture. It is in this literate border space, Lam argues, that Willis "exercises agency in defining his subject positions" and in reflecting critically "on the different social systems and ways of life around him."

There are three aspects of interest in this border space: It is mediated by text; it is a hybrid linguistic space; and it enacts an oppositional stance vis-à-vis dominant discourses.

It seems at first sight paradoxical that Willis would find his social identity in textual productions of a caricatural kind rather than in live interactions with his peers. What this and similar immigrant experiences suggest is the importance of literacy as the symbolic mediation between who you are and who you might become. But there is more. Paraphrasing Ricoeur (1981: 220), one could say that understanding oneself has nothing to do with an immediate grasping of one's identity or with an emotional identification with a hero in a comic book. It is entirely mediated by the interpretive procedures used by youngsters engaged in critiquing, evaluating, and commenting upon a common text; in this case, Japanese comics. It is within this dialogue on a common text that the sense of self emerges. This self is a symbolic self (Deacon, 1997: 452), to whom the text holds up, like a mirror, vicarious experiences and future potentialities, but with the critical distance that enable the reader to grow into his or her own.

The brazen juxtaposition in these comic books of an American doughnut and a Japanese school uniform, of English, Mandarin, and Cantonese words, of Chinese, Japanese, and Arabic characters, gives a select community of multilingual readers and speakers access to the cosmopolitan exclusivity of linguistically hybrid Selves. It offers them the pleasures of forbidden crossings into foreign linguistic territories (Rampton, 1995). Through the multimodal semiotic channels of image, representations of sound (WHACK! ZAPP!), and text, readers can fashion for themselves a rich cultural environment free from the competitive pressures of school and society, and from the commercial pressures of television and other media.

Ultimately, we have to ask ourselves whether the reading of Japanese comics is a strategy of resistance on the part of these youngsters or whether it is not, rather, an oppositional tactic (de Certeau, 1980, 1984). Lam endows Willis with "agency...to resist subordination." But what kind of agency is this? Because these youngsters do not have a "proper locus" of belonging, and because they feel disenfranchised in mainstream American society, they do not strive to fight against the discrimination they encounter in school, but, rather, they attempt to neutralize it by finding their gratification elsewhere. Such manoeuvers, one might argue, are less strategies of resistance and more the calculated applications of tactics within and through the cracks and gaps of dominated spaces (de Certeau, 1980, 1984). They leave the current ethnic discrimination intact. In fact, it is this very discrimination that gives the community of Japanese comics readers its sense of (oppositional) pride and identity. But these tactics are not without risks. The Japanese comic book industry is a thriving commercial affair. It enables Willis and his friends to resist, as Lam points out, both their "wholesale assimilation into U.S. society" and any kind of nostalgia for China; but, at the same time, it makes them vulnerable to the commercial practices of the global corporate economy. The fact that they reconstitute on a global plane the community that failed them on the local plane can make them easy targets for multinational take-overs. One can imagine a day when Willis and his friends, disenchanted with the global commercialization of their favorite comic books, might return to regional or local ways of acquiring the profit of distinction they are now seeking on the transnational level.

The competitive struggle in the field of cultural (re)production (Bourdieu, 1993) is a reminder of the extent to which discourses and identities have to be constantly redefined and renegotiated—not through heroic deeds and subversive strategies, but through short-term tactics that seize the opportunities such as those given by the comic-book industry to divert the products of that industry for their own use. Willis's tactics are part of the identity formation of a transnational youth culture that has now embraced the global without rejecting its local affiliations. But this identity can hardly be called a *place* of one's own, it is more an art of making-do between places—comic books' no-place, a *utopia*.

✱ BAND-AID for problem ✱

Works Cited

Bourdieu, P. (1993). *The field of cultural production. Essays on art and literature*. Edited and Introduced by Randal Johnson. New York: Columbia University Press.

Chambers, R. (1991). *Room for manoeuver: Reading (the) oppositional (in) narrative*. Chicago, IL: University of Chicago Press.

de Certeau, M. (1980). On the oppositional practices of everyday life. *Social Text*, 3, 3–43.

———. (1984). *The practice of everyday life*. Berkeley: University of California Press.

Deacon, T. W. (1997). *The symbolic species*. New York: W.W. Norton.

Rampton, B. (1995). *Crossing language and ethnicity among adolescents*. London: Longman.

Ricoeur, P. (1981). *Hermeneutics and the human sciences*. (J.B. Thompson, Ed. & Trans.). Cambridge: Cambridge University Press.

CHAPTER FIVE

"I used to go to school. Now I learn." Unschoolers Critiquing the Discourse of School

Beth Lewis Samuelson

lthough rare even thirty years ago, today homeschooling is the choice of approximately 1.5 million children and their families (Golden, 2000; Krantrowitz and Wingert, 1998). They are part of a growing phenomenon—parents choosing to remove their children from the compulsory public school system and educate them at home. Their reasons for this choice are extremely varied. Although the early pioneers of the movement were mostly Protestants or persons of libertarian persuasions, many families from other walks of life are also joining the homeschooling community. A quick survey of the bibliography of *Growing Without Schooling*, a major bimonthly newsletter devoted to homeschooling, features "Russian homeschoolers," "Japanese school refusers," and "Homeschoolers of color," among others. Despite legal challenges and opposition from public school interests, the movement appears to be set to grow substantially.

The small-scale ethnography reported here is not intended to argue for or against homeschooling. While the topic is admittedly controversial, it holds an attraction because it has received relatively little attention from education researchers. This silence is similar to the silences of the absent students who leave the public school system, many of whom eventually find alternative modes of education, including unschooling, but whose experiences remain largely unrecorded. In part, these are the silences Lauryn Hill hinted at in the introduction to her compact disk and referred to in the introduction to this book. This study addresses such a silence, a gap in our understanding of the goals and concerns of the education research, much of which has focused on teaching and learning in school. Homeschoolers, and especially the unschoolers who are the focus of this study, believe they learn in a way that is radically different from school learning. The experiences of those who have chosen to take full responsibility for their learning have important lessons to teach us about what we assume is necessary for education.

The stories behind the silences and reported in this chapter focus on two of unschooled young people who are learning independently in nontraditional ways. They call themselves "unschoolers" because their philosophy of education does not require that they follow the schedules and rhythms of traditional schooling practices. We will listen to their voices as they discuss their views of schooling in their online journals. The online journals provide a rich source of information for answering some key questions about these teenage unschoolers: What goals do they pursue when they are free from the constraints of compulsory schooling, when they can choose what they will learn and who will teach them? What projects do they choose? How do they go about realizing them? And most importantly, what do they think of themselves in relation to this process? To borrow Sheffer's (1995) phrase from her study of the self-esteem of homeschooled girls, what is their "sense of self"?

This project is conducted in the spirit of the new interest in nonschool literacy practices of a wide variety of communities, prompted by the New Literacy Studies of Street (1993), and by Gee's work with social discourses (Gee, 1991, 1996). Ethnographers of educational practices who have been inspired by the New Literacy Studies take us to worlds we would never be able to visit without their help. Recent studies have already examined communities similar to unschoolers in their distinctiveness and relative inaccessibility. These include ethnographies of the literate culture of traditional Amish communities (Fishman, 1988); the long-distance letter-writing and literacy learning practices of migrant Chicano Mexicanos workers in the United States (Guerra, 1998); and the distribution of English and Navajo literacy practices in Navajo Nation schools (McLaughlin, 1994). Such ethnographies challenge the "commonsense" notion of what literacy is and what forms are important, and have broad implications for the uses of schooling. This study also examines the ways in which unschoolers posting online journals engage in literacy practices and form a unique discourse community. According to Gee (1996: 128), discourses are "ways of displaying (through words, actions, values, and beliefs) membership in a particular social group or social network, people who associate with each other around a common set of interests, goals, and activities" and they "create, produce, and reproduce opportunities for people to be and recognize certain kinds of people."

Definitions of Homeschooling

While homeschooling has become common enough that almost everyone in the United States knows of someone who is involved in it, homeschoolers often remark that definitions provided by outsiders are often limited and misleading. This problem is further compounded for unschoolers since they are fewer in number and are less well known. Therefore, the definitions of unschooling provided here are derived from unschooling and homeschooling sources. Unschooling is technically a subset of homeschooling. Families identify themselves as unschooling when they do not follow traditional school curricula and schedules. Children decide what they wish to explore, and whom they wish to be their teachers, and parents serve as resources to help locate tutors, community college classes, books, equipment, or whatever the child requires for pursuing his or her studies. The Homeschool Association of California clarifies the uniqueness of unschoolers by distinguishing them from homeschoolers and adherents of various well-known alternative modes of education in this definition provided on its website:

> Some homeschooling families operate like small-scale versions of conventional schools, with textbooks and tests and traditional grades. Other families freely adapt ideas from other alternative educational philosophies such as Waldorf, Montessori, Reggio Emilia, or the Sudbury model, while still more give their children considerable control over what is learned and how learning takes place. (Homeschool Association of California, 2000: 1)

what are benefits of limits to this?

While many families educating at home mimic the rhythms and structures of school, unschooling families allow their children a great deal of freedom in planning and implementing their own learning projects until, as they claim, learning and living become indistinguishable. *Growing Up Without Schooling*, Holt (1979), emphasizes that unschooling means "allowing for children's natural learning rather than giving them unasked-for teaching." Sheffer, author of two books on homeschoolers, points out that this means children can choose who will teach them and also decide how they will make use of their teachers' skills and knowledge (Sheffer, 1992). This idea challenges traditional, basic assumptions about teaching and learning.

Perhaps the best definitions of unschooling come from the learners themselves and their parents:

> Imagine, waking up in the morning and having all day, all tomorrow, and every-day, to learn what you choose. Imagine, being able to direct your own life. Unschooling is self-directed. You choose what, when, how, why, and to what depth you learn.
>
> I consider myself Unschooled. I learn what I want, and how, when, and why I want to learn it. I am a 15-year-old college student. I have time for college because I don't go to compulsory schools. I made a choice not to attend com-pulsory school. I am now in control of my learning. I have the choice, to spend my day reading philosophy or play the guitar for eight hours. (Mona)

For Sandy Keane, a Canadian mother homeschooling her three children, learning occurs through doing. The family makes no distinction between teacher and learner, and no one is forced to study something because it is prescribed as appropriate for their developmental stage:

> To me, unschooling is more of an attitude than a system. The lion's share of the learning is incidental, i.e. inherent in our day-to-day activities. Some of the learning is conscious and some isn't. We don't separate ourselves into teachers and learners, but rather consider that we're all learning and sharing all the time. (Keane 1999: 1)

Learning at home in the fashion of unschoolers will not resemble learn-ing in school, nor will teaching. Keane describes an innovative math workshop taught by a local math teacher who was trying out ideas and concepts he could not implement at school: logic puzzles, games, manip-ulatives, and the like. Keane describes how the activity differs from a school lesson: The children are there by choice; they are free to get up and leave at any time, but they don't because they enjoy the class and because they are learning to stick with a task, even if it is frustrating (Keane, 1999).

Learning at home does not resemble the managed child development neatly laid out in stages or grade levels by professional teachers and edu-cation researchers. Nonetheless, when explaining their choices to state education officials or outsiders, parents learn to speak of their children's activities in curricular terms, as a program they are administering to their children, when in reality much of the learning taking place through much more mundane activities.

Contrary to the connotations evoked by Howard Gardner in his book, *The Unschooled Mind* (1991: 5), "unschooled" does not mean that students have retained "the initial conceptions, stereotypes, and 'scripts'" they brought to school when they were five years old. With such potent definitions lurking in the public consciousness, it is no wonder that home-schoolers and unschoolers wish to define themselves as they see fit. Perhaps the best synonym for the unschooler is the *autodidact;* someone who is self-educated.

Literature on Homeschooling

The modern homeschooling movement is a relatively recent phenomenon within the U.S. educational scene (Divoky, 1983). A handful of recent studies have examined parental motivations for removing their children from public schools (Gray, 1992; Hetzel, 1998; Krupnick, 1980; Van Galen and Pitman, 1994), the development of self-concept in home-schooled children (Sheffer, 1995; Taylor, 1987), and parent and administrator perceptions of homeschooling (McGraw, 1990).

A small number of research reports have examined various aspects of the practices of homeschooling families, but very few have looked at the literate practices of homeschooled or unschooled children. In the area of early literacy development, Hetzel (1997) surveyed homeschooling families to learn the amount of time they spent on literacy or literacy related activities each day. Literacy-related activities targetted by Hetzel included reading (together or alone), writing instruction, solitary writing, and phonics instruction. Results showed that homeschooled children spend between 2.25 and 3.75 hours per day on literacy-related activities. She also surveyed the parents on their methodologies for teaching reading and found that approximately 52 percent employed a combination of phonics and whole language. Since these terms in themselves are highly controversial, it is doubtful that Hetzel's results illuminate anything useful because she did not define what the terms might have meant to the parents she surveyed.

A study focused on older students, and published under the title *Writing Because We Love to: Homeschoolers at Work*, documents Sheffer's correspondence with several teenage girls engaged in writing projects of their own choosing (Sheffer, 1992). As the editor of *Growing Without Schooling*, Sheffer printed a notice to adolescent writers inviting them to send her their work for reading and comment. She reports that her writing apprentices did not find writing an onerous or boring task, but instead devoted much time to doing their work. This attitude toward work, a theme that is common to many of the pieces in this volume, is central to the production of online journals as well. The students whose views are in this chapter did not write their journals in order to complete a set assignment.

In a separate study, Sheffer also interviewed homeschooled teenage girls to get a sense of their developing self-confidence and independence and noted that the homeschooled girls she knew "didn't sound like people who were losing their self-confidence or distrusting their own voices or burying their hopes and dreams under a façade of compliance" (Sheffer, 1995).

Unschoolers as a Discourse Community

Unschoolers share a discourse community that is distinguished by a strong sense of freedom or liberation. This theme runs through a number of publications and journals that serve as identifying hallmarks for the group. Likewise, the teenage unschoolers whose journals are surveyed here share a sense of belonging to a meaningful group or social network that Gee (1991: 3) describes as so necessary to a discourse community. Their centers of discourse and the themes of interaction described here constitute part of the "identity kit" of unschooled teenagers.

Several printed media and meeting places help to build the cohesiveness of the community and its outlook. One of the central publications defining the unschooling movement is the bimonthly newsletter already mentioned: *Growing Without Schooling*. Founded in 1977 by John Holt, one of the thought-leaders of the homeschooling movement,[1] the magazine serves as a forum where parents and children can find ideas, activities, research, and resources for home education.[2] *Growing Without Schooling* also publishes first-person accounts of learning and teaching at home. The publication draws its readership from both parents and children and caters to the broad spectrum of choices available to homeschooling families.

While *Growing Without Schooling* is a forum for both adults and children, for unschooled teenagers two particular centers for information and meeting provide additional input. A book titled, *The Teenage Liberation Handbook: How to Quit School and Get a Real Life Education*, by Grace Llewellyn (1998), gives teenagers practical advice for taking control of their own education through non-traditional learning, early enrolment in college, and apprenticeships. This book contributes to the "liberation" terminology that is common in the discourse of the unschooled teenagers by providing detailed descriptions of how to manage self-education

liberation /Discourse practices [margin note]

("Unschooling Math," "Unschooling Foreign Languages"), how to get into college without going to high school, and how to manage doubtful parents. The *Liberation Handbook* also contains detailed advice on learning to write that doesn't accord great importance to teachers: "Take a writing course—*if* you trust the teacher" (original emphasis; Llewellyn 1998: 240). Also included is a lengthy excerpt from the journal of one of Sheffer's correspondent writing apprentices.

Llewellyn also operates the annual Not Back to School Camp in rural Oregon, which attracts teenagers from around the country. Many unschoolers write enthusiastically about Not Back to School Camp on their listserves and in chatrooms. They attend every year and friendships made there are maintained by means of email correspondence. While they normally do not have difficulties establishing active social lives in their hometowns, the camp fills their need for a group of peers who fully share their unique perspectives and attitudes.

This community of unschoolers would be less well defined without digital communication technologies such as email, listserves, and Internet relay chatrooms. Homeschoolers report that contrary to the popular impressions that homeschoolers lack socialization, they have rich contacts with children of all ages, both homeschooled and non-homeschooled. However, they frequently have limited face-to-face contact with other unschoolers of the same age, people who share their attitudes regarding school and the importance of being independent. They meet online, where their discussions frequently center on the distinctiveness of their experiences as unschoolers, their sense of distance from public school practices, their vocal independence and freethinking spirit, and their aspirations, dreams and plans for pursuing their learning goals.

Despite its commitment to learning and other socially valued norms and mores, this discourse community is nevertheless very different from most other discourse communities. Liberation from school means that these youngsters have not acquired the secondary discourse of formal schooling that is shared, to some degree, by most Americans. What happens when children don't acquire this secondary discourse? Gee (1996: 140) specifically mentions autodidacts as persons unlikely to ever be accepted into mainstream discourses because of their non-conformist education. The emphasis on individualism in American culture makes it easy to forget the importance of a "proper socialization." However, even though unschoolers and home-schoolers have removed themselves from public school socialization, this quick dismissal of their potential seems ill advised. While it is most likely true that they will always be on the outside of certain discourse communities, their critique of the discourse of schooling makes them possessors of a "powerful discourse." Just as powerful critiques of American culture coming from other sectors have the potential to bring about changes for the better in mainstream culture, the discourse of these unschoolers has the potential to help bring about changes for the better in the way people in the United States talk about and do education.

Indeed, unschoolers have situated themselves in a "community of practice" that shares a set of social or cultural practices that is remarkable for the way it critiques the discourse of schooling (Reder, 1994: 33). They have acquired a distinctive voice—one that many outsiders might consider arrogant in its sense of self-assurance and purposefulness. In contrast to many of their public school counterparts also keeping online journals, they do not seem to express a great deal of angst and aimlessness.

Their discourse is ideological, as are all discourses (Street, 1993). Many of them are activists and espouse favorite causes, such as youth rights, gay rights, and environmentalism. They make use of their literacy skills to write articles, publish newsletters and fliers, and create websites promulgating their positions.

The Online Journals

The most important source of initial information for this study has been the online journals of two unschooled teenage girls: Jasmine and Ellen.[3] The phenomenon of the online journal is itself an interesting site for study since it has occurred relatively recently and is by no means limited to unschooled and homeschooled teenagers. Many public schoolers are also posting regular journal entries and linking together in elite "webrings." Jessica Wilber, a homeschooled teenager, has published her own how-to book on journaling: *Totally Private and Personal: Journaling Ideas for Girls and Young Women* (1996). Since a major feature of journaling is its privacy, it is fascinating to consider the reasons why these journals—or *web logs*—appear on the Internet at all. Jasmine's and Ellen's journals differ significantly from their public schooling counterparts as they reflect the distinctive experience of unschooling, but their online world is by no means separate. Online journalers read each other's sites, create links to their favorite sites, and respond to each other in their posting.

Jasmine's and Ellen's journals have been analyzed for their attitudes about learning and schooling, their descriptions of their projects and interests, and for their sense of self; that is, their self-concepts. These girls have served as my primary informants. A brief bio on each is listed below.

> Jasmine: I am a teenager who sleeps too much, stays up too late, reads too much, listens to too much music, checks my e-mail too much;) and daydreams WAY too much. I am a libertarian, unschooler, autodidact, and believe in equal rights for teenagers. And that's not all. Because I am also an artist, writer, musician, and a free person who loves outdoors and animals. And I'm only 14 years old. I live with my mom, dad, and brother in New England, in a pretty rural town. I used to go to school. Now I learn.

Jasmine reports that she left school because she didn't believe that "learning takes place in a specific place at a specific time and in a specific way." She believes that she will learn no matter what she is doing. She sees one of the great advantages of unschooling as not having to separate school from the "real world," since they live in the real world all the time:

> Jasmine: When you're an unschooler, like me, you learn how to live in the "real world" before you have to live on your own. Ever notice how after people graduate they have a hard time adjusting? Well, unschoolers don't have to adjust, because they're already living in the "real world."

[handwritten margin note: Good point? But... socialization?]

Jasmine frequently expressed very strong objections to public school although she once attended school.

Ellen and her family are observant Jews living in New Haven, Connecticut.

> Ellen: I am a *homeschooled teenager* who lives in one of those tiny little states in New England, USA. [...] *Writing* is a big part of my life, and I am constantly thinking up stories and writing *essays*, thoughts, and more. I have a mailing list for young writers on the Internet, called *MUSE*. Of course, since I write, I also read a lot. I am reading more nonfiction now—I'm into books about physics, and the universe. I'm practically devouring them! It's so much fun. Reading books makes me ask questions, and really think about the world and about myself.

The italicized portions of Ellen's bio signify hyperlinks to other webpages she has constructed and are part of a key feature of her website, which she uses as a forum for her many interests and pursuits. She enjoys fashion, so she made a page on her site to cover her interests. She also has pages on her two favorite activist causes: unschooling and youth rights.

Unschoolers Liberated: Attitudes About School

The sentiments these young people express about compulsory schooling are often similar to their counterparts who are still attending school. A major difference, however, is their sense of liberation, which is a major theme in their writing. Jasmine's words capture some of the jargon that these unschoolers often use to express their sense of freedom (March 22, 1999):

> I was thinking about school earlier today. That's not that unusual for me though. It's not like I want to think about school, but for some reason I do anyway. It's kinda strange really, that a true 100% unschooler would think of such things. No, wait. Maybe it isn't. If other unschoolers never thought about school then there would be no books and websites and essays on it that are written so powerfully. Reading those makes me proud to be one of the few who have managed to escape.

Unschoolers often reflect on how their public school friends seem to be "brainwashed" about the importance of school, especially in relation to the social activities attached to school, such as the prom or a school fieldtrip. They complain about how difficult it is to explain to their public school friends how content they are with their learning projects and their freedom. Jasmine's anecdote conveys this frustration quite strongly.

> I got a letter from my friend today.... Well anyway she still has to go to school (the poor thing). She's the one...that said she wanted to go to high school because of The Almighty Prom. I'm sad to say she's still brainwashed.
>
> "High school is going to be so much fun. I have these little visions of me like this super jock and really popular. I'm at a prom or something and I see [you] and I'm like: look what you're missing out on. My fantasy."
>
> I read that and I could hardly believe my eyes. Look what I'm missing out on?? She's the one who's missing out. On life. I mean, is that all she has to look forward to? A PROM? A stupid DANCE!?!?...I sit there and think about it and I want to run all the way across two states to her house and scream at her and tell her that high school will NOT be fun, and that there is so much more to life then The Almighty Prom. I want to drag her back to my house and show her my life, and show her my freedom, and then scream at her some more that she can have it too, that it's not that hard once you realize what school does to you. I want to figuratively smack her upside the head with the truth and make her look at it. And if I did that and she understood, if she really understood, and she still wanted to go to high school I would let her. But she can't even see the truth, never mind understand it. I want to help her. But I don't know how.
>
> How do you un-brainwash a person you can hardly talk to, and who can't see the truth? (April 16, 1999)

Unschoolers Learning: Projects and Interests

Both girls frequently describe their daily activities in journals. I combed their entries for details on their learning work. Both girls seem to be inclined towards writing and artistic expression through music, art, and computer-generated graphics.

In one entry, Ellen described a book she found at the bookstore, *The Physics of Star Trek*. She spends her days working on her website, writing (a novel, essays for her webpage, poetry), painting, babysitting, and reading. Her reading interests cover philosophy (*Sophie's World* seems to be a favorite among unschoolers), "physics and the universe," and political satire. She plans to work on an organic farm this summer, and of course go to the Not Back to School Camp. She's thinking about starting a babysitting service and advertising with a flier. She plans to redecorate her room to make it look more "alternative."

Ellen uses her website as a forum for other writing besides her journal. When she has ideas for projects, she starts a new page for the topic. Her website is therefore a true web of interconnecting links. She has named one of her current research projects "Project S" ("S" for "shyness"). Since she feels that she struggles with shyness, she is surveying homeschoolers and public schoolers to see if this is a bigger problem for homeschoolers than it is for public schoolers. She plans to start a zine on computer art and rediscovering math entitled *Atonal Geometry*, for "bringing the arts, math, and the universe all together." On her "philosophy" page she has created a Book of Questions with questions such as "What is a chair?" and "What's in a book?" She also runs her own listserve for teenage girls' writing.

Writing is a common activity for both Jasmine and Ellen. Both write novels, short essays, and poetry. Jasmine takes advantage of friendships to get feedback on her writing and discuss plots:

> So I've got this idea for a novel, see, and I'm trying to type it, but I'm not sure what should happen next. I know what I want to have happen later in the story but I'm stumped as to what should happen NOW.
>
> This happens every time I start to write a novel. I get this wonderful idea on how to start it and what should happen later in the book, and it's the middle I always get stumped on.
>
> The last time this happened was around my birthday, and on my birthday my two lifelong friends came over, so I was able to ask them what they thought should happen. And they would help me every time they came and after they left I would always be re-inspired. This time I've got a huge chunk of that novel that I want to ask them about, and the beginning of this new one, but they're not going to BE here for who knows how long. (March 27, 1999)

Unschoolers Growing:"A Sense of Self"

In talking about her life as an unschooler, Ellen describes a great deal of pride and joy in her activities, even though she feels slightly guilty. She knows that her schooled friends are not having a comparably smooth transition through adolescence:

> I love my life now. Sometimes I feel kind of guilty for that. A lot of my friends are going through hell, or at least confusion, right now. Their lives are not going as well as mine is going now. I wonder what's going on. I wonder what happened. I wonder what is happening. I wonder what is going to happen.

[handwritten margin note: yeah bc they're dealing w/ ppl and real world]

Jasmine's following entry on trying to be invisible in school gives us a glimpse of how she sees herself differently since she left school. It also provides a taste of the type of inter-journal dialogue that occurs as the girls read each other's work and respond in their own journals. The next bit is from the same journal, but a different entry.

> The girl was shy and withdrawn, but then she had a drastic change, and became this huge party girl. When the author was describing the way that girl used to be I felt like she was really talking about me. There was one sentence—one little sentence—that really got me. She said that the girl used to try to make herself invisible in class.
>
> I used to do that. I would sit there tensed up whenever I might get called on, trying to make myself invisible. When I DID get called on I tensed up even more, got it over with as quickly as possible, and hoped no one would notice or care what I said. Even outside of school I didn't say much to people unless I really knew them. As I read that I thought—Have I really changed? (March 25, 1999).

Jasmine also describes her growing self-confidence in her writing.

> I'm also beginning to feel like my writing is good. Really good, I mean. I was reading over my novels today I was thinking something like "I wrote that? That is incredible!" I never give myself enough credit. It's times like this that I really can't figure out why. I mean, I've got talent! I can do this! That makes me so happy. (May 2, 1999).

[handwritten margin note: ignorance is it bliss? ignorance or reality?]

This expression of delight and joy in her work is the type of response that was common in Sheffer's interviews with homeschooled girls. Since they did not have to deal with pressures from the culture regarding stereotypes for girls, they were freer to develop their interests and believe in themselves.

Conclusion

Gee (1991) argues that discourses resist internal criticism since utterances that reflect opposing or critical viewpoints define the speaker as outside the discourse community. With the unschoolers I studied, I found this is true only to a certain extent. Discourses undergo change that is brought about due to internal change and critique. Sometimes internal criticism is heeded, and changes occur. Sometimes criticisms do go unheard and ignored, but the speaker still maintains a sense of membership and involvement in the community. Sometimes the speaker *exits* the community, as is demonstrated by these unschooled girls and their families. The literacy that these unschooled girls exhibit is not dissimilar to the secondary discourses we learn in school, even though they have distanced themselves from school in many significant ways. They use their secondary discourse as a powerful literacy to criticize the discourse of school in ways that would not be tolerated in school-based literacy practices. Thus, although their secondary discourse resembles school literacy, it is already a "powerful literacy" that they use in critical ways to interrogate the power that schooling has over the lives of their friends (Gee, 1991: 8).

I have attempted to provide insights into aspects of the community of unschooled teenagers: their attitudes towards school, their learning pursuits, and their developing self-confidence. I have also tried to describe what I believe is a discourse community that is serious about critiquing the discourse of compulsory schooling. Further research is necessary to understand the experiences of homeschooled children and the unique perspectives they develop as a result. What motivates them to learn when no one is pushing them. Is there any way that this kind of self-directed learning can be promoted in public schools? In the area of literacy, how differently do young people approach reading and writing when they haven't learned in the ways structured by teachers and schools?

Unpopular ideas often follow a predictable course on their way to acceptance by the general public. First they are ignored, then misrepresented and ridiculed. Third, they are denounced, but finally their detractors accept them and say, "we knew that all along." Homeschooling is probably in the second and third stages. It will likely never be a real option for most families, nor should it be. But the lessons to be learned from the children who have taken active responsibility for their learning are valuable for improving education for all children. In a period of declining faith in our public schools, we would do well to listen to those who have chosen to do without them. Their lessons may help us find ways to remake schools into places where, like unschooling, the boundaries between learning and teaching are blurred and the youth have a greater say in what they will learn.

Challenges agency in education systems

Notes

1. John Holt worked for many years in the area of public school reform before turning to homeschooling. His philosophical writings are a source of inspiration for many homeschoolers. See, for example: Holt, 1983, 1989, and 1995.
2. Each issue contains short news items and reports on home schooling, letters from parents, letters on the challenges and concerns of home schooling, and book and resource reviews. Feature topics cover a wide range of interests such as "Homeschoolers in College," "When Kids Ask to Homeschool," "Russian Homeschoolers," "Japanese School Refusers," "Homeschoolers of Color," and "Homeschooling Group Activities." Other issues have included learning languages from native speakers, compliance with state regulations, homeschooling with a non-parental adult, compliance issues, mathematical thinking, doctors' prejudice, outdoor programs for homeschoolers, Christian unschooling, and using experiential learning to change self-perceptions.
3. Not their real names.

Works Cited

Divoky, D. (1983). The new pioneers of the home-schooling movement. *Phi Delta Kappan*, 64, 395–399

Fishman, A. (1988). *Amish literacy: What and how it means*. Portsmouth, NH: Heinemann.

Gardner, H. (1991). *The unschooled mind*. New York: Basic Books.

Gee, J. (1991). What is literacy? In C. Mitchell and K. Weiler (Eds.), *Rewriting literacy: Culture and the discourse of the other* (pp. 3–12). New York: Bergin & Garvey.

———. (1996). *Social linguistics and literacies: Ideology in discourses* (2nd ed.). London: Taylor & Francis.

Golden, D. (2000, April 24). Homeschoolers learn how to gain clout inside the Beltway. *The Wall Street Journal*, A1, A6.

Gray, S. (1992). *Why families home school*. Unpublished Dissertation, Thesis (Ph.D). University of California, Los Angeles, CA.

Guerra, J. (1998). *Close to home: Oral and literate practices in a transnational Mexicano community*. New York: Teachers College Press.

Hetzel, J. (1997). *Literacy in the homeschool setting, Literacy: Building on what we know: Proceedings of the Claremont reading conference* (pp. 60–81). Claremont, CA: Claremont Reading Conference, Institute for Developmental Studies, Claremont Graduate University.

———. (1998). *Factors that influence parents to homeschool*. Unpublished doctoral dissertation, Claremont University, Claremont, CA.

Holt, J. (1979). *Growing up without schooling: A record of a grassroots movement*. Washington, D.C.: Education Reform Books.

———. (1983). School and home schoolers: A fruitful partnership. *Phi Delta Kappan*, 64, 391–394.

———. (1989). *Learning all the time*. Reading, MA: Addison-Wesley.

———. (1995). *How children learn*. Reading, MA: Addison-Wesley.

Homeschool Association of California. (2000). Homeschooling questions and answers. http://www.hsc.org/facofficial.html.

Kantrowitz, B., and Wingert, P. (1998, October 5). Learning at home: Does it pass the test? *Newsweek*, 64–70.

Keane, S. (1999). A typical unschooling day. mypage.direct.ca/s/skeane/unschool.html (accessed 25 July 1999).

Krupnick, L. (1980). *The psychology of compulsory schooling and the emergence of strategies for coping and change*. Unpublished doctoral dissertation. University of Northern Colorado, Greeley, CO.

Llewellyn, G. (1998). *The teenage liberation handbook: How to quit school and get a real life and education*. Revised edition. Eugene, OR: Lowry House.

McGraw, R. (1990). *Selected aspects of homeschooling as reported by homeschooling parents and reported with perceptions of Indiana public school superintendents and principals of homeschooling in Indiana*. Unpublished doctoral dissertation. Ball State University, Muncie, IN.

McLaughlin, D. (1994). Toward a dialogical understanding of literacy: The case of Navajo print. In B. Moss (Ed.), *Literacy across communities* (pp. 85–119). Cresskill, NJ: Hampton Press.

Reder, S. (1994). Practice engagement theory: A sociocultural approach to literacy across languages and cultures. In B. Ferdman, R. Weber, and A. Ramirez (Eds.), *Literacy across languages and cultures* (pp. 33–74). Albany, NY: State University of New York Press.

Sheffer, S. (1992). *Writing because we love to: Homeschoolers at work*. Portsmouth, NH: Boynton/Cook.

———. (1995). *A sense of self: Listening to homeschooled adolescent girls*. Portsmouth, NH: Heinemann.

Street, B. (1993). *Cross-cultural approaches to literacy*. New York: Cambridge University Press.

Taylor, J. (1987). *Self-concept in homeschooling children*. Unpublished doctoral dissertation, Andrews University, Berrien Springs, MI.

Van Galen, J. and Pitman, M. A. (Eds.) (1994). *Homeschooling: Political, historical, and pedagogical perspectives*. New York: Ablex.

Wilber, J. (1996). *Totally private and personal*. Minneapolis, MN: Free Spirit Publishing.

Response to

"I used to go to school. Now I learn."

Carol D. Lee

Beth Lewis Samuelson has provided the reader with a glimpse into a world of literate practices that is largely invisible in both public discourses on education as well as in the education research literature. She turns an intense gaze on adolescents and their families who have chosen not to follow the path of traditional public education. The road not taken includes not only the physical space of the public school facility, but also the prescribed standards, objectives, scope and sequence, standardized and other forms of assessments that currently hold an almost pentecostal grip over the public imagination, and the stimulus-response matrix of grades. The population of her focus is not only homeschooled, but explicitly "unschooled."

Over the past thirty years, I have dedicated my attention as a parent, an educator, an administrator, and as a member of boards of directors to another movement that also stands in contrast to and tension with public schooling. Independent Black Institutions, or "IBIs" as they are often called, have a long history in the United States. African Americans have historically seen education as a tool in the struggle for political, ideological, economic, and cultural liberation. During the African Holocaust of Enslavement,[1] it was illegal for Africans in America to learn to read and write. There are stories of enslaved Africans in America, during the dark of the night, pulling up wooden slats in the floors of their meager cabins to bring out books to read by candlelight under the threat of physical dismemberment (cutting off hands or fingers) or even death (Harding, 1993). Because education, and literacy specifically, was seen as so central to the future well-being of the community, among the very first institutions these Africans established in the United States were schools (Anderson, 1988). Because they saw literacy as liberating for both individuals and communities, it was of central importance that they controlled their educational institutions. Thus when representatives from the Freedman's Bureau came South to help the newly "emancipated slaves," they were shocked to find these freedom-loving human beings already had established their own schools and had no intentions of sharing the administration of these institutions with others. In that same tradition, thousands of Independent Black Institutions flourish throughout the United States today: as full time schools, as after school programs, and as community-based programs, such as Rites of Passage programs.

I have taken some time to describe this independent school movement among African Americans because I needed an anchor to connect my personal history to Samuelson's analysis of communities of homeschooled and unschooled families. Through the lens of my own history, I could empathize with the critique of public education in the United States represented by these families and with their decisions to take an active stance in support of their convictions. These convictions are hallowed territory when the subject is one's children. As Samuelson accurately points out, such communities of conviction and practice develop unique discourses that convey to themselves and others a bounded identity and sense of shared values.

At the same time, my personal history, not only as an advocate and long-time participant in a movement that stands in tension with public education, but also as an African American female, growing up during the Civil Rights Era in U.S. history, growing up in public housing in Chicago on what was then and now known as the notorious west side of Chicago, I cannot help but acknowledge what I perceive (rightly or wrongly) as the very middle-class and individualistic orientation of the homeschool/unschooled movement. Families must be in a position, both economically and in terms of other resources, to make the choice to keep their children out of public schools and to educate them at home. Literate practices, as described by Samuelson, of adolescents who establish websites and communicate with one another and others through online journals are hardly available to the poor or working poor. In low-income communities—whether they be the neighborhoods of concentrated poverty in large cities or the deep stretches of rural poverty in Appalachia or the Mississippi Delta—there are scores of "unschooled" who are in school, and scores of "unschooled" who are out of school. Both of these groups of "unschooled" also engage in unique literacy practices that are more invisible than those of the populations Samuelson describes. While I absolutely agree with Samuelson that there are stances and epistemologies evident in the discourses of the students she describes that are fundamentally different from the inherent discourses promulgated by five paragraph themes and research papers that are expected to be nothing more than regurgitations of somebody else's authoritative words, I suspect that Ellen and Jasmine are still fundamentally closer to the kinds of Discourses and epistemologies found in the Harvards and Princetons of the world.

I do not mean to suggest by my critique, however, that there are no lessons to be learned from the middle-class homeschool movement and the specific orientation of the "unschooled" Samuelson discusses. Inherent in the activity structures of the "unschooled" is the assumption of the value of play, of engaging in learning activities that are intrinsically motivating to participants. Even for the teenagers she describes, the choices of what they select to investigate and pursue have a play-like quality. Developmentally, across cultures, play has intrinsically motivating qualities for human beings, most certainly for children, as well as across the life cycle (albeit with less intensity as we age). Michael Cole and colleagues at the Laboratory of Comparative Human Cognition, along with colleges across the University of California system (and other institutions nationally and internationally) over the past 11 years, have run the Fifth Dimension. The Fifth Dimension is an after school club for children where they play games (some computer-based and some not), engage with peers and adults (many of whom are local area college students) on equal footing, in a magical world occupied by an invisible Wizard/ess who helps mediate questions and problems that participants have. Cole (1998) offers longitudinal data on the positive learning outcomes for these children, not only in terms of their "school" achievement, but equally if not more importantly of their sense of efficacy as whole human beings and problem solvers. Thus the power of play in its many instantiations could prove a robust lever for schools and open up a liberating discourse for learning.

Let me conclude by applauding Beth Samuelson for opening a window into the stance-taking and epistemologies of these young people who themselves and whose families have taken bold moves to resist the hegemony of much of public education. I have attempted briefly in my commentary to link their moves with those of others. Let me also in closing say to Jasmine, I, as a mother of three adult children, *do not believe* "in equal rights for teenagers."

Note

1. In this volume, we are concerned with new literacies and discourse practices that inscribe perspective and position. I have chosen to use the terms "African Holocaust of Enslavement," "Africans in America," and "enslaved persons" precisely because the normative discourse of slavery and slaves inscribe conditions of servitude as inherent characteristics of the people, rather than conditions to which they were subjected against their will. That is, the people were slaves, not human beings subjected to conditions of enslavement. The people were not U.S. citizens, but were Africans (Akan, Yoruba, Igbo, etc.) forced to live in the Americas. In addition, these normative terms do not communicate the gravity of the conditions to which they were subjected. Holocaust does.

Works Cited

Anderson, J. (1988). *The education of blacks in the south, 1860–1935*. Chapel Hill: University of North Carolina.

Cole, M. (1998). *Cultural psychology: A once and future discipline*. Cambridge, MA: Belknap

Harding, V. (1993). *There is a river: The black struggle for freedom in America*. San Diego, CA: Harvest Books.

CHAPTER SIX

Critical Cyberliteracy:
Reading and Writing *The X-Files*

Jennifer Seibel Trainor

arbara is a participant in an informal online fan club and a regular contributor to *The Gossamer Project*, an online fiction archive housing over 5,000 short stories and novellas on its U.S. website (it maintains similar archives in Britain, Finland, and Australia), all centered on the popular television science fiction drama, *The X-Files*. As a member of this fan club, Barbara reads and writes what's known as "fan fiction"—stories based on the characters, plots and themes of a television show or film. Fan fiction is not a new phenomenon—underground fan magazines have published take-offs on popular science fiction for a number of years—but the nature of *The Gossamer Project* makes it somewhat unusual. In fact, it has come under the scrutiny of FOX Network, which "owns" *The X-Files*, and which has repeatedly threatened cyber-archivists and writers with copyright infringement lawsuits. As one network executive commented, "the creators of popular television shows have certain approval rights over what is done [with the characters of a show]...they have a profit participation interest and [the Internet] is actually taking the creative approval away from [the network and the original creators of the show]." However, network efforts to block fan fiction writing have resulted only in more and more sarcastic "disclaimers" from the writers, like the following one written by Barbara and which was posted along with one of her stories.

> Okay, I know I haven't posted in a while—I've been really thinking about Memento Mori. Finally, it looks like Chris Carter is realizing what we've known

all along:). This is my Post-Memento Mori attempt, and it's definitely MSR [Mulder/Scully Romance] but nothing too explicit. I'm rating it PG-13.

Thanks Rhonda, Sarah S. and Megan for your inspiration and Paula for your editing! And congrats Rhonda on your Morley! [A fan fiction award]

By the way, I watched Momento Mori 17 times last week before I wrote this. Can you say _addicted_???

Disclaimer: I don't own these characters. I'm *only* "borrowing" them. There is no reason to sue me. Really. No copyright infringement is intended, and more to the point, I am not making a profit by my efforts (as if!!).

BUT: feedback is a form of payment Fox *can't* sue over! Please. Let me know what you think. Email me at...

Television network efforts to block the writing of fans like Barbara have also culminated in a movement on the Internet, accessible from the Gossamer pages as well as from a host of other sites, to protect fans from intellectual property lawsuits. A clear objective of this movement is to force television networks and others seeking to control the content of the Internet to recognize the rights of fans to participate in the creation of popular culture.

What makes *The Gossamer Project* so threatening to television networks is the communications technology of the Internet that collects and disseminates "the commodity" in question—in this case, creative license with a television show. Consisting of an electronic interconnection of thousands of computer networks and millions of computers, the Internet is a vast database of information, and an environment in which to communicate electronically—in real or virtual time—with a vast number of people. This number continues to grow exponentially. As such, the Internet is at the forefront of a communications revolution, and it is having a profound impact on our notions and practices of literacy.

We are living through one of the dramatic transformations in human society that has only happened a few times in the past 10,000 years. Schlender captures something of the significance of this critical "shift."

> Following on the older networks that have reshaped our world by tying us together over the past two centuries—railroads, highways, airports, oil and gas pipelines, TV broadcasting, the electric power grid, and, of course, global telecommunications—now comes the most protean and potentially the most powerful network of all: the Internet. In [the past] five years more than 200 million people have plugged computers into the Net, by far the fastest spread of a new communications technology ever. (2000: 90)

Several noteworthy features of Barbara's participation in *The Gossamer Project* demonstrate some of the questions this new technology raises. The nature of Barbara's participation also suggests some of the ways we will need to alter, modify, and extend existing theories and paradigms of literacy if we are to understand adequately the social meanings of reading and writing in cyberspace. Questions include:

1. How are literacy communities configured in cyberspace?
2. What kinds of literacy practices does cyberspace make possible?
3. What are the implications of cyberliteracies for traditional literacy gatekeeping structures—editors, producers, owners, publishers?
4. What are the connections between cyberspace, literacy and popular culture?
5. How is gender enacted in cyberspace?
6. What are the access issues, and the corresponding race, class and nation issues involved?
7. What do the literacy practices in cyberspace mean for school literacies and formal literacy instruction?
8. How will technology, especially its alliances with aspects of popular culture, alter school literacy instruction?

C/Sites of Resistance and Change

The Internet is a primary signifier of the much-touted shift in the late twentieth century to an information economy, and websites like *The Gossamer Project* neatly highlight the corresponding new social relations—between labor, commodity, producer, owner, and consumer—that this shift has ushered in.[1] As technology becomes more and more sophisticated, the changes—and the threats—to traditional vestiges of power, such as television networks, become more and more immediate. As *Web Magazine* (1997: 28) writes in connection with Fox's attempt to quash sites like *The Gossamer Project*: "just imagine ten years from now:…the Internet looks more and more like television, only every user has a channel. Static fan sites with pictures [of stars] become full-motion shows. Would-be Matt Groenings are animating their own acerbic adventures and distributing them online."

Barbara's disclaimer regarding copyright infringement signifies this shift: She has in effect claimed control of a popular medium—television—and in the process redefined the intellectual property laws and conventions that govern literacy practices in our culture. She publishes, yes, but not for profit, which removes her from the traditional marketplace and its rules. Publishing on the Internet, as Barbara well knows, involves a whole new set of codes and she is scornful of FOX Network's anachronistic faith in old paradigms. The issue, then, that the Internet raises for traditional vestiges of power is essentially one of ownership and property, and

Barbara's disclaimer demonstrates just how tricky the issue promises to be. As Poster (1995: 29) writes, property rights are put into doubt "when information is set free of its material confinement to move and multiply in cyberspace with few constraints.... The problem for capitalism is how to contain the word and the image, to bind them to proper names and logos when they flit about at the speed of light and procreate with indecent rapidity."

This breakdown of traditional hierarchical boundaries between producer and consumer manifests itself in another form as well. Barbara, for example, is also a prolific writer of reviews of *The X-Files*. On her webpage, one can find in-depth and detailed commentaries on each episode including analyses of cinematography, character studies, plot predictions and examinations of the themes of the show. Fan reviews are sometimes read by Chris Carter, the original creator of *The X-Files*, who has mentioned in interviews that he takes fan reviews into account and values their insights into the show's themes. Thus Barbara is a consumer of popular culture, but because of the Internet, she also participates in the production of that culture. The seemingly monolithic and impenetrable television industry is accessible to her in an entirely new way. Theorists who have tried to understand the role of the individual in the creation of mass culture now have a window into just how consumers not only receive but also transform and recreate the messages sent to them via popular forms.

Disembodied Postmodern Pleasures

Although reviews and discussions of *The X-Files* constitute a portion of the literacy practices revolving around *The Gossamer Project*, the fan fiction is the project's raison d'être and the source of the project's attraction for the 8,000 or so web users visiting the site weekly. Barbara herself has written over 25 short stories, some of them serials, and which are posted every four or five days. In return for serial postings, Barbara receives fan email, as her own audience clamors for the latest installment of her narrative. She has become, in effect, a postmodern Dickens, contributing to the explosion of narrativity, the turn to the "little story" that Lyotard (1984) identifies as fundamental to postmodern culture.

Barbara shares her obsession with the officially non-existent Mulder-and-Scully romance with several cyber-friends and with fan readers and writers from around the world. The four women she mentions in her note, for example, are also regular *Gossamer* writers. Barbara has never met any of them in person, but she knows them well and has communicated with them since the beginning of *The Gossamer Project* five years ago. They regularly edit each other's work, recommend new writers, and exchange information and opinions about the show. *The Gossamer Project*, then, constitutes a multilayered literacy community configured in an entirely new way. It allows Barbara to write to specific cyber-friends made through her participation in the archive, to the larger *X-Files* fan community and to web users in general; indeed, to virtually anyone who may be cyber-traveling through.

In addition to her writing, Barbara estimates that she has read nearly everything on the Internet concerning *The X-Files*, but now keeps up only with the postings of her 30 or so favorite authors. She spends between 2 and 5 hours a day reading and writing *The Gossamer Project* and is a self-described "media junkie" who rents four to five video films a week and watches 15 weekly television shows.

This incredible amount of disposable time is made possible, presumably, by the fact that Barbara is college-educated, single, childless, and has a white-collar day job. In addition, she is highly literate in the traditional sense of the word, sometimes using canonical poetry as epigraphs for her fan fiction. In these ways she is typical of *The X-Files'* fan fiction writers, who are generally professional white women ranging in age from 17 to 45 years.

Barbara writes exclusively about *The X-Files*, a show that centers on unexplained phenomena, extra-terrestrial and futuristic life forms and sinister government conspiracies. The main characters are FBI agents Dana Scully and her partner, Fox Mulder, whose obsession with finding his long-vanished sister drives the overarching plot. The obsession signals, for both characters, a rupturing of the certainty and security of childhood, and their pursuit of the mystery of the sister's disappearance becomes a desperate quest for "the truth"—a truth the show steadfastly refuses to supply. Episodes usually end by raising more questions than they answer, weaving a web of interconnected mysteries the solution to which is always just out of Mulder's, and the viewer's, reach. The show thus operates in some ways like a science fiction soap opera, refusing closure in an endless narrative tease of deferred resolution. But the unresolved plots of *The X-Files*, unlike those of soap operas, deal with fairly hefty epistemological questions about the unknowability of the universe, the limits of rational inquiry, the unreliability of traditional structures of authority and the elusive—even illusory—nature of reality and truth.

The X-Files, then, is a postmodern text, centered around the characters' ineffective quest for certitude and truth in a world that continually deconstructs that truth, demonstrating that it is, at best, ephemeral, at worst, misleading, even dangerous. (One episode, for example, consists entirely of witness accounts of the same event, told repetitively from different perspectives, the story transmorphing each time, so that interpretation fragments and recent history deteriorates into nothing more authoritative than individual points of view.) The show juxtaposes the characters' beliefs in the possibility of finding an answer—through science, through investigation, through faith—with the absolute inexplicability of the cases they face. Thus the epigraph at the beginning of each show—"The truth is out there"—becomes an ironic anti-motto, reminding the audience of the void at the center of Mulder's and Scully's quest.

Interestingly, Barbara, like most Gossamer writers, chooses to diffuse these darker complexities by adding, as she indicates in her note, a somewhat controversial although seemingly entirely conventional element to her story. This is known among Gossamer reader-writers as "MSR," or Mulder-Scully Romance. In this, she is typical of about 70 percent of the fan fiction writers archived in *The Gossamer Project*. These fans, as one put it, "are intrigued by the bond Mulder and his partner have on the show and want to explore where this bond might go if we got to see more." As a result, their fiction either peripherally includes or focuses exclusively on the development of a sexual romantic relationship between the partners. The focus on romance is controversial because of a small but vocal contingent of readers and writers in *The Gossamer Project* who feel that taking the strictly platonic relationship the characters share on TV any farther than friendship is a betrayal of the intent of the original show. The producers of the show agree, and they never allow the two characters to share more than friendship, though they are not above teasing the large numbers of romance fans with the subtle and often sexually charged dynamics between the two characters.[2] Like print romance novels, the romance stories in the *Gossamer* archive have developed certain conventions that are ritualistically incorporated into each narrative and that have been appropriated from the print romance genre, from *The X-Files* TV episodes and from other *Gossamer* writers' stories, creating a pastiche of blurred popular forms.

I mention these details in part because they are illustrative of several important features of the Internet and highlight several of the pressing questions that new technology raises in terms of our understanding of the social meanings of literacy: questions of ownership, authorship, and access, questions of pleasure, play, and power. But I also mention them because I believe these details speak to a larger debate within literacy education about the role of theories of culture and language in understanding the social and political dimensions of literacy. Specifically, as I hope to make clear in the remainder of this chapter, the Internet, as a postmodern writing space with far-reaching political, social, and economic implications, complicates critical educators' concerns with the political dimensions of reading and writing.

Any discussion of cyber cultural practices, especially those that coincide with popular media, as *The Gossamer Project* does, must take into account the fractures postmodernism has introduced into social theories of literacy because, as many have already argued, cyberspace itself is a postmodern space, a validation of postmodern theory and a product of the late capitalist economic practices that postmodernism mirrors. In short, electronic communications technology—and in particular, the Internet— manifests the direction of literary theory for the past 25 years. The death of the author that Roland Barthes (1974) predicted seems to have literal significance in cyberspace, where anyone can publish, or add to an already posted text, spawning endlessly proliferating narratives and suggesting that, as Derrida famously remarked, there is nothing outside the text (1966/2000). In addition, Wolfgang Iser's (1978) understanding of the reader as constituting the text in the act of reading becomes more than theoretical speculation in cyberspace, where interactive users read, write, modify, link, and interweave texts. The Internet breaks down the distinction between reader and writer, and implicitly calls into question all forms of authorial control, challenging our sense that each book is a complete, separate and unique expression of its author (Tuman, 1992a, 1992b). Finally, the Internet makes identity fluid and multiple, offering users a chance to re-examine, play, experiment with, and ultimately transform, their own subjectivities. In this way, cyberspace conforms to postmodern notions of both text and identity.

Critical Literacy and Postmodernism

Critical literacy, derived as it is from a modernist tradition of critical social theory, has tended to falter around the question of postmodernity. Specifically, critical literacy theory has ruptured along a modernist/postmodernist binary that produces what Sholle and Denski (1993) call "schizophrenia," and that threatens to undermine the project of critical literacy altogether. To put it simply, postmodern deconstructions of master narratives of truth, of the rational, autonomous subject and of the authority of the text have called into question the viability of critical theory and the political projects it sustains. Because of this, critical theorists have critiqued and rejected many of the major tenets of postmodernism.

Frederic Jameson (1984), for example, has forcefully argued that postmodernism coincides with and helps to define late capitalist consumer society, where the surging images of the media have created what Voss and Schutze (1989: 120) call "a world blanketed with signs and texts, image and media of all kinds and which has brought forth a culture...based on an overproduction of sensations that dulls our sensory faculties." From this standpoint, postmodernism represents a "cultural logic," to use Jameson's phrase, that correlates with economic changes in late capitalism.

In addition, postmodernism is often accused of never going beyond the text, of depoliticizing social action, of theorizing only an endless play of discourse. As McLaren and Lankshear (1993: 401) write, the reading practices postmodernism celebrates produce

> a mode of subjectivity that can participate gleefully in troubling the hegemony of social silence while avoiding the task of reconstructing the social practices which produce such silence. They can create an optimism that is strictly personal, removed from historical context...the act of reading itself can be reduced to a textual palliative in which the material conditions of existence, the suffering of certain groups in our society, can be turned into a fantasy of personal resolution.

Postmodernism and its corresponding mode of meaning-making, they seem to suggest, can *appear* politically progressive while still serving the interests of the dominant culture. It privileges individual experience over political critique, an accomplishment made possible by postmodernism's penchant for pleasure and play. Such playfulness, McLaren and Lankshear contend, contains and subverts political action, yielding a politics of liberation that, while at odds with bourgeois norms and practices, doesn't seriously challenge the social logic of those norms.

James Berlin (1993: 251) takes the rejection of postmodernism a step farther when he writes that "both the fragmented, disconnected nature of postmodern experience and the use of poststructuralist and deconstructionist conceptions of language in considering these conditions have led to the denial of the adequacy of any metanarrative to account for contemporary economic and political events." If we cannot even explain the larger power relations of the present, Berlin asks, how can we ever begin to explain these relations over time? He argues that to abandon the attempt to make sense of history is for the vast majority of people to accept being victimized by it. Indeed, as he sees it, the master narratives that postmodernism deconstructs are necessary if history and politics are to serve the interests of democracy, equality, and justice, and not simply the interests of a wealthy and powerful ruling class. Similarly, Sholle and Denski argue that it would be foolish to reject entirely the truths after which modernism sought, and caution against the potential within postmodern theory for it to lead to *"fatal strategies*, wherein resistance is replaced by refusal, and critique by play" (original emphasis; 1993: 305). Finally, Giroux (1993, 1996) has argued that literacy researchers and educators carefully need to separate out those elements of postmodernism that enhance the goals of democracy, such as its celebration of difference, while avoiding and rejecting its nihilism and its tendency toward uncritical pleasure and play.

We can hear in these voices a distrust of the pleasures of language and popular culture, perhaps stemming from a fear that such pleasure is merely palliative, distracting individuals from more pressing matters at hand. We can also hear in them a fear that the endless theorizations of sign and symbol postmodernism is rooted in may lead us away from a more grounded perspective on the material problems that call for social action, a fear that the materiality of the body on which such problems are inscribed has been "maligned...liquidated to the currency of signs" (McLaren, 1991: 150).

But any attempt to describe and explain media literacy and, I would add, cyberliteracy falls short without recourse to postmodern theory. For example, Sholle and Denski in an article outlining in broad strokes a theory of critical postmodern media literacy are not able to dismiss even the regressive tendencies of postmodernism outright. Their discussion brings together discourses on critical literacy and theories of popular culture, and tries to bridge these two fields while simultaneously taking into account the ruptures postmodernism has produced within them. Sholle and Denski make clear that the creation of new theories and paradigms accounting for cultural practices and technology must somehow more thoroughly explain and incorporate postmodernism. They imply that to extend critical literacy beyond the word and into the media and, I would add, technology forces us to contend more fully with those regressive elements of postmodernism that many have rejected. Their critical postmodern media literacy thus centers on a pedagogy that entails reading not only the ideological meanings popular culture may impose on audiences, but also the ways in which audiences find pleasure, resistance, and play within that culture.

But despite Sholle and Denski's willingness to embrace postmodernism, they too eventually pull back from it. While they attempt to situate critical postmodern media literacy within the rupture between modernist discourses of critical literacy and postmodern understandings of the fluidity of subjectivity and the deconstruction of master narratives, they, like the critical educators cited above, caution against succumbing to Jean Baudrillard's "fatal strategies" (1983), urging educators to reject the most radical elements of postmodern theories.

If, however, cyberspace embodies both postmodern meaning-making methods and mirrors postmodernism's corresponding relationship to what Poster (1995) calls "high-tech" capitalism, then it seems risky to abandon those theorists, like Baudrillard, who have tried to articulate an understanding of that culture. In fact, the powerful combination of technology and popular culture manifest in *The Gossamer Project* makes a rejection of Baudrillard's postmodernism impossible if we want to articulate socially responsible critiques of cyberliteracy practices.

I would like to argue that, postmodernism, as Angela McRobbie suggests, helps us shift our gaze away from a totalizing search for meaning and toward an understanding of the play between images and different cultural forms and institutions. We need, as McRobbie (1994) urges, to pay more, not less, attention to the social practices of consuming and—thanks to new technologies—producing media culture.

"The Truth Is in Me": A Critical Reading of *The Gossamer Project*

I'd like to begin my analysis of the *Gossamer* romances with the postmodern theorist who critical literacy educators have most assiduously avoided: Jean Baudrillard, whose revision of Marxism and theory of the self-referentiality of language and truth make him crucial to my reading. One of Baudrillard's basic premises, as Poster reminds us, is that Marxism mistakenly overlooks the role of language in the production of social relations under capitalism. For example, in a consumer culture, according to Baudrillard, the *meanings* of commodities, rather than the commodities themselves, are consumed. Baudrillard's work highlights an important flaw in Marxist analysis for late capitalist culture, demonstrating that the privileging of labor and class is inadequate for the analyses of postmodern media practices. Because Baudrillard argues that the world "is only the effect of the sign" (1983: 185), the centerpiece of his social theory is symbolic exchange, not the production of goods. Value is created, for

Baudrillard, not in the labor process but in communication structures themselves.

Thus, for Baudrillard, language replaces, even erases, the body in postmodern culture; "the change from human scale to a system of nuclear matrices is visible everywhere: this body, our body, often appears simply superfluous, basically useless in its extension, in the multiplicity and complexity of its organs, its tissues and functions, since today everything is concentrated in the brain and in genetic codes" (1983: 128). It is this erasure that critical literacy advocates have tried to resist. Like the Marxists on whom their educational theories are based, critical educators focus their analysis on the social, political and economic relations that language obscures and mystifies, rather than on how language itself, manifest in the proliferation of signs and images produced by the media, seduces by constructing those images.

For example, when Sholle and Denski argue that one of the first steps of media analysis is to help students make the "invisible visible," they miss an essentially postmodern understanding of how language works. As Baudrillard makes clear, one of the ways in which postmodern popular media has so easily defied critique is that it has already made the invisible visible, and in fact incorporates the invisible as visible right into its text. This is how, as Sholle and Denski themselves acknowledge, one can see the message in the media, refuse or reject it and go on watching anyway (1993: 313).

I would argue that rather than reading Baudrillard's erasure of the body as an abandonment of the project of material critique, as critical Marxist educators are apt to view his work, we read it instead as an attempt to understand the ways in which the culture of late capitalism ushers in new kinds of domination generated by the code or sign of the media. This domination can be revealed by analyzing not the relations of production or critiquing the social deprivation of certain groups in our society but by unraveling the code, and hence recovering the body, upon which the appeal of domination is based.

Baudrillard's understanding of the way postmodern culture replaces the body with the sign helps us to understand both the ideology of *The X-Files* and *Gossamer* readers'/writers' reconstitution of that ideology into romance. Thematically, *The X-Files* is a postmodern text. As such, it offers viewers an ambivalent, sometimes contradictory vision of the body and of heterosexual love: The show simultaneously reminds its viewers of both the importance and the irrelevance of corporeality. In one episode, Scully gets a tattoo; in another Mulder's identity is stolen by a man who assumes his physical form. Several of the show's overarching themes deal with genetic cloning, alien hybridization, and futuristic reproductive techniques.

Anchored in the midst of these ambivalent but suggestive themes is Mulder and Scully's relationship. They are intimately involved in each other's lives—they know each other well, spend hours of time together, care deeply for each other, even write love letters to each other—but, for reasons the show never explains, they do not express this intimacy in physical terms. However, while their relationship on the show is entirely cerebral, their relationship in the *Gossamer* archives is decidedly physical, echoing the genre of print romance novels where love is always at least partially physical —manifesting itself in textual descriptions of corporeal pleasures—and where identity is always stable, rooted in the body, heavily dependent, for example, on the overdetermined physical attributes of its heroine and hero.

It may be that the sexual elements that *Gossamer* writers continually rewrite into the show constitute not only a desire to return to a more familiar genre but also a kind of resistance to cyber, sexual, and gender relationships of the future. In this way, the *Gossamer* archive can be seen as an attempt to come to terms with the erasure of the physical through literacy practices made possible, ironically, by a postmodern communications technology that, of course, constitutes identity in precisely the same way *The X-Files* does. It can be seen, in other words, as an attempt to reconstitute the self through and beyond its erasure on the show and in the technology that produces the archive.

Thus the pleasures Barbara, our postmodern Dickens, provides for her fans is a return to the body that postmodernism erases; a return mediated, ironically, by the technology that both literally manifests disembodiedness and that simultaneously allows Barbara a forum to voice her distress over it. And thus the significance of *The X-Files*, the element of its text that returns fans obsessively to the 5,000 romance stories archived in cyberspace, is the show's refusal, for all its modernist longing, to provide anything more than a cerebral, non-physical relationship between its characters. It is this refusal that spawns the fan fiction, where romance writers reject the superfluity of the physical in Mulder and Scully's quest, and then ironically reproduce it in the very cerebrality of the medium through which they communicate.

Gossamer writers aren't alone in their resistance to the erasure of the body, of course. Critical theorists rally around the cry for a return to the materiality of social and political critique. For example, McLaren offers an interesting critique of postmodernism and its over-reliance on signs:

> [Postmodernism] is a position which maligns the lived body as a material referent for the construction of oppositional subjective forms, material practices, and cultural formations...in effect, postmodern culture has taken the body in custody where it has become liquidated to the currency of signs. It is as if the flesh has been numbed in order to avoid the unspeakable terror of its own existence. (1991: 150)

These theorists long for firm ground on which to stand as they analyze the conditions of our world. The terms they employ revolve around the physical: they caution against theories that too easily forget, in Teresa Ebert's (1996) phrase, "the material suffering of third world bodies," reject the replacement of the material with the purely textual, and speak in metaphors of illness and invasion.

This longing for a return to a stable identity rooted in the body is echoed in one of the themes of *The X-Files*. In a series of episodes, Scully has contracted cancer, possibly as the result of her contact with futuristic hybridized alien-human life forms. The cancer, growing ominously in her brain, may contain the secret truths about these other life forms that Mulder and Scully have sought after. "The truth," Scully tells Mulder referring to her cancer, "is in me, and that's where I have to find it." But as is typical of *The X-Files*, Scully can't control the "dark stranger" that has invaded her—doesn't know where it came from or how to rid herself of it.

Gossamer writers, like the literacy theorists who cry for a return to material critique, long for the certainty that comes when individuals are owners and agents of their bodies—an ideology, they suspect, that is as anachronistic as the futile lawsuits Fox continues to lob at them. We can read their romance writing on the Net as an attempt to return to that ideology, to reconfigure the materiality of the self they feel they have lost.

Conclusion

I have tried to demonstrate that the social meanings of cyberliteracy, and hence the ability to make any kind of social or political critique based on those meanings, will allude us until we come to a fuller understanding of the relationship of postmodern theories of language and culture to the project of progressive social change. Without recourse to Baudrillard's allegedly "pessimistic" and "nihilistic" postmodernism, we would still be fumbling with awkward and ill-fitting understandings of the social meanings of *The Gossamer Project*, understandings that figure *Gossamer* romance reader/writers as resisters or producers of oppressive patriarchal ideologies. In actuality, Barbara, her cyber-fans and cyber-friends seem untouched by the social conditions that make up reality for the romance readers in studies of print romance communities. Instead, they are seeking to understand the implications of cyberspace and all its postmodern ramifications, for the body, for the self.

Having identified the possible source of the pleasure *Gossamer* writers and readers derive from their participation in popular culture and literacy, we are now in a position, as Sholle and Denski suggest, to begin the project of reconstructing our postmodern reading so that it contains the possibility of political critique and action. We can now see how popular cultural forms like *The X-Files* invite viewers to construct different understandings of self by inviting them to understand the body in fundamentally different ways. We can further connect these new understandings of our physical selves to new ways of communicating and to larger trends in the global economy. Now we are in a position to understand some of the political and social implications of *The X-Files'* erasure of the body and the Gossamer readers'/writers' reconstitution of it, mediated as it is by the fundamentally disembodied space of the Internet.

Notes

1. For a detailed description of this shift and its relationship to literacy, see Mark Poster's work (e.g., 1995). Poster aligns the current changes in communications technology with a similar and equally profound change in the Middle Ages, as the new practice of exchange of commodities required individuals to act and speak in new ways. The new merchants required written documents guaranteeing spoken promises and an "arms length distance" attitude even when face-to-face so as to afford a space for calculations of self-interest. A new identity thus was constructed around simultaneous and interdependent practices of commodity exchange, burgeoning merchant capitalism, and literacy. In the late twentieth century, according to Poster, electronic media are supporting an equally profound transformation of cultural identity as new economic practices usher in corresponding changing literacy practices: "If modern society may be said to foster an individual who is rational, autonomous, centered, and stable (the 'reasonable man of law,' the educated citizen of representative democracy, the calculating economic man of capitalism, the grade-defined student of public education), then a postmodern society is emerging which nurtures forms of identity different from, even opposed to, those of modernity" (1995: 24).

2. An episode entitled "Small Potatoes," for example, is considered among Gossamer writers to be a direct response to the romance writers/readers on the Internet and a gentle parody of their obsession with the relationship between Mulder and Scully.

Works Cited

Barthes, R. (1974). *S/2*. (R. Miller, Trans.). New York: Hall and Wang. (Original work published in 1970).

Baudrillard, J. (1983). The ecstasy of communication. In H. Foster (Ed.), *The anti-esthetic*. Port Townsend, WA: Bay Press.

Berlin, J. (1993). Literacy, pedagogy, and English studies: Postmodern connections. In C. Lankshear and P. McLaren (Eds.), *Critical literacy: Politics, praxis, and the postmodern* (pp. 247–270). Albany, NY: State University of New York Press.

Carter, C. (Creator/Executive Producer). *The X-Files* [TV series]. Beverly Hills, CA: Fox Communications.

Derrida, J. (2000). Structure, sign and play in the discourse of the human sciences. In C. Kaplan and W. Anderson (Eds.), *Criticism: Major statements* (4th edition). New York: Bedford/St. Martin's. (Original work published in 1966).

Ebert, T. (1996). For a red pedagogy: Feminism, desire and need. *College English*, 58, 7.

Giroux, H. (1993). Literacy and the politics of difference. In C. Lankshear and P. McLaren (Eds.), *Critical literacy: Politics, praxis, and the postmodern* (pp. 367–378). Albany, NY: State University of New York Press.

———. (1996). Slacking off: Border youth and postmodern education. In H. Giroux, C. Lankshear, P. McLaren and M. Peters, *Counternarratives: Cultural studies and critical pedagogies in postmodern spaces*. New York: Routledge.

The Gossamer Project. (1997). The X-Files fan fiction archive. http://www.gossamer.org/

Iseke-Barnes, J. (1996). Issues of educational uses of the Internet: Power and criticism in communications and searching. *Journal of educational computing research*, 15 (1), 1–23.

Iser, W. (1978). *The act of reading*. Baltimore, MD: Johns Hopkins University Press.

Jameson, F. (1984). Postmodernism, or the cultural logic of late capitalism. *New Left Review*, 146.

Lyotard, J.-F. (1984). *The postmodern condition*. Minneapolis: University of Minnesota Press.

McLaren, P. (1991). Schooling the postmodern body: Critical pedagogy and the politics of enfleshment. In H. Giroux (Ed.), *Postmodernism, feminism, and cultural politics: Redrawing educational boundaries*. Albany, NY: State University of New York Press.

——— and Lankshear, C. (1993). Critical literacy and the postmodern turn. In C. Lankshear and P. McLaren (Eds.), *Critical literacy: Politics, praxis, and the postmodern* (pp. 379–420). Albany, NY: State University of New York Press.

McRobbie, A. (1994). *Postmodernism and popular culture*. London: Routledge.

Poster, M. (1995). *The second media age*. London: Polity Press.

Schlender, B. (2000 October). Enter here. *Fortune*, 142 (8), 90–91.

Sholle, D. and Denski, S. (1993). Reading and writing the media: Critical media literacy and postmodernism. In C. Lankshear and P. McLaren (Eds.), *Critical literacy: Politics, praxis, and the postmodern* (pp. 297–322). Albany, NY: State University of New York Press.

Tuman, M. (1992a). First Thoughts. In M. Tuman (Ed.), *Literacy online: The promise (and peril) of reading and writing with computers*. Pittsburgh, PA: University of Pittsburgh Press.

———. (Ed.). (1992b). *Literacy online: The promise (and peril) of reading and writing with computers*. Pittsburgh, PA: University of Pittsburgh Press.

Voss, D., and Schutze, J. (1989). Postmodernism in context: Perspectives of a structural change in society, literature and literary criticism. *New German Critique*, 47.

The Web Magazine. (1997). http://govt.ucsd.edu/newjournal/w/msg02299.html

Response to

"Critical Cyberliteracy"

Andrea Abernethy Lunsford

eading Jennifer Seibel Trainor's fascinating meditation on post-modernism, *The X-Files*, and the work of its fans makes me wish I'd been paying more attention to television lately. Searching my memory yields only one vaguely recalled episode featuring the adventures of Mulder and Scully, although even that vague memory confirms what Trainor says about the jittery uncertainty and fluidity of selfhood the show promulgates—its own particular version of (disembodied) post-modernity. *The Gossamer Project* and the work of Barbara and her colleagues are much more familiar, especially their resistance to traditional copyright and focus on collaboration, issues I see as crucial to expanding definitions of literacy and of self/selves in current "new times."

What does copyright and its infringement have to do with literacy, cyber or otherwise? As it turns out, a great deal. For the last 300 years in the West, the increasingly powerful concept of copyright (which grants "creators" the right to ownership of intellectual property) has regulated the fruits of literacy, the *expression* of ideas in a form that can then be commodified, bartered, sold, and protected. England's first copyright law (the 1710 Statute of Anne) gave authors 14 years of exclusive rights to their works, a time span that has consistently been lengthened. This network of protectionism has grown steadily from the Enlightenment through Romanticism and Modernism, and right on into Postmodernism. In fact, as many now recognize, during the three decades that theorists have declared the death of the author and debated the very concept of "author-ship" and ownership of what I've been calling the fruits of literacy, the ideology of the author continues to circulate powerfully through legal and corporate as well as academic worlds, where the concept of the solitary and sovereign "author" still holds sway. As a result, copyright cannot exist in a work produced as a true collective enterprise; copyright does not hold in works that are not "original" (which, as Peter Jaszi demonstrates, rules out protection for "nonindividualistic cultural productions, like folkloric works, which cannot be reimagined as products of solitary, originary authorship," 1994: 38); and copyright does not extend to what the law sees as the basic components of cultural production (the rhythms of traditional musical forms, for example). What the law *does* protect is "author's rights," which have been repeatedly expanded during the last thirty years (in spite of postmodern tenets), effectively keeping a great deal of cultural material out of the public domain and further restricting the fair use of copyrighted (or copyrightable) works.

In a particularly ironic turn of events, corporate entities assuming the mantle of the author now lead the way in a kind of gold rush attempt to extend traditional copyright in all directions. Bill Gates is trying to corner the world's market of images; Disney is working to extend the limits of copyright to well over a hundred years before Mickey Mouse moves into the public commons; drug companies are patenting and copyrighting chemicals found in the plants of third-world countries in order to process and sell them as "cures"—and for a great profit; and scientists, the U.S. government, and large corporations are locked in debate over who will "own" various parts of the human genome.

Most recent has been the move in legal and corporate worlds to apply the mantle of proprietary authorship to hardware and software. In spite of their wide public use and the fact that they are the products of a highly collaborative process, computer programs (with a few notable exceptions) are increasingly defined in the law and in the economy as works of "originality" and "creative genius"; that is, as works that fall within the ever-expanding protection of copyright and authors' rights. In short, the old cloak of the author/genius who owns his (and traditionally, it has been *his*) intellectual property—this old cloak has been spruced up and donned by corporate entrepreneurial interests, and the bigger and more global, the better. Today, the same old cloak is being stretched to cover emerging Internet policies regarding authors' rights, although the recent suits and countersuits associated with Napster and other sites for downloading and copying music have revealed some holes in the fabric. Nonetheless, as James Porter (1999) points out in examining the ethical frameworks available for use in Internet policy, the individualist frame of traditional authorship, which is decidedly NOT postmodernist, is almost universally accepted as the only valid choice.

Barbara and her friends in *The Gossamer Project* know enough of this history to be actively resisting the ways in which traditional concepts of individual authorship and ownership have regulated literacy. The Project front page, for example, carries the following notice: "DISCLAIMER: FOX Network owns The X-Files. No copyright infringement is intended and no money is being made from the use of these characters." Interestingly enough, this statement is immediately followed by another statement: "Image copyright CloverBlue," suggesting the extent to which copyright rules even where it is being firmly resisted. In fact, I wonder what kind of ownership Barbara feels for the texts she (re)writes based on *The X-Files* model, just as I wonder what kind of ownership Chris Carter and *The X-Files* writers feel for the texts they write that are owned by the "author," FOX Network. In the case of Barbara and other Gossamer writers, it may be one thing to work collaboratively and to reject FOX claims to ownership and quite another to disentangle themselves from the ideological entailments of authorship and copyright. (In the same way, Jennifer Seibel Trainor suggests, it's one thing to declare the body ephemeral, attenuated, distributed, or erased—and quite another to act, in everyday life, as if that was the case.)

For all their explanatory power, postmodern theories have not displaced the pervasive ideologies of individualism, including those related to regulating literacies through copyright and other regimes of ownership. One result is the "Identity Crisis" identified and explored by Sherry Turkle (19950 in *Life on the Screen* and numerous essays; works in which she demonstrates both the potential for collaborative and multiple ways of knowing and being as well as the dangers attendant on them. "The final contest," she says, concerns the notion of the "real" in the face of virtual experience and virtual selves—and, she observes with no little irony, "the notion of the real fights back" (1995: 267). Given Turkle's trenchant analysis, it seems altogether fitting that *X-Files* fan fiction explores fluidity of selfhood while reinstating the body by way of master narratives of romance, or carries out deeply collaborative practices while participating in the ideologies of individualism. We are, as Trainor's essay makes strikingly evident, at an "in-between" time for literacy in general and cyberliteracy in particular; a liminal moment full of tension, contradiction, and opportunity. Out of such a moment may grow new understandings of the relationship among self/selves, text(s), and ownership necessary to the kind of critical cyberliteracy Trainor invokes.

Works Cited

The Gossamer Project. (2000). krycek.gossamer.org/gossamer/index.html (accessed 20 Dec. 2000).

Jaszi, P. (1994). On the author effect: Contemporary copyright and collective creativity. In M. Woodmansee and P. Jaszi (Eds.), *The Construction of authorship: Textual appropriation in law and literature.* Durham: Duke University Press.

Porter, J. (1999). Liberal individualism and internet policy: A communitarian critique. In G. Hawisher and S. Selfe (Eds.), *Passions, pedagogies, and 21st century technologies* (pp. 231–248). Logan: Utah State University Press.

Turkle, S. (1995). *Life on the screen: Identity in the age of the internet.* New York: Simon and Schuster.

CHAPTER SEVEN

Learning to Serve:
The Language and Literacy
of Food Service Workers

Tony Mirabelli

itterwaitress.com is one of the newest among a burgeoning number of worker-produced websites associated with the service industry.[1] The menu on the first page of this website offers links to gossip about celebrity behavior in restaurants, gossip about chefs and restaurant owners, accounts from famous people who were once waitresses,[2] and customer-related horror stories. There is also a forum that includes a "hate mail" page that posts email criticisms of the website itself, as well as general criticisms of waitressing, but the criticisms are followed by rebuttals usually from past or present waitresses. Predictably, most of the criticisms either implicitly or explicitly portray waitresses as ignorant and stupid. One email respondent didn't like what he read on the customer horror story page and sent in this response:

> If you find your job [as a waitress] so despicable, then go get an education and get a REAL job. You are whining about something that you can fix. Stop being such a weakling, go out and learn something, anything, and go make a real contribution to society.... Wait, let me guess: you do not have any marketable skills or useful knowledge, so you do what any bumbling fool can do, wait on tables. This is your own fault.

This response inspired a number of rebuttals of which the following two best summarize the overall sentiment expressed in response to the rant above. The first is from the webmaster of *bitterwaitress.com*:

Is it possible that I have an education, maybe I went to, oh say, Duke, and I just waitressed for some free time? Or that there are very many people in the industry who do this so that they CAN get an education? Not all of us were born with a trust fund.—There is, I might add, considerably more or less to a job than a "clear cut" salary. If you...live in New York, ...you'll know that empty stores and un-crowded subways are half the reason to work at night. By the way, what are the three Leovilles? What are the two kinds of tripe? Who was Cesar Ritz' partner? What is the JavaScript for a rollover? I guess I would have to ask a bumbling fool those questions. So, tell me then.

The second is from a mother of four:

I might not have a college education, but I would love to see those so called intelligent people get a big tip out of a bad meal, or from a person who is rude and cocky just because that's the way they are—that takes talent and its not a talent you can learn at any university. So, think about it before you say, "poor girl—to dumb to get a real job...."

Assumptions that waitresses (and waiters) are ignorant and stupid and that waiting on tables contributes little to society are not new. The rebuttals to commonplace, pejorative understandings of the food service industry suggest, however, that there is complexity and skill that may go unrecognized by the general public or institutions such as universities. Indeed institutions, particularly government and corporate entities in the United States, like the Bureau of Labor Statistics or the National Skills Labor Board, define waiting on tables as a low skilled profession. By defining this kind of work as low skilled, there is a concomitant implication that the more than one-third of America's work force who do it are low skilled.

Service occupations, otherwise known as "in-person" services (Reich, 1992) or "interactive services" (Leidner, 1993; MacDonald and Sirianni, 1996), include any kind of work which fundamentally involves face-to-face or voice-to-voice interactions and conscious manipulation of self-presentation. As distinguished from white-collar service work, this category of "emotional proletariat" (Macdonald and Sirianni, 1996) is comprised primarily of retail sales workers, hotel workers, cashiers, house cleaners, flight attendants, taxi drivers, package delivery drivers, and waiters, among others. According to the U.S. Bureau of Labor Statistics (1996), one-fifth of the jobs in eating, drinking, and grocery store establishments are held by youth workers between the ages of 16 and 24. While this kind of work is traditionally assumed to be primarily a stop-gap for young workers who will later move up and on to other careers, it also involves youths who will later end up in both middle- and working-class careers. It should not be forgotten that more than two thirds of the workers involved in food service are mature adults—many or most who began their careers in the same or similar industries. Interactive service work is a significant part of the economy in the U.S. today, and the Bureau of Labor Statistics predicts that jobs will be "abundant" in this category through 2006.

Economists such as Peter Drucker (1993) suggest that interactive service workers lack the necessary education to be "knowledge" workers. These economists support general conceptions that service work is "mindless," involving routine and repetitive tasks that require little education. This orientation further suggests that these supposedly low skilled workers lack the problem identifying, problem solving, and other high level abilities needed to work in other occupations. However, relatively little specific attention and analysis have been given to the literacy skills and language abilities needed to do this work. My research investigates these issues with a focus on waiters and waitresses who work in diners. Diner restaurants are somewhat distinct from fast food or fine-dining restaurants, and they also epitomize many of the assumptions held about low skilled workplaces that require interactive services. The National Skills Standards Board, for instance, has determined that a ninth-grade level of spoken and written language use is needed to be a waiter or a waitress. Yet, how language is spoken, read, or written in a restaurant may be vastly different from how it is used in a classroom. A seemingly simple event such as taking a customer's food order can become significantly more complex, for example, when a customer has a special request. How the waitress or waiter understands and uses texts such as the menu and how she or he "reads" and verbally interacts with the customer reflect carefully constructed uses of language and literacy.

This chapter explores these constructed ways of "reading" texts (and customers) along with the verbal "performances" and other manipulations of self-presentation that characterize interactive service work. In line with Macdonald and Sirianni (1996), I hope this work will contribute to the development of understandings and policies that build more respect and recognition for service work to help ensure it does not become equated with servitude.

Literacy and Contemporary Theory

In contrast to institutional assessments such as the National Skills Standards Board (1995), current thinking in key areas of education, sociology, anthropology and linguistics views language, literacy, and learning as embedded in social practice rather than entirely in the minds of individuals (Street, 1984; Gee, 1991; Lave and Wenger, 1991; Kress, 1993, 1995; Mahiri and Sablo, 1996; New London Group, 1996; Gee, Hull, and Lankshear 1996). As earlier chapters in this book have noted, Gee (1991: 6)—a key proponent of this conception of literacy—explains that to be literate means to have control of "a socially accepted association among ways of using language, of thinking, and of acting that can be used to identify oneself as a member of a socially meaningful group or 'social network.'" In a similar fashion, research work located explicitly within workplace studies proposes that literacy is "a range of practices specific to groups and individuals of different cultures, races, classes and genders" (Hull et al., 1996: 5).

In most societal institutions, however, literacy, continues to be defined by considerations of achievement and by abstract, standardized tests of individual students. Also, there is a decided focus on printed texts over other mediums of communication like visual and audio. Such a focus limits our understanding of literacy in terms of its use in specific situations in multiple modes of communication. The New Literacy Studies orientation that shapes the work reported in this book argues that literacy extends beyond individual experiences of reading and writing to include the various modes of communication and situations of any socially meaningful group or network where language is used in multiple ways. The New London Group (1996), for example, claims that due to changes in the social and economic environment, schools too must begin to consider language and literacy education in terms of "multiliteracies." The concept of multiliteracies supplements traditional literacy pedagogy by addressing the multiplicity of communications channels and the increasing saliency of cultural and linguistic diversity in the world today. Central to this study is the understanding that literate acts are embedded in specific situations and that they also extend beyond the printed text involving other modes of communication including both verbal and nonverbal. In this chapter, I illustrate something of the character of literacies specific to the "social network" of waiting on tables and show how they are distinct from the conceptions of literacy commonly associated with formal education. This is not simply to suggest that there is a jargon specific to the work, which of course there is, but that there is something unique and complex about the ways waiters and waitresses in diners use language and literacy in doing their work.

Methodology

Taken together, extant New Literacies Studies research makes a formidable argument for the need to re-evaluate how we understand literacy in the workplace—particularly from the perspective of interactive service workers. The research reported here is modeled after Hull and her colleagues' groundbreaking ethnographic study of skill requirements in the factories of two different Silicon Valley computer manufacturing plants (1996). Instead of studying manufacturing plants, the larger research study I conducted and that underpins the study reported here involves two diner restaurants—one that is corporately owned and one that is privately owned. In this chapter, however, I focus only on the one that is privately owned to begin addressing the specific ways that language use and literacy practices function in this kind of workplace.

To analyze the data, I relied on some of the methodological tools from the work of Hull and her colleagues (1996). In short, I looked at patterns of thought and behavior in the setting; I identified key events taking place; I did conversational analysis of verbal interactions; and, I conducted sociocultural analyses of key work events.

The data used in this chapter came from direct participation, observation, field notes, documents, interviews, tape recordings, and transcriptions, as well as from historical and bibliographic literature. I myself have been a waiter (both part-time and full-time over a ten-year period), and I was actually employed at the privately owned restaurant during my data collection period. In addition to providing important insights into worker skills, attitudes, and behaviors, my experience and positioning in this setting also enabled access to unique aspects of the work that might have otherwise gone unnoticed. The primary data considered in this chapter were collected during eight-hour periods of participant observation on Friday and/or Saturday nights in the restaurant. I chose weekend nights because they were usually the busiest times in the diner and were therefore the most challenging for the workers. Weekend shifts are also the most lucrative for the restaurant and the workers.

Lou's Restaurant

Lou's Restaurant[3] is a modest, privately owned diner restaurant patterned in a style that is popular in the local region. It has an open kitchen layout with a counter where individual customers can come and sit directly in front of the cooks' line and watch the "drama" of food service unfold while enjoying their meals. The food served at Lou's is Italian-American and it includes pastas, seafood, and a variety of sautéed or broiled poultry, beef, and veal. As is often the case with diner restaurants, Lou's has over ninety main course items, including several kinds of appetizers and salads, as well as a number of side dishes. The primary participants focused on in this chapter are three waiters at Lou's: John, Harvey, and myself.

After finishing my master's degree in English literature and deciding to move out of the state where I taught English as a Second Language at a community college, I ended up working as a waiter for two years at Lou's. This work allowed me to survive financially while further advancing my academic career. At the time I began my study at this site, the only waiter to have worked longer than two years at Lou's was John. Like myself, John began working in the restaurant business to earn extra money while in school after he had been discharged from the Marines, where he had been trained as a radio operator, telephone wireman, and Arabic translator. Two days after his honorable discharge, he started working in the restaurant that four years later would become Lou's. He subsequently has worked there for ten years. John also is the most experienced waiter at Lou's, and although the restaurant does not have an official "head" waiter, John is considered by his peers to be the expert. In an interview, he noted that it took almost ten years before he felt that he had really begun to master his craft.

Harvey might also be considered a master waiter, having been in the profession for over thirty years. However, at the beginning of the study he had been with Lou's for only two weeks. He was initially reticent to participate in the study because he said he lacked experience at this restaurant, and "didn't know the menu." Having left home when he was 14 years old to come "out West," over the years he had done a stint in the Air Force, held a position as a postal clerk, worked as a bellhop and bartender, and even had the opportunity to manage a local café. He decided that he did not like managerial work because he missed the freedom, autonomy, and customer interaction he had as a waiter and took a position at Lou's.

The Menu

Harvey's concern over not knowing the menu was not surprising. The menu is the most important printed text used by waiters and waitresses, and not knowing it can dramatically affect how they are able to do their work. The menu is the key text used for most interactions with the customer, and, of course, the contents of menus vary greatly from restaurant

menu literacy

to restaurant. But, what is a menu and what does it mean to have a literate understanding of one?

The restaurant menu is a genre unto itself. There is regularity and predictability in the conventions used such as the listing, categorizing, and pricing of individual, ready-made food items. The menu at Lou's contains ninety main course items, as well as a variety of soups, salads, appetizers, and side dishes. In addition, there are numerous selections where, for example, many main course items offer customers a choice of their own starch item from a selection of four: spaghetti, ravioli, french fries, or a baked potato. Some of the main course items, such as sandwiches, however, only come with french fries—but if the customer prefers something such as spaghetti, or vegetables instead of fries, they can substitute another item for a small charge, although this service is not listed in the menu. In addition to the food menu, there is also a wine menu and a full service bar meaning that hard liquor is sold in this restaurant. There are twenty different kinds of wine sold by the glass and a selection of thirty-eight different kinds of wine sold by the bottle, and customers can order most other kinds of alcoholic beverages.

In one context, waitresses and waiters' knowing the meaning of the words in the menus means knowing the process of food production in the restaurant. But this meaning is generally only used when a customer has a question or special request. In such situations the meaning of the words on the page are defined more by the questions and the waiters or waitresses' understanding of specific food preparation than by any standard cookbook or dictionary. For example, the *Better Homes and Gardens New Cook Book* (1996) presents a recipe for marinara sauce calling for a thick sauce consisting of tomatoes, tomato puree, peppers, carrots, celery, and garlic all sautéed and simmered for over thirty minutes. At Lou's, a marinara sauce is cooked in less than ten minutes and is a light tomato sauce consisting of fresh tomatoes, garlic, and parsley sautéed in olive oil. At a similar restaurant nearby—Joe's Italian Diner—marinara sauce is a seafood sauce, albeit tomato based. Someone who is familiar with Italian cooking will know that marinara sauce will have ingredients like tomatoes, olive oil, and garlic, but, in a restaurant, to have a more complete understanding of a word like *marinara* requires knowing how the kitchen prepares the dish. Clearly, the meanings of the language used in menus are socially and culturally embedded in the context of the specific situation or restaurant. To be literate here requires something other than a ninth-grade level of literacy. More than just a factual, or literal interpretation of the words on the page, it requires knowledge of specific prac-

[margin annotations: "how rhetorical / socially constructed menus are"; "Hm. Never realized how"]

tices—such as methods of food preparation—that take place in a particular restaurant.

On one occasion Harvey, the new but experienced waiter, asked me what "pesto" sauce was. He said that he had never come across the term before, and explained that he had never worked in an Italian restaurant and had rarely eaten at one. Pesto is one of the standard sauces on the menu, and like marinara, is commonly found on the menus of many Italian-American restaurants. I explained that it comprised primarily olive oil and basil, as well as garlic, pine nuts, Parmesan cheese, and a little cream. Harvey then told me that a customer had asked him about the sauce, and since he could not explain what it was, the customer did not order it.

On another occasion a mother asked Harvey if her child could have only carrots instead of the mixed vegetables as it said in the menu. Although he initially told her this was not possible, explaining that the vegetables were premixed and that the cooks would have to pick the carrots out one by one, the mother persisted. After a few trips from the table to the cooks' line, Harvey managed to get the carrots, but the customer then declined them because everyone had finished eating. Later, I explained to Harvey that it would have been possible to go to the back of the restaurant where he could find the vegetables in various stages of preparation. While the cooks only have supplies of pre-mixed vegetables on the line, Harvey could have gone to the walk-in refrigerator and picked up an order of carrots himself to give to the cooks.

Harvey's interactions with his customers highlight how much of what he needs to know to be a good waiter is learned within the specific situations and social networks in which that knowledge is used. The instantiation of the meaning of words like *pesto* and *marinara* often occurs in the interaction between co-workers as well as with customers. Conversation becomes a necessary element in achieving an appropriately literate understanding of the menu.

Harvey's understanding and use of the menu and special requests also involves more than his knowledge of food preparation. It involves the manipulation of power and control. Sociocultural theories of literacy consider the role of power and authority in the construction of meaning (Kress, 1993). From his perspective, the order of carrots was not simply an order of carrots, but a way of positioning one's self in the interaction. The customer saw her desire for the carrots as greater than what was advertised in the menu and thus exercised authority as a customer by requesting them despite Harvey's attempt to not make the carrots an option. While such a request might seem fairly innocuous in isolation, when considered in the specific situation of Lou's at that time—that is, peak dinner hour—it becomes more complex.

Special requests and questions can extend the meaning of the menu beyond the printed page and into the conversation and interaction between the waiter or waitress and the customer. Furthermore, special requests and questions can be as varied as the individual customers themselves. The general public shares a diner restaurant menu, but it is used by each individual patron to satisfy a private appetite. How to describe something to an individual customer and satisfy their private appetite requires not only the ability to *read* the menu, but also the ability to *read* the customer. This is achieved during the process of the dinner interaction, and it includes linguistic events such as greeting the customer or taking food orders and involves both verbal and non-verbal communication. In such events the meaning of the menu is continually reconstructed in the interaction between the waitress or waiter and the individual customer, and as a text functions as a "boundary object" that coordinates the perspectives of various constituencies for a similar purpose (Star and Griesmer, 1989); in this case the satisfaction of the individual patron's appetite. The degree to which private appetite is truly satisfied is open to debate, however. Virtually everyone who has eaten at a restaurant has his or her favorite horror story about the food and/or the service, and more often than not these stories in some way involve the menu and an unfulfilled private appetite.

In addition to being a text that is shared by the general public and used by the individual patron to satisfy a private appetite, the menu is also a text whose production of meaning results in ready-made consumable goods sold for a profit. The authors of a printed menu, usually the chefs and owners of the restaurant, have their own intentions when producing the hard copy. For example, it is common practice to write long extensively itemized menus in diner restaurants like Lou's. As was pointed out earlier, Lou's menu has over ninety selections from which to choose, and many of these can be combined with a range of additional possible choices. Printing a large selection of food items gives the appearance that the customer will be able to make a personal—and *personalized*—selection from the extensive menu. In fact, it is not uncommon for patrons at Lou's to request extra time to read the menu, or ask for recommendations before making a choice. The authors of the printed menu at Lou's constructed a text that appears to be able to satisfy private appetites, but they ultimately have little control over how the patron will interpret and use the menu.

The waiters and waitresses, however, do have some control. While customers certainly have their own intentions when asking questions, waitresses and waiters have their own intentions when responding. When customers ask questions about the menu, in addition to exercising their own authority, they also introduce the opportunity for waiters and waitresses to gain control of the interaction. A good example of how this control could be manipulated by a waiter or waitress comes from Chris Fehlinger, the web-master of *bitterwaitress.com*, in an interview with *New Yorker* magazine:

> "A lot of times when people asked about the menu, I would make it sound so elaborate that they would just leave it up to me," he said, "I'd describe, like, three dishes in excruciating detail, and they would just stutter, 'I, I, I can't decide, you decide for me.' So in that case, if the kitchen wants to sell fish, you're gonna have fish." He also employed what might be called a "magic words" strategy: "All you have to do is throw out certain terms, like *guanciale*, and then you throw in something like *saba*, a reduction of the unfermented must of the Trebbiano grape. If you mention things like that, people are just, like, 'O.K.!'" (Teicholz, 1999)

The use of linguistic devices like obfuscating descriptions and "magic words" is not unusual—particularly for waiters in fine dining restaurants. In *The World of Waiters* (1983), Mars and Nicod examined how English waiters use such devices to "get the jump" and gain control of selecting items from the menu. Their position of authority is further substantiated in fine dining restaurants by the common practice of printing menus in foreign languages, such as French, because it shifts the responsibility of food ordering from the customer, who often will not understand the language, to the waiter.

[margin handwritten note: Wow! Again Power/control!]

While diner restaurants generally do not print their menus in incomprehensible terms, they do, as at Lou's, tend to produce unusually long ones that can have a similar effect. But, diner menus like Lou's which offer Italian-American cuisine do use some language that is potentially unfamiliar to the clientele (e.g., *pesto*). The combination of menu length and potentially confusing language creates frequent opportunities for waiters and waitresses to get a jump on the customer. Customers at Lou's tend to ask questions about the meaning of almost every word and phrase in the menu. Not being able to provide at least a basic description of a menu item, as shown by Harvey's unfamiliarity with pesto, usually results in that item not being ordered.

Knowing what a customer wants often goes beyond simply being able to describe the food. It also involves knowing which descriptions will more likely sell and requires being able to apply the menu to the specific situation. For instance, in the following transcription I approach a table to take a food order while one customer is still reading the menu (Customer 3b). She asks me to explain the difference between veal scaloppini and veal scaloppini sec.

Tony:	(to Customer 3a and Customer 3b) hi
Customer 3b:	what's the difference between scaloppini and scaloppini sec?
Tony:	veal scaloppini is a tomato-based sauce with green onions and mushrooms / veal scaloppini sec is with marsala wine green onions and mushrooms
Customer 3b:	I'll have the veal scaloppini sec
Tony:	ok / would you like it with spaghetti / ravioli / french fries
Customer 3b:	ravioli
Customer 3a:	and / I'll get the tomato one / the veal scaloppini with mushrooms
Tony:	with spaghetti / ravioli / french fries
Customer 3a:	can I get steamed vegetables
Tony:	you want vegetables and no starch? / it already comes with vegetables / (.) (Customer 3a nods yes) ok / great / thank you
Customer 3a:	thanks

The word *sec* functions not unlike one of Fehlinger's "magic" words. Customers who are interested in ordering veal frequently ask questions about the distinction between the two kinds of scaloppini. I discovered over time that my description of the veal scaloppini sec almost always resulted in the customer ordering the dish. It seemed that mentioning marsala wine piqued customer interest more than tomato sauce did. One customer once quipped that marsala was a sweet wine and wanted to know why the word *sec*—meaning *dry*—was used. I replied that since no fat was used in the cooking process, it was considered "dry" cooking. In situations like this the menu is situated more in a conversational mode than a printed one. The transition from print to spoken word occurs due to the customer's inability to understand the menu, and/or satisfy his or her private appetite which results in a request for assistance. As a result the waiter or waitress can become the authority in relation to not only the printed text, but within the interaction as well. Eventually, I began to recommend this dish when customers asked for one, and the customers more often than not purchased it.

waiter is the authority

This particular food-ordering event also is interesting with regard to the customer's request for steamed vegetables. When I asked what kind of pasta she would like with her meal, she asked for steamed vegetables. The menu clearly states that vegetables are included with the meal along with the customer's choice of spaghetti, ravioli, or french fries. When she requested steamed vegetables, I simply could have arranged for her to have them and persisted in asking her which pasta she would like, but instead I anticipated that she might not want any pasta at all. I knew that, while it was not printed in the menu, the kitchen could serve her a double portion of steamed vegetables with no pasta. Most importantly, this customer's ability to order food that would satisfy her private appetite depended almost entirely upon my suggestions and understanding of the menu. Mars and Nicod (1984: 82), discussing a situation in a similar restaurant noted a waiter who would say, "You don't really need a menu... I'm a 'walking menu' and I'm much better than the ordinary kind... I can tell you things you won't find on the menu." Examples like this illustrate not only how waitresses and waiters gain control of their interactions with customers, but also how other modes of communication—such as conversations—are used to construct complex forms of meaning around printed texts like menus. Thus, the meaning of words in a menu are embedded in the situation, its participants, and the balance of power and authority, and this meaning manifests itself in more than one mode of communication.

Reading menus and reading customers also involves a myriad of cultural distinctions. Although there is not the space to discuss them here, age, gender, race, and class are all relevant to interactions between customers and waiter or waitress. The argument can be made that diner restaurants like Lou's promote a friendly, family-like atmosphere. Historically diners in the U.S. have been recognized as being places where customers can find a familial environment. Popular media today support this characteristic—particularly via television—where restaurant chains explicitly advertise that their customers are treated like family, and a number of television situation comedies have long used restaurants, diners, bars, and cafés as settings where customers and employees interact in very personal and intimate ways. This cultural atmosphere can have a tremendous impact on interactions with the customers. There is sometimes miscommunication or resistance where a customer may or may not want to be treated like family, or the waitress or waiter may or may not want to treat a customer like family. At Lou's, in addition to having an intimate understanding of food production and being able to describe it to a customer in an appealing fashion, reading a menu and taking a customer's food order also requires the ability to perform these tasks in a friendly, familial manner.

The following example reveals the complexity of meanings involved in taking a customer's food order and the expression of "family." Al is a regular customer who almost always comes in by himself and sits at the counter in front of the cooks' line. He also always has the same thing to eat, a side order of spaghetti Marinara, and never looks at the menu. Perhaps more important to Al than the food he eats are the people he interacts with at Lou's. He will sit at the counter and enjoy the badinage he shares with the other customers who sit down next to him at the counter, the waitresses and waiters as they pass by his seat, and the cooks working just across the counter. On this particular evening, however, he was joined by his son, daughter-in-law, and young adult granddaughter, and rather than sitting at the counter, he sat in a large booth. Although I immediately recognized Al, I had never waited on him and his family before, I was not sure how informal he would like the interaction to be. So I began with a fairly formal greeting saying "hello" instead of "hi" and avoided opportunities to make small talk with Al and his family:

Tony: hello::=
Customer 2d: =hello
Al: hey (.) what they put in the water? / I don't know / is it the ice or what is it?
Customer 2s: (chuckles from Customer 2d, Customer 2s and Customer 2c)
Tony: does the water taste strange?
Customer 2s: no
Tony: do you want me to get you another water?
Al: no / I don't want any water
Tony :   ok
Al: I had a couple of drinks before I came
Customer 2s: (chuckles)=
Tony: (in reference to the water tasting strange) =it could be / it could be/ I don't know
Customer 2d: (to Customer 2s) are you having anything to drink?
Customer 2s: I'll have a beer / American beer / you have miller draft?
Tony: (while writing down the order) miller genuine
Customer 2d: and I'll have a tequila sunrise
Al: (to Customer 2d) what are you having?
Customer 2d: tequila sunrise
Al: oh / you should fly / you should fly
Tony: (to Customer 2a) al / you want anything
Customer 2s: (to Customer 2a) a beer? / or anything?
Al: no / I've had too much already
Customer 2s: are you sure
Customer 2d: we'll get you a coffee later
Tony: (nod of affirmation to daughter-in-law)
Al: I've been home alone drinking
Tony: ugh ogh:: / (chuckles along with Customer 2s)

Al's comments about the water tasting funny and his drinking at home alone both provided opportunities for me to interact more intimately with Al and his family, but instead I concerned myself solely with taking their drink orders. Al's desire for me to interact in a more familial manner became more apparent when I returned to take their food order.

Customer 2d: (as the drinks are delivered) ah / great / thank you
Tony: (placing drinks in front of customers) there you go / you're wel-come
Al: (to Customer 2s) so we're flying to vegas (mumbles)
Tony: all right / you need a few minutes here?
Customer 2s: no / (to Customer 2a) are you ready or do you want to wait?
Customer 2d: you made up your mind yet?
Al: (mumble) made up my mind yet
Customer 2d: oh / ok
Tony: al / what can I get for you?
Al: I said I haven't made up my mind yet
Tony: oh / ok (everyone at the table chuckles except Al)
Al: I always have pasta you know / I would walk out there (points to the counter) the guy says / I know what you want
Tony: ok / I'll be back in a few minutes
Customer 2d: come back in a few minutes / thanks

While I misunderstood Al when I asked if he was ready to order, for him the greater transgression was simply asking if he was ready to order. Al expected me to know what he was going to eat because he's a regular; he's like family. He wanted a side order of spaghetti marinara and didn't want to have to speak regarding his food order. To be successful in fulfilling Al's private appetite required more than the ability to describe food according to individual customer preferences. A side order of spaghetti marinara represents not merely a food item on a menu, nor a satisfying mix of pasta and tomatoes, but also, depending on the way it is ordered and served, a gesture of friendliness: "I always have pasta you know / I would walk out there (points to the counter) the guy says / I know what you want." To be literate with a menu also means knowing when and how to express emotion (or not express emotion) to a customer through its use.

Being able to take a customer's order without him or her reading the menu or being able to fulfill a special request not printed in the menu are important ways of expressing friendliness and family at Lou's. John, the most experienced waiter on staff, often can be found running to get an order of homemade gnocchi from the back freezer and delivering them to the cooks when they are too busy to get back there themselves. Or, he might step in behind the bar to make his own cappuccino when the bartender is busy serving other customers. On one occasion, like many others, John had a customer request a special order called *prawns romano*, a pasta dish consisting of fettuccine with prawns in a white sauce with green onions, tomatoes, and garlic. This is not listed on any menu in the restaurant, but it is something that the cooks occasionally offer as an evening special. John politely asked whether or not the cooks could accommodate his customer's request, and they complied. One can frequently hear John greeting many of his customers with some variation of, "Can I get you the usual?" Alternatively, in the case of special requests, some variant of, "That's no problem" is an often used phrase. Just like a friend for whom it would be no problem, John attempts to satisfy his customer's special requests in a similar fashion.

Yet, friendliness is often a feigned performance. Being friendly is an experiential phenomenon that is learned through participation. To be a good waitress or waiter generally requires being able to perform friendliness under any number of circumstances. To be successful at the practice of being friendly requires performing certain techniques over and over until they can be performed on an unconscious level. Referred to as emotional labor (Hochschild, 1983: 6–7) this kind of work "requires one to induce or suppress feeling in order to sustain the outward countenance that produces the proper state of mind in others." Emotional labor also is an integral part to how a waitress constructs meaning in a menu. While emotional labor may not yield the same monetary results in restaurants like Lou's, it is still essential to the work. For example, John is masterful in the way he utilizes emotional labor. On one particularly busy evening John was trapped in a line at the bar waiting to place his drink order. He was clearly anxious, and was looking at his food order tickets to see what he needed to do next. The crowd of customers waiting to be seated spilled out of the foyer and into the aisle near where the waitresses and waiters where waiting to place their drink orders. One customer, who recognized John, caught his attention:

John:	hi=
Customer:	=hi can I get a glass of wine
John:	sure (.) what do you want
Customer:	are you busy
John:	NO (.) I got it (.) what do you want

John's friendly "hi" and over emphatic "no" were intended to suggest to the customer that he was not busy, when he clearly was. As he later explained, he knew that the customer knew he was really busy, but he also knew that if he was friendly and accommodating, the customer probably would give him a nice tip for his trouble, which the customer did. His feigned amiability in agreeing to get the customer a drink was more or less a monetary performance. John had learned to use language for financial gain. One should not be fooled by the apparent simplicity in the preceding interaction. While it may be brief, being able to be friendly and accommodating under extreme circumstances like the "dinner rush" requires years of practice in a real work setting learning to be able to say, "hi—sure—NO, I got it."

Although interactions with customers have been presented individually, the reality of how these events occur is quite different. Unlike fine-dining restaurants where the dinner experience can extend over a few hours, diners operate on high volume serving to a great number of patrons in a short amount of time. George Orwell, reflecting on the difficulty involved in this work, wrote, "I calculated that [a waiter] had to walk and run about 15 miles during the day and yet the strain of the work was more mental than physical.... One has to leap to and fro between a multitude of jobs—it is like sorting a pack of cards against the clock" (Orwell, 1933). Because one person may be serving as many as ten tables or more at one time, the process of serving each individual table will overlap with the others. Food orders are taken numerous times in a half-hour period during busy dinner hours at Lou's. The preceding transcriptions were taken from tape-recorded data collected on Friday evenings around 7 o'clock. My own interactions were recorded during a period when I had what is referred to as a *full station*, meaning that all of the tables under my supervision were filled with customers. By this point in the evening I had two customers at the counter, a party of four and six parties of two, for a total of eighteen customers—all of whom were in the process of ordering their meals within the same half-hour to forty-five minute period.

Literacy practices in this environment are nothing like those found in traditional classrooms, but they might be more comparable to those found in the emergency ward of a hospital or an air-traffic controller's tower. Interaction with texts and participants takes place in a rapid succession of small chunks. During the dinner hours, there are no long, drawn out monologues. Time is of the essence during the busiest dinner hours for all participants involved: from the waiters and waitresses to the cooks, bartenders, and busboys. In two hundred lines of transcribed dialogue during a busy dinner period, for example, I never paused longer than thirty-nine seconds, and no participant spoke more than forty-one words in one turn. Even these pauses were usually the result of other work being completed, such as preparing a salad or waiting to order a drink. During this period, virtually all the conversation, reading, and writing were related to the immediate situational context. As this research has shown, language use was far more complex than one might assume in situations and events that involve taking a customer's food order. In addition to knowing how food is prepared, what will appeal to specific customers, and how to present this information in a friendly manner, the waiter or waitress must also remain conscious of the number of other tables waiting to have their orders taken and the amount of time that will take. Reading menus and reading customers requires the ability to think and react quickly to a multitude of almost simultaneously occurring literate events.

Conclusion

Menus at Lou's are texts that are catalysts for interaction between staff and customers, and their meaning is firmly embedded in this interaction. Meaning is constructed from the menu through more than one mode of communication and between a variety of participants. This process involves knowledge of food preparation, use specific linguistic devices like magic words and other ways of describing food, the ability to read individual customers' tastes and preferences, the general expectation to perform in a friendly manner, and all during numerous virtually simultaneous and similar events. Yet, there is much left unconsidered in this chapter, particularly regarding the nature of power and control. While waitresses and waiters are frequently able to manipulate control over customer decisions while taking a food order, this control is often tenuous and insignificant beyond the immediate interaction.

Little also has been said in this chapter about the role of management. Extensive research has already been done in the area of management control, literacy, and worker skills (Braverman, 1974; Hochschild, 1983; Kress, 1993; Leidner, 1993; Hall, 1993; Hull et al., 1996; Macdonald and Sirianni, 1996; Gee, Hull, and Lankshear, 1996). These researchers consider how literacy practices are manipulated by management to maintain control over the worker. Whether it be scientific management where workers are deskilled and routinized, or Fast Capitalism where forms of control are more insidious and shrouded in the guise of "empowering" the worker, there is little research on interactive service work beyond the fast food industry that explores how this rhetoric plays itself out in a real world situation. This leaves open to debate questions regarding the effectiveness of Fast Capitalism as a form of control over the worker. While my research has shown that waiters and waitresses can exercise some level of authority, skill and wit through their use of language with customers, they must also interact with management and other staff where authority and control plays out in different ways.

In the end, however, the customer has ultimate authority over the waiter or waitress. Diner waitressing has a long history of prejudice dating back to the beginning of the industrial revolution and involves issues of gender regarding our general perceptions and ways of interacting (Cobble, 1991; Hall, 1993). Waitressing is integrally tied to domesticated housework and likewise has historically been treated as requiring little skill or ability. In fact, the stigma of servitude that plagues waitressing and other similar kinds of work are not only the result of less than respectable treatment from management, but from customers as well. In her sociological study of diner waitresses in New Jersey, Greta Paules sums it up best:

> That customers embrace the service-as-servitude metaphor is evidenced by the way they speak to and about service workers. Virtually every rule of etiquette is violated by customers in their interactions with the waitress: the waitress can be interrupted; she can be addressed with the mouth full; she can be ignored and stared at; and she can be subjected to unrestrained anger. Lacking status as a person she like the servant, is refused the most basic considerations of polite interaction. She is, in addition, the subject of chronic criticism. Just as in the nineteenth century servants were perceived as ignorant, slow, lazy, indifferent, and immoral (Sutherland 1981), so in the twentieth century service workers are condemned for their stupidity, apathy, slowness, competence, and questionable moral character. (1991: 138–139)

The low status of waitressing and waitering belies the complex nature of this kind of work and the innovative and creative ways in which such workers use language.

Notes

1. Some of the more than 20 websites I have found so far like waitersrevenge.com are award winning. They include sites for taxi drivers, hotel workers, and the like.
2. How to appropriately refer to waitresses and waiters is not a simple decision. Terms like *server* and *food server* are alternatives, but all are problematic. I personally do not like *server* or *food server* because they are too closely related to the word servitude. The waiter/waitress distinction is problematic not simply because it differentiates genders, but also because it is associated with a kind/class of service. Often in fine-dining restaurants today both men and women are referred to as waiters, but it is

more commonly the practice in the "diner" style restaurant to maintain the distinctive terms. This is historically connected to the diner waitressing being regarded as inferior to fine-dining waitering because it was merely an extension of the domesticated duties of the household.

3. Pseudonyms have been used throughout this chapter.

Works Cited

Better homes and gardens new cook book. (1996). New York: Better Homes and Gardens.

Braverman, H. (1974). *Labor and monopoly capital: The degradation of work in the twentieth century.* New York: Monthly Review Press.

Bureau of Labor Statistics. (1996). Washington, D.C.: U.S. Department of Labor.

Drucker, P. (1993). *Innovation and entrepreneurship: Practice and principles.* New York: Harperbusiness.

Cobble, S. (1991). *Dishing it out: Waitresses and their unions in the 20th century.* Urbana: University of Illinois Press.

Gee, J. (1991). *Sociolinguistics and literacies: Ideology in discourses.* New York. Falmer.

———, Hull, G., and Lankshear, C. (1996). *The new work order: Behind the language of the new capitalism.* Sydney: Allen & Unwin.

Gowen, S. (1992). *The politics of workplace literacy.* New York: Teachers College Press.

Hall, E. (1993). Smiling, deferring, and good service. *Work and occupations,* 20 (4), 452–471.

Hochschild, A. (1983). *The managed heart.* Berkeley: University of California Press.

Hull, G. (Ed.). (1997). *Changing work, changing workers: Critical perspectives on language, literacy, and skills.* New York: State University of New York Press.

——— et al. (1996). *Changing work, changing literacy? A study of skills requirements and development in a traditional and restructured workplace. Final Report.* Unpublished manuscript. University of California at Berkeley.

Kress, G. (1993). Genre as social process. In B. Cope and M. Kalantzis (Eds.), *The powers of literacy: A genre approach to teaching writing* (pp. 22–37). London: Falmer.

———. (1995). *Writing the future: English and the making of a cultural innovation.* London: NATE.

Lave, J. and Wenger, E. (1991). *Situated learning: Legitimate peripheral participation.* New York: Cambridge University Press.

Leidner, R. (1993). *Fast food, fast talk: Service work and the routinization of everyday life.* Berkeley: University of California Press.

Macdonald, C. and Sirianni, C. (Eds.). (1996). *Working in the service society.* Philadelphia, PA: Temple University Press.

Mahiri, J. and Sablo, S. (1996). Writing for their lives: The non-school literacy of California's urban African American youth. *Journal of Negro Education,* 65 (2), 164–180.

Mars, G. and Nicod, M. (1984). *The world of waiters.* London: Unwin Hyman.

New London Group. (1996). A pedagogy of multiliteracies: Designing social futures. *Harvard Educational Review,* 66 (1), 60–92.

NSSB (National Skills Standards Board). (1995). *Server skill standards: National performance criteria in the foodservice industry.* Washington, DC: U.S. Council on Hotel, Restaurant and Institutional Education.

Orwell, G. (1933). *Down and out in Paris and London*. New York. Harcourt Brace.

Paules, G. (1991). *Dishing it out: Power and resistance among waitresses in a New Jersey Restaurant*. Philadelphia, PA: Temple University Press.

Reich, R. (1992). *The work of nations*. New York: Vintage.

Star, L. and Griesmer, J. (1989). Institutional ecology, translations and boundary objects: Amateurs and professional in Berkeley's Museum of Vertebrate Zoology, 1907–1939. *Social Studies of Science*, 19.

Street, B. (1984 April 5). *Literacy in theory and practice*. London: Cambridge University Press.

"Learning to Serve"

Stuart Tannock

If the interactional study of science and technology has often worked to make the labor of scientists and technicians appear less specialized and more everyday and mundane, the interactional study of low-end service work has frequently taken the form of a "recovery project," seeking to make that which we see as everyday and mundane seem instead to be special, skilled, and indeed, "literate." Such symbolic leveling can be immensely and aesthetically appealing in the halls of academe: with our own hands—that is, with our own specific forms of social scientific literacy—we can begin to erase the vast inequalities that exist between contemporary knowledge and service workers. Service workers now appear to us as highly knowledgeable; knowledge workers as merely serviceable.[1]

In this response, I do not wish to focus so much on the core arguments of Tony Mirabelli's chapter, for these I find to be persuasive. Mirabelli produces a deft analysis of the precise ways in which the literate work of diner waitstaff is locally and collaboratively accomplished, embedded in social networks, and closely tied to individual waitstaff identities. From the vantage point of literacy studies (and critical discourse analysis), Mirabelli produces an excellent example of the value of moving beyond simple text analysis to study how actual written texts are produced, read, and negotiated in real time, ongoing interaction between diverse social actors.

My focus in this response is instead on the frame that Mirabelli uses to argue for the larger social value of his chapter: specifically his desire to erase the "stigma of servitude" by demonstrating the "complex," "innovative," "creative," and "literate" nature of service work, as represented here by the labor of two waiters, Harvey and John, as well as by Mirabelli himself, in a privately owned dinner house named "Lou's Restaurant." I have much sympathy for such desire and effort—and indeed, have made similar efforts in my own writing on service workers. What I wish to emphasize here, however, is that the academic documentation of literacy among social groups and individuals for whom such literacy has previously been left unrecognized is not in and of itself an automatically enabling or progressive move, but can in fact be extremely disempowering for the subjects of our research.

The point of the following discussion is to remind ourselves (as literacy researchers) of the constant need to think carefully about "what's at stake for whom" in the analyses we make, and to situate our analyses precisely in specific social settings, political contexts, and ideological discourses. It is also to remind us of the fundamental ambiguity and polysemy—and consequent possibility of unintended and unanticipated treachery—of all symbolic and intellectual endeavor: what we think of as symbolic leveling can all too often turn out to be retrenchment of symbolic stratification. I focus my remarks here on the possible implications of Mirabelli's analyses for three areas of social and political concern: the empowerment of service workers; the training of service workers; and the empowerment of (urban) youth. The first two areas of concern I take directly from Mirabelli's chapter; the third I take from the title of this book and Jabari Mahiri's introduction to it.

Food Service Literacies and the Empowerment of Service Workers

From unionization to professionalization to pay equity (comparable worth) efforts, claims of the complex and valuable skills embedded in socially devalued occupations have been at the center of workers' efforts to demand more respect, status, and wealth for themselves. Mirabelli's careful analyses of the emotional labor, local and general background knowledge, and complex "menu work" enacted by diner waitstaff clearly could be of great value in supporting such worker empowerment efforts. But is this how such analyses will actually be used? We cannot be certain.

There is a risk that claims of finding high levels of skill in the work of supposedly unskilled workers may impose an element of condescension on such workers, and serve to undermine or displace attention from these workers' complaints of the unskilled nature of their work. Many low-end service occupations, after all, have not only been *devalued*; they have often been deliberately *deskilled* by management as well. Moreover, encouraging low-end service workers to think of themselves as already being skilled (professional, empowered) workers can and very often does serve as a "disciplinary mechanism" to raise worker morale and extract higher levels of effort from them. Mirabelli acknowledges these phenomena of deskilling and disciplining in a brief discussion of "scientific management" and "Fast Capitalism" at the end of his chapter, but he does not explore how his own analyses could themselves be implicated in such processes.

Even if Mirabelli's analyses could be used by waiters such as Harvey and John in local self-empowerment efforts to lay claim to greater status and wealth, there is the further concern that such efforts, based on the authoritative (academic) documentation of previously unrecognized skills in their jobs, could simultaneously *dis*empower other workers. The reason is that (ostensibly) skill-based worker empowerment efforts implicitly embrace an ideology of meritocracy—an ideology that posits that workers who are unable to demonstrate high levels of skill to outside audiences have little or no claim to increasing their status or income. I return to this point in my discussion of youth workers below.

Food Service Literacies and the Training of Service Workers

In the opening sections of his chapter, Mirabelli critiques the representations of service work by the National Skills Standards Board (NSSB, 1995)—an organization created by U.S. Congress in 1994 to oversee the development of skills standards for various occupational clusters that would help improve worker training and development throughout the country. Mirabelli's careful and detailed analyses of how restaurant waiting work is actually performed (in the context of one privately owned dinner house) represent a vast improvement over the acontextual and apolitical descriptions of such work contained in the NSSB's "Server Skill Standards." Mirabelli's analyses could quite conceivably contribute to efforts to rethink, reform and improve the training of new workers coming into restaurants such as "Lou's."

But how might John and Harvey, the two waiters discussed in Mirabelli's chapter, respond to such endeavors? Mirabelli tells us that these two men have worked in the restaurant industry for fourteen and thirty years, respectively, that both are deeply invested in a craft identity, and that both are committed to a sense of expertise that can be built only through years of on-the-job work experience. John tells Mirabelli that "it took almost ten years before he felt that he had really begun to master his craft," while Harvey, despite three decades of working in the restaurant industry, was "initially reticent to participate" in Mirabelli's study because he had only recently started at Lou's Restaurant.

Attempts to capture informal worker-based expertise and translate such expertise into training programs (which in the restaurant industry, are almost universally run by management) that quickly reproduce highly skilled new workers could be seen not only as doing violence to Harvey and John's sense of work identity, but as part of a process that shifts control over the workplace from worker to manager, and that makes workers such as Harvey and John more expendable. In the local context of Lou's Restaurant and Mirabelli's research presence there, such a reading may seem farfetched and even absurd. But in our era of reengineering, downsizing, and general job instability, these sorts of disempowering uses of academic "recovery projects" of hidden and informal worker knowledge, skill, and institutional memory are, of course, by no means unheard of.

Food Service Literacies and the Empowerment of Youth

Mirabelli frames his chapter as a study of service workers *in general*, while the book's editor, Jabari Mahiri, in titling and introducing this book as a collection of studies of literacies among *urban youth*, suggests that Mirabelli's chapter can contribute to a collective effort to understand and empower contemporary urban (especially minority and working class) youths. But what exactly is the significance of Mirabelli's analyses for youth—in particular, for those youths working in the food service industry?

Mirabelli's study documents the skilled nature of the work of two *adult, long-term, craft-oriented* waiters in a *privately owned dinner house*. It is almost certain that Harvey and John would deny claims by *younger, newer*, and *temporary* waitstaff at Lou's Restaurant to have equal or parallel levels of skill. It is also quite likely that Harvey and John would deny claims of equal levels of skill among waitstaff in *corporate-owned chain diners* (where waiting work is generally seen—whether justifiably or not—as being more routinized) or among food service workers in *fast food restaurants*. Youth workers, of course, are far more likely to work in corporate-owned fast-food and dinner house chains than they are in privately owned diners (or upscale restaurants).

It is not clear how Mirabelli himself would want to represent "skill" among these other populations and settings—although my guess is that

Mirabelli would most likely want to show that food service work among other social groups and in other settings also contains unrecognized levels and types of skill (literacy). But how would Mirabelli compare the nature of "skill" across different social groups and settings within the restaurant industry as a whole? Are some social groups and settings "more" or "less" skilled? Here the social scientific representation of skill (or literacy) may run into problems. Were Mirabelli to represent other settings and social groups in the restaurant industry as being "equally" skilled to Harvey and John, he risks imposing symbolic violence on the identities and self-professed expertise of these two waiters; yet if he represents Harvey and John as having "more" skill than others, he equally risks imposing symbolic violence elsewhere.

What is fundamentally at issue here is that claims of skill are usually exclusionary—that is, they are based on the assertion that certain abilities and knowledges are special or rare, and that other groups of people do not have them. In the food service industry, historically, upscale restaurant workers have been more able to assert the skilled nature of their work than have dinner house workers, while dinner house workers have been positioned as more "skilled" than fast food workers. Similarly, long-term or career restaurant workers have generally been more able to assert the high level of their skills than short-term, temporary workers; and adult restaurant workers have been more able to position themselves as "skilled" than youth restaurant workers.

All of this brings us to the question: how might *temporary, stopgap, youth* food service workers—*in particular*—from their position at the bottom of this "food chain," seek to erase the "stigma of servitude" and lay claim to higher wages and greater status in the workplace? In part, I would guess, they could do so through precisely the kind of project in which Mirabelli is engaged—that is, through showing the value, difficulty, skill or literacy inherent in their work. And in part, they could publicize the deskilled and impoverished nature of the workplaces in which they work, seeking to change and improve such conditions. But above and beyond such skill-based strategies, I would think that youth workers would need to challenge the misleading notion of meritocracy itself: to reject the embrace of a mythical skills-and-wages hierarchy; and to point to how wages and statuses in our workplaces are more likely to be set by the identities of *who* is working in a particular job than by any neutral and universal (academic) assessment of differential (or parallel) skill levels across jobs.

In this country, the "stigma of servitude" that is experienced by youth service workers is often based, in part at least, upon an amazingly open and unconcealed age-based prejudice against the young. As Mahiri points out in the introduction to this book, youth—especially minority and working class youth—in the United States are often pathologized and "inscribed by stigmatized images." In the context of the workplace, this means that youths are often not seen as deserving the same working conditions as are adults, and that youths are "inscribed" in a tautology that conflates youth with low value and with low skill—and consequently, with low status and low wages. To transform and improve the working lives of youths in this country, therefore, we need to do more than "upvalue" and "upskill" the workplaces in which youths tend to work. We need also to confront head-on the debilitating effects of age-based prejudice against the young.

Note

1. *Acknowledgment*: My opening comments on symbolic leveling, recovery projects, and especially on the interactional study of science and technology draw on conversations with Roger Hall.

Works Cited

NSSB (National Skills Standards Board). (1995). *Server skill standards: National performance criteria in the foodservice industry*. Washington, DC: U.S. Council on Hotel, Restaurant and Institutional Education.

CHAPTER EIGHT

Practicing for Romance: Adolescent Girls Read the Romance Novel

Jane Stanley

In one short day I had turned pretty... Just the night before I'd been practicing my smile, and it had been just as rigid as it had always been. But Paul had said my smile was beautiful—sure enough, now it was. (Conklin, 1981: 57)

In one short paragraph, the 350,000 adolescent female readers of the bestseller, *P.S. I Love You* (Conklin, 1981: 57), have learned not to blink under the potent beam of the male gaze. But chances are good that they already knew this from their reading, if not yet from their experiences in life. A 1993 survey of the reading habits of seventh-graders indicates a strong preference for romance novels, some sixty-one percent of the girls nominating romance as their first choice among thirteen genres (Willinsky and Hunniford, 1993). While young readers' preferences have certainly shifted to themes more Harry-Potteresque since that survey was conducted, romance novels still continue to enjoy breathless readership among girls. The publishing industry counts mightily upon this loyalty, numbering adolescent girls among its favorite customers. Serial romances for teens and pre-teens enjoy massive sales. Bantam's Sweet Valley High series, for example, has printed over twenty-six million books (Cooper, 1993).

However, while girl readers and publishers are floating on a cushy cloud of romance, many parents and educators are searching in vain for the silver lining. The Council of Interracial Books for Children finds that these novels teach girls to put boys' interests above their own, and that, by and large, they show only the lives of white suburban middle-class families (Christian-Smith, 1993a). In fact, amid all this middle-class abundance the only thing that is impoverished is the range of options available to the female protagonists in these stories.

> What options are you doing at school next year?" he asked as his hand circled her shoulder blades. Jilly hadn't really thought about it. It felt good having him stroke the suntan cream into her skin. Choosing options was the last thing on her mind. "I don't know," she said, "maybe…astronomy." She sounded as though she were asking a question. "Astronomy!" said Tom. "I didn't know they were offering it. *That'd be great.* You know, there was an explosion up there in one of the galaxies hundreds of years ago. It left a black hole." "A black hole? [she responded,] What's that got to do with horoscopes?" "Horoscopes? [he asked,] Oh, you mean *astrology.*" "Astrology, astronomy [she replied,] What's the difference?" (Vaughan, 1988: 72, cited in Gilbert and Taylor, 1991: 91)

For some teachers, however, the difference between romance and other reading is moot. Faced with a classroom of "reluctant readers," teachers have welcomed, albeit wanly, the girls' keen interest in romance.

In giving themselves over so passionately to romance, these girls have pressed their teachers into embracing—however uneasily—an autonomous model of literacy. That is, the consequences of their literacy practices are seen strictly in cognitive terms: Increased exposure to texts leads to increased mastery of the technical skills of decoding and drawing inferences, and this results in a heightened interest in the act of reading. However, those of us not confronted daily with a class full of reluctant readers have the luxury of asking for more for the girls. We can afford to ascribe to the view endorsed by Brian Street (1993), among others, of literacy practices as ineluctably ideological; that is, they are profoundly coupled with cultural and power structures. For us, the consequences of this kind of literacy are the reproduction of a culture that instructs girls that the quest for romance is in and of itself a career (Gilbert, 1993).

In fact, these girls are characters in a story that is far more complex than the stories they read. The plot line here is not simply the tension between the ideological and autonomous views of their literacy practices. They use their romances as a resource for cracking the cryptic code of male behavior. They subvert their teachers' delivery of "pedagogized literacy" (Street and Street, 1991: 158), presenting an example of oppositional behavior at least as compelling as that of the "lads" in Willis's classic tale of resistance in *Learning to Labour* (1977). Significant labor, too, is invested in this campaign for the girls' hearts and minds by the publishing industry which goes to inordinate lengths to secure the girls' continued romance readership.

This chapter tells the story of these girls' unyielding loyalty to the genre of romance. It considers the role of the publishing industry in nurturing this market, and it revisits, in some detail, two important ethnographic studies made of young romance readers and their responses to their texts. Additionally, it considers resistance theory in light of the girls' assertion of their right to read the romance. Throughout this piece, I offer conjectures as to why reading the romance is so compelling a literacy practice.

The Book Trade: Romancing the Consumer

It is not possible to discuss the girls' agency in selecting romances as their preferred genre without considering the assiduous marketing efforts undertaken by publishers. The past twenty years have seen the rise of media giants, a conflation of the apparatus of book production and marketing/ distribution. In the book trade, this has resulted in editorial decisions that tend away from untried literary formulations, and toward quick turnover of product, big press runs, and "sure bets." Thus, it is not surprising that teen romances are written to narrowly conceived, and heavily market-researched specifications. They are designed to appeal to the "lowest common denominator of reader to attract the largest possible audience" (Coser et al., 1982: 1).

In a book chapter titled, "Retailing Gender," Cooper considers the commodity function of popular literature, arguing persuasively that publishers undertake to create a product as well as to create the desire for more products like it. She maintains that this process develops in the consumer a "hunger for redundancy" (Eco, 1979, cited in Cooper, 1993: 14). In the case of the teen romance novel, Cooper argues that it is this very sameness that leads to passivity and non-critical reading. Luke (1993: 10) sees such "texts of desire" as providing females with "scripts for rehearsing gender relations, marriage, sexuality, and work."

Many schools do their part in sounding the casting call by their participation in book clubs. Cooper (1993) characterizes teachers as acting as sales representatives in the schools, passing out promotional brochures, persuading parents to underwrite purchases, processing students' orders, and generating enthusiasm for the companies' promotional schemes, such as trips to Disneyland. In return for sales, teachers and their schools receive incentives such as books for the library or class collection. This process results in a Tupperware model of commodification of literacy, with institutional legitimacy conferred by educators. This textual merchandise, like Tupperware, is very popular; book clubs in schools had by the early 1990s accounted for 47 million book sales (Cooper, 1993: 9).

The Readers

Street (1990) urges a careful analysis of individual reading practices in their various settings in order fully to comprehend the ideological character of literacy and its role in cultural reproduction. This section will briefly report two specific researchers' findings, and then will discuss in some detail both of the groups of girls studied and their engagement in romance.

In *Private Practices: Girls Reading Fiction and Constructing Identity*, Cherland (1994) studied the literacy practices of a group of 11-year-olds in a small Canadian town. These girls read both romances and other books. In her inquiry into *what* books the girls read and *how* they read them, Cherland found the reading of romance fiction to be a highly social practice as well as an important component in the girls' construction of a gendered identity.

In *Becoming a Woman Through Romance*, Christian-Smith sought to understand what perspectives of femininity popular romance fiction presented to a group of working- and middle-class girls, aged 12 to 15 years old, from the inner city and near-suburbs of a large U.S. city. That is, she hoped to gain insight into how these girls interpreted romance novels, and what social, economic, and political implications their readings carried for them. Although the texture of life was very different for these girls compared with the small-town Canadian girls, the consequences of their literacy were the same. Their reading of romance "reconciled them to the prevailing social arrangements" (Christian-Smith, 1991: 9).

Reading the Romance in a Small Town

The girls in Cherland's study led wholesome, comfortable, enviable lives in a small-town setting. They were good students and good readers. They compliantly read all the books their teacher assigned, even though these were all books about males' adventures and experiences. Their teacher felt that boys would not be willing to read books featuring girls as central characters. So confident was she of this opinion that when offered the option of assigning a science fiction title with a female lead, she declined, even though science fiction was a genre that the boys liked, sighing: "Too bad it's got a girl as the main character" (Cherland, 1994: 149). Siegel's

Also, times have changed

(1986) study of teacher education texts offers some insight into this attitude. She found in these texts copious advice on the importance of selecting books with "male themes" and male characters. Teachers-in-training were instructed explicitly that boys *should not* be asked to read books about females for fear of the potential damage to their emerging gender identities. There does not seem to be a corollary fear for girls. *?? what*

The girls in Cherland's study first read these assigned books about boys and their lives, and then—perhaps because they found no character resembling themselves in the pedagogized literacy—they turned to romances. They were avid consumers of romance on the side, many of the girls reading romances several hours a day. They read in the car, and they kept romances tucked into their desks at school for a bit of surreptitious reading when the lesson became boring. Another reason why the romance *#2* appealed to these girls, maintains Cherland, is that it gave them cues about how to behave with boys when their turn came for romance. In much the same way that the curriculum in nineteenth-century Canada provided students with a "middle-class training camp" (Graff, 1979, quoted in Street, 1993: 8), the extracurriculum in this twentieth-century Canadian setting provided the girls with a gender training camp. *Discourse Comm*

These girls formed a literacy community, an elaborate social network built largely around learning romance. They talked at length with each other about the books, they made recommendations about specific titles, and they eagerly anticipated the forthcoming number in their favorite romance series. They borrowed and loaned these books, and gave each other romance novels as birthday presents. Cherland saw that reading and sharing romances was a way to demonstrate affection and maintain nurturing social relationships.

The girls' well-developed social practice created an exchange of what Cherland calls "emotional currency" (1994: 101). This construct resonates with the observations of conversation analysts who have described the ways in which the maintenance of social interaction through conversation is gendered work (Fairclough, 1989; Fishman, 1978).

Reading the Romance in the Inner City

The girls in Christian-Smith's study enjoyed less success in school. Their teachers characterized them as "more interested in boys than academics" and as being at risk of dropping out (Christian-Smith, 1993b: 50). They had been tracked into the lowest level of reading instruction, and had been identified as reluctant readers. Yet these girls were anything but reluctant to read romance.

The girls in Christian-Smith's study, however, were much more willing to voice opposition to their teacher than the girls studied by Cherland. They demanded the right to read romances during independent study period, and their teacher, feeling that "any reading is better than no reading" (1993b: 50), capitulated to their demand. The teacher's sanctioning of romance reading may also have been driven by the fact that this was a Chapter I classroom, and thus she felt herself under particular pressure to deliver improved reading scores. As the following extract from Christian-Smith's transcripts show, this teacher was well aware of the ideological power of the girls' preferred genre, but she bowed, understandably, I think, to the exigencies of her difficult teaching situation:

> I feel guilty about letting the girls order these books through TAB [a school book club]. I read a couple of them once. They are so simple and the characters in them are stereotypes. You know, Mom at home in her apron, Dad reading the paper with his feet up. But the girls seem to like the books, and the classroom sure is quiet when they're reading them. (1993b: 50)

Not only did the girls read the romances quietly in class, they kept the stories to themselves. Unlike the girls in Cherland's study, these girls did not share speculations on the characters or reflect on the plotlines. For them, like the adult romance readers in Janice Radway's (1984) study, romance reading was a private, individualized act. The only sense of shared desires vis-á-vis romance reading surfaced in another class where four girls—also participants in Christian-Smith's study—banded together to overturn their teacher's very strong objection to romance reading. This teacher made a point of allowing only "quality literature" in her classroom; ultimately, however, the girls prevailed. Christian-Smith does not report the teacher's rationale for her capitulation, but she does note that an important element of the girls' argument was that their mothers were avid romance readers. This identification with their mothers' literacy practices may well have made further condemnation of romance novels awkward for the teacher. It also may be that she changed her policy without engaging the girls in any kind of critical dialog about the implicit messages in romance.

When asked about their reasons for preferring romances, these girls, like the others, reported finding them far more engaging than teacher-sponsored reading. Additionally, they found the books instructive about romance itself. However, their interest was generally not as hypothetical as was that of the younger girls. Many of these older girls had boyfriends. The romance in these books seemed to offer them a more sanguine view of male-female relationships. Noted one of the girls:

> Nobody has these neat boyfriends. I mean most of the guys boss you around...and bash you if you look at somebody else. But it's fun to read the books and think that someday you'll meet a nice guy who'll be good to you. (Christian-Smith, 1993b: 53)

[handwritten margin notes: wow; so reading for hope?; imagination]

This comment is important in another way: it suggests that this girl at least was willing to engage in a critical consideration of her romances, both the ones she read and the ones she experienced in real life.

Other girls saw a difference between what was possible for the characters in their novels and what was possible for them as they negotiated real-life relationships. When talking with the researcher about the steps a female character had taken to get even with a boy who catcalled and constantly harassed her, they commented that such revenge would not be possible for them. When the researcher asked the girls if they would do the same thing that the character had done, one girl was simply incredulous: "Are you kidding? No way!" another was wistful: "Well, I'd like to do something like that with some of the boys in my class who are real pains. But I'd get chicken and probably just fume" (Christian-Smith, 1993b: 57). She went on to articulate a sophisticated view of female subjectivity:

> It's kinda difficult, I mean, well, I guess I don't want to be seen as a girl who's too pushy with boys. You have to be careful about that (1993b: 57).

[handwritten margin note: wow]

The girls in both studies pored over the romance texts as instruction manuals. Even the 11-year-olds had read—and lived—enough to understand that doing gender is fraught with contradictions: be assertive enough to attract male attention, but not too assertive; be smart, but not too smart (see also Holland and Eisenhart, 1990). For the younger girls, romances are a vital guide to the future. Unlike Radway's (1984) adult readers who see romances as vicarious pleasure, an escape from daily routine, the younger adolescent readers seem to articulate an expectation that their life will unfold just as the heroine's does (Willinsky and Hunniford, 1993). Given this clear warrant, the young reader learns that she has only to wait. And attend to her looks.

*[handwritten margin note: * MANUAL on GENDER]*

For the slightly older girls whose own romantic lives had already begun to unfold in ways not as roseate as in the romance novels, the persistent appeal of this genre may be due to a more complex set of reasons. A girl may believe that her *next* real-life romance will more closely conform to her readings, or perhaps that some remediation in romance will help her to do gender more successfully. In some part, her motivations may be closer to those of Radway's adult women whose romance reading was an act of opposition, however temporary, against the social structure that demands great outlays of nurturance from women, but offers little in return. Radway's adult women, and perhaps Christian-Smith's adolescents, use the romance when they're short of emotional currency. However, to anyone who has had the experience of working with adult females, this portrait of passivity isn't wholly satisfying. Another way of understanding the girls' unflagging loyalty to the romances is in terms of resistance theory.

Romance and Resistance

Both groups of girls exercised agency as they resisted the imposition of teacher dictates regarding classroom literacy practices. For the girls in Cherland's study, resistance was extremely mild—a romance hidden in a desk as an antidote to a boring lesson. However, for the girls in Christian-Smith's study, resistance—staging a classroom mutiny—was much more overt and carried higher stakes for them. Giroux (1983) argues that the model of schools as units of cultural reproduction is inadequate in that it fails to explain the oppositional behaviors of students. Rather than viewing the girls as "passive role bearers," Giroux's approach would lead us to see the girls' demand to choose their own "texts of desire" as an exercise of agency, a resistance to the hegemony of the school (1983: 75). The question remains, of course, whether in resisting the local hegemony, they are facilitating the reproduction process of a larger, patriarchal ideology. The gendered reading that these girls engaged in has the characteristic of being both "conservative and liberating" (Freire, 1983: 15).

The resistance of the girls in Christian-Smith's study has parallels in the oppositional behavior of the lads in Willis's (1977) ethnographic work. These working-class boys read the "mental work" of the school curriculum as female, and thus, unsurprisingly, inferior to manual work. Perceiving that their class-bound chances for upward mobility within the economy were nonexistent, they read status into the work done by their fathers and brothers on the shop floor. Thus they aspired to factory occupations. Apple (1982: 99) explains the lads' resistance succinctly: "Their rejection of so much of the content and form of day-to-day educational life bears on the almost unconscious realization that, as a class, schooling will not enable them to go further than they already are." By the same token, Christian-Smith's girls might have developed an "almost unconscious" realization that their access to economic and cultural authority can be gained almost solely through male intervention in the prevailing ideological framework. The "quality literature" that their teacher is offering them just might not seem in any way relevant to this ideology.

Another interesting picture of resistance was sketched by McRobbie (1978). The adolescent girls in her study regarded romance reading as axiomatic of their femininity. Their particular reading of the genre informed them that femininity was expressed not in diligence and compliance, but in overt displays of sexuality. Their expression of feminized agency lay in resisting their teachers' demands that they not wear such revealing clothing, that they not engage in public "primping," and so forth. More than twenty years later, this form of resistance seems not very resistant at all, but rather quaint. The fact remains, though, that however much clothing styles have changed and sexual expressiveness has increased, the appeal of romances has persisted.

What's Love Got to Do With It?

Even though the general discourse of desire has expanded to consider a broader range of views on female sexual choices, as well as issues of consent and coercion, the school discourse is still substantially structured to situate females as *victims* of sexuality. Fine (1993: 77) argues that sex education curricula focus on teaching females to defend themselves against AIDS, sexually transmitted diseases, pregnancy, and "being used." Curriculum frameworks include discussions of the social and emotional risks of sexual involvement, and variations on the "just say no" theme. Attention is focused on the female's role in putting the brakes on male sexuality, and this denies females the acknowledgment of their own patterns of desire. The school sex education discourse, ostensibly open, is a closed text for females. Their bodies are the object of the discourse, but their desires are not the subject.

In romance novels, as in sex education class, girls are presented as the sexual police who must suppress the boys' dangerous urges. Even in the more liberal, contemporary romance novels, girls discover their sexual feelings only in reference to the romantic potential that a special boy represents. But that is, of course, not how sexual development occurs. As the girls read and respond to the texts, they come to understand this. As a teen in Christian-Smith's study puts it:

> My favorite part is when the girl and the guy first kiss. That gives me a squishy feeling in my stomach. (1993b: 59)

At this crucial moment, the adolescent reader interacts with the text in a very different way. It is at this point that the young reader's feelings powerfully contradict the message she reads. For a moment, her feelings go beyond what the text authorizes, and what the culture authorizes for her. I believe that it is for the power conferred in these brief, subversive moments that she returns again and again to the romance novel.

Conclusion

Romance reading exerts such a strong pull on adolescent girls for a variety of reasons. The books offer guidance to the girls as to what kind of behavior is culturally permissible for them. Romances offer them insight into the inexplicable behavior of adolescent boys. These texts feature female protagonists, something their school-sponsored reading doesn't often do. They're simple to read, and predictable; this is comforting in a world that changes particularly rapidly for adolescents. These novels are a site for the exchange of emotional currency.

Importantly, romance novels serve as a rallying point for resistance, through which the girls can demonstrate opposition to a literacy curriculum that does not engage them, nor does it fit with their notion of preparation for an adult future. Romance reading offers them a chance to contradict their image as reluctant readers. Finally, these books offer a venue for the girls to acknowledge an agency in terms of their own sexuality that exists independent of male authorization.

Clearly, the romance has a lot to offer adolescent girls. But these texts of desire offer the girls something else: what Lankshear and Lawler (1987) call "improper literacy." In their study of the nationwide literacy campaign conducted in Nicaragua in the mid-1980s, these researchers came to see that subordinate groups were acquiring particular forms of literacy that had the effect of undermining their own interests, and of preserving the dominant ideology. Such is the case with the girls' reading of the romance. The more they come to accept the gendered subject position that has been apportioned to them as natural or "voluntary" (Davies, 1993), the less chance there is for individual empowerment or broader social change.

Bourdieu (1977) argues that a person's aspirations in life are based not on anything faintly resembling a rational assessment of her prospects, but rather on the *habitus* of her group, that is, on the durable attitudes, beliefs, shared myths, and accommodations that she holds in common with her peers. Although the romance novel is only one factor in the formation of an adolescent girl's habitus, it is a powerful one.

Resistance theory would suggest that some of the girls in the studies discussed in this chapter "saw through" the pedagogized literacy on offer, and thus behaved oppositionally: demanding to choose their own texts. It may be useful for theorists to posit that subordinate groups like Willis's lads or these adolescent girls have the insight to recognize and resist the dominant ideology. However, this resistance is not particularly useful to the real people involved. It may be briefly empowering for these groups to exercise agency. Yet, the end result of the girls' resistance was that they hewed even more closely to the extant order. Their resistance perpetuated their identities as at-risk students. Their teacher's acquiescence in this program of lowest-common-denominator literacy, coupled with her inability, or unwillingness, to engage the girls in a critical look at the values enshrined on those pages had the result of excluding these readers from what Baker and Luke (1991) refer to as discourses of power. The consequences of literacy—however complex—were not weighted in these girls' favor. Admittedly, they traded emotional currency in their romance reading. But, by all accounts, emotional currency is the small change of cultural capital.

[handwritten marginalia: Again, feeds patriarchy AND capitalist publishers]

Works Cited

Apple, M. (1982). *Education and power*. Boston, MA: Routledge.

Baker, C. and Luke, A. (1991). Towards a critical sociology of reading pedagogy. In C. Baker and A. Luke. (Eds.), *Towards a critical sociology of reading pedagogy* (pp. xi-xxi). Philadelphia, PA: John Benjamins.

Bourdieu, P. (1977). *Outline of a theory of practice*. Cambridge: Cambridge University Press.

Cherland, M. R. (1994). *Private practices: Girls reading fiction and constructing identity*. London: Taylor & Francis.

Christian-Smith, L. (1991). *Becoming a woman through romance*. New York: Routledge.

———. (1993a). Constituting and reconstituting desire: Fiction, fantasy, and femininity. In L. Christian-Smith (Ed.), *Texts of desire: Essays on fiction, femininity and schooling* (pp. 1–8). London: Falmer.

———. (1993b). Sweet dreams: Gender and desire in teen romance novels. In L. Christian-Smith (Ed.), *Texts of desire: Essays on fiction, femininity and schooling* (pp. 45–68). London: Falmer.

Conklin, B. (1981). *P.S. I Love You*. New York: Bantam's Sweet Dreams.

Cooper, D. (1993). Retailing gender. In L. Christian-Smith (Ed.), *Texts of desire: Essays on fiction, femininity and schooling* (pp. 9–27). London: Falmer.

Coser, L. et al. (1982). *Books: The culture and commerce of publishing*. New York: Basic Books.

Davies, B. (1993). Beyond dualism and toward multiple subjectivities. In L. Christian-Smith (Ed.), *Texts of desire: Essays on fiction, femininity and schooling* (pp. 145–173). London: Falmer.

Fairclough, N. (1989). *Language and power*. London: Longman.

Fine, M. (1993). Sexuality, schooling and adolescent females: The missing discourse of desire. In L. Weis and M. Fine (Eds.), *Beyond silenced voices: Class, race and gender in United States schools* (pp. 75–100). Albany, NY: State University of New York Press.

Fishman, P. (1978). Interaction: The work women do. *Social problems, 25,* 397–406.

Freire, P. (1983). The importance of reading. *Journal of Education, 165,* 9–15.

Gilbert, P. (1993). Dolly fictions. In L. Christian-Smith (Ed.), *Texts of desire: Essays on fiction, femininity and schooling* (pp. 69–86.) London: Falmer.

———— and Taylor, S. (1991). *Fashioning the feminine: Girls, popular culture and schooling.* Sydney: Allen & Unwin.

Giroux, H. (1983). *Theory and resistance in education.* New York: Heinemann.

Holland, D. and Eisenhart, M. (1990). *Educated in romance: Women, achievement and college culture.* Chicago, IL: University of Chicago Press.

Lankshear, C. with Lawler, M. (1987). *Literacy, schooling and revolution.* London: Falmer.

Luke, A. (1993). Series Editor's Introduction. In L. Christian-Smith (Ed.), *Texts of desire: Essays on fiction, femininity and schooling* (pp. vii–xiv). London: Falmer.

McRobbie, A. (1978). Working class girls and the culture of femininity. In Women's Study Group (Eds.), *Women take issue: Aspects of women's subordination* (pp. 96–108). London: Hutchinson.

Radway, J. (1984). *Reading the romance: Women, patriarchy, and popular literature.* Chapel Hill: University of North Carolina Press.

Siegel, E. (1986). "As the twig is bent..." Gender and childhood reading. In E. Flynn and P. Schweickart (Eds.), *Gender and reading: Essays on readers, texts, and contexts.* Baltimore: Johns Hopkins University Press.

Street, B. (1990). *Literacy in theory and practice.* Cambridge: Cambridge University Press.

————. (Ed.). (1993). *Cross-cultural approaches to literacy.* Cambridge: Cambridge University Press.

Street, B. and Street, J. (1991). The schooling of literacy. In D. Barton and R. Ivanic (Eds.), *Writing in the community* (pp. 158–181). London: Sage.

Willinsky, J. and Hunniford, R. M. (1993). Reading the romance younger: The mirrors and fears of a preparatory literature. In L. Christian-Smith (Ed.), *Texts of desire: Essays on fiction, femininity and schooling* (pp. 87–105). London: Falmer.

Willis, P. (1977). *Learning to labour.* Aldershot, UK: Gower.

"Practicing for Romance"

Gesa E. Kirsch

ane Stanley offers a rich and thoughtful examination of the diverse factors that go into adolescent girls reading romance novels—both as resistance to school-sponsored literacy activities and as a reproduction of heterosexism, cultural norms, and gender expectations. Reading her chapter, I was reminded of the complexity that often informs out-of-school literacy practices and encouraged to learn that adolescent girls often find ways to resist, challenge, or subvert the curriculum. Stanley's chapter raised several questions for me—questions about the nature of the trend of young girls reading romance novels, about whether there are parallel trends affecting adolescent boys, and finally, how educators and parents should respond to girls "practicing for romance."

My first question concerns the nature of the trend over time—have adolescent girls always "fallen for" romance novels, reading in clandestine places and at clandestine times, or has this trend changed over time? To be sure, female audiences have been singled out as consumers of special literacy for a long time: whether they were encouraged to read books on moral virtues, on manners and etiquette, on home economics, on child care, or on the performance of gender roles as depicted in novels, romances, and women's magazines, the first of which were published more than 200 years ago. (For historical work in this area see Davidson, 1986; Eldred and Mortensen, 2002; and Radway, 1984.)

Perhaps the attraction between young women and romance novels is not new at all, but what is new, as Stanley suggests, are the publisher-sponsored book-clubs which relentlessly promote the reading of romances by providing powerful incentives for students and teachers to use their materials inside and outside the classroom. As Mortensen (2002) suggests, "publishers, because of certain monopolistic and collusive possibilities in the book market today, can much more effectively than ever before play both sides of the double bind: they can enable resistance to school reading (for a price), while cultivating uncritical orientations toward the performance of gender and the habits of expression and consumption that attend such performances. But the bind itself—and public worry about it—is not new" (personal correspondence).

What we ought to examine, then, I want to propose, are corporate-school partnerships which are springing up at all levels of education—kindergarten through university—whereby large companies offer incentives for school boards and administrators to purchase their products and services. I suggest that we consider establishing ethical standards which can guide educators' decisions regarding school-corporate partnerships. We need to develop creative ways to envision how such partnerships can work without compromising the best interests of students, teachers, and the goals of the curriculum. Furthermore, we need models for ethical practices which help educators respond to the persistent requests made by publishers and sales representatives. I predict that in the next decades, we will see more, rather than fewer, proposals for school-corporate partnerships. Perhaps, then, educators need to worry more about the nature of such partnerships than about the content of romance novels.

Reading Stanley's essay, I also wondered whether there are out-of-school literacy practices that largely affect young adolescent males. I realize that this question exceeds the scope of Stanley's work, but I would like to raise it nevertheless in the context of this edited collection. Are there school-corporate partnerships which target the interests and literacy practices of young men, practices such as reading comic books and sport magazines, playing computer and video games, and participating in hip-hop music and culture? If such trends exists, do they perpetuate gender roles and the dominant ideology in similar ways that romance novels do?

Finally, I wanted to know more about Stanley's thoughts on how educators and parents should respond to girls reading the romance. In her conclusion, the author seems to imply that teachers, even if they tolerate the reading of romance novels in their classrooms or study halls, should teach girls how to respond critically to, if not resist, the gender roles depicted by the characters and narrative plots in romances. Stanley is careful not to lay blame on over-taxed teachers who are eager to see reluctant readers pick up books. Still, she suggests that "those of us *not* confronted daily with a class full of reluctant readers have the luxury of asking for more for the girls." I wanted to know what Stanley had in mind here, what the "more" would look like, and how she would attempt to implement her vision in a classroom full of adolescent girls and boys.

As the questions I have raised imply, Stanley's discussion engaged me as a reader, a feminist, and an educator, and provides important insight into the literacy practices and gender roles performed by students of all ages. Stanley's essay leaves me hopeful that adolescent girls, in their quest for finding an identity, use predictable materials in unpredictable ways, ways which enable them to resist teachers, to change the curriculum, to explore their sexual identity and agency, to challenge young boys in critical ways, to bond with their peers, and last, but not least, to practice their literacy skills.

Works Cited

Davidson, C. (1986). *Revolution and the word: The rise of the novel in America*. New York: Oxford University Press.

Eldred, J. and Mortensen, P. (2002). *Composing women of the early United States: Rhetoric, education, and schooling fictions, 1798–1859*. Pittsburgh: University of Pittsburgh Press.

Mortensen, P. Personal Correspondence. Dec. 15, 2000.

Radway, J. (1984). *Reading the romance: Women, patriarchy, and popular literature*. Chapel Hill: University of North Carolina Press.

CHAPTER NINE

Negotiating Gender Through Academic Literacy Practices

Amanda Godley

She walked in with this big, sincere smile on her face. As she made her way to her seat, she exchanged greetings with practically the whole class, smiling all the while.... Being the naive, self-absorbed teenager that I was, I immediately labeled her. "So that's who I have to interview, miss popularity, homecoming princess, the all-star basketball player...." It was then that we started the conversation that forever changed my views about her...the person I knew ten minutes ago no longer existed, instead she was replaced by someone new, by someone whom I could relate to, but someone I could understand, someone with a story. This is her story.

Thus begins *Refuge*, an essay based on a student-to-student interview conducted during an eleventh-grade English honors class at Montana High School. The author of the essay, Keri, goes on to describe her classmate Paula's background as a first-generation Cambodian-American, born to Cambodian political refugees. The bulk of the essay describes Paula's strength in standing up to traditional Cambodian culture and the role of women within it:

In her [Paula's] culture, a woman was expected to behave a certain way, to act in such a way that prevented her from being an independent person. In the midst of all these problems and expectations, Paula slowly tried to distance herself, not so much as from her family but from her culture, and in the end, the same way that her family had once turned to America for refuge, Paula turned to the American culture for a chance at being free.

Sociocultural studies of literacy (Dyson, 1995; Gee, 1996; Heath, 1983; Street, 1984) have shown us that literacy not only represents the skills of reading and writing, but reflects particular social and cultural values and relationships. In this chapter, I show how two students, Keri and Paula, used school-based literacy practices to negotiate their in-school and out-of-school relationships with others. In particular, I demonstrate the ways in which these students negotiated their positions as gendered beings through the literacy practices of their eleventh-grade English class. In the excerpt above, Keri uses her interview essay to question cultures that limit women's independence. By representing Paula as a female who has had gender-specific challenges in her life and who has worked for independence, Keri calls into question Paula's school-based reputation as "Miss Popularity," "homecoming princess," and "all-star basketball player." Literacy also becomes a means through which Keri can question and negotiate her own position within an Iranian home culture and imagine different life possibilities for herself as a female.

At times during the six months I observed this class—English 3H—as part of a larger ethnographic study, in-school literacy practices served not only as means through which to explore the meanings of femaleness and maleness, but also as social events shaped by the way participants "did gender." West and Zimmerman (1987: 126) use the term "doing gender" to define gender as a form of social interaction rather than a natural difference. In this view, gender is not an innate state of being, but rather a relation constituted through interaction with others. As this chapter shows, the ways in which students read, wrote, and talked about literature in the eleventh-grade honors class at Montana High School were shaped by the notions of gender they brought with them to school and to the classroom.

Drawing on feminist poststructuralist as well as practice-based theories of gender and literacy, this chapter demonstrates how literacy is a gendered social practice, both because students negotiate their views of gender through literacy and because literacy practices are shaped by the notions of gender students bring to class. As mentioned before, my discussion focuses on two students, Paula and Keri, and the ways in which their out-of-school gender and literacy practices shaped their in-school literacy. While this case study approach may seem to forefront personal views and experiences of gender and literacy, I demonstrate that at the heart of the sociocultural practices of gender and of literacy lies interpersonal, social interaction. Indeed, both Paula's and Keri's "personal" views about literacy and about gender were shaped by their interactions with friends, school administrators, and family. Keri's essay—quoted from at the start of this chapter—signals that Paula's view of what it means to be a female Cambodian-American is very much shaped by her interactions with her parents, other Cambodian immigrants, and more mainstream American culture. The cases of Paula and Keri compel us to view school-based literacy as intimately connected with other social practices, such as gender, that may have their roots in out-of-school settings. School-based literacy, then, becomes not just a set of skills that students learn in order to succeed academically or financially, but rather a means through which they reassess and practice other kinds of social interaction.

Gender and Literacy as Sociocultural Practices

The theoretical framework that informs this study recognizes both literacy and gender as contextualized social practices. In their 1991 report for the Center for the Study of Writing at the University of California, Berkeley, Dyson and Freedman call for a more expansive framework for the study of literacy that "include[s] more analytic attention to how the complex of sociocultural experiences enters into literacy learning, experiences that have roots in social class, ethnicity, language background, family, neighborhood, *gender*. Without serious attention to the unfolding of this wider cultural frame in literacy learning, our vision of the whole remains partially obscured" (1991: 4; emphasis added). In the past decade or so, however, few studies in the U.S. have directly addressed the intersection of gender and literacy practices, and of those that have, many have posited gender as a "natural" biological or social dichotomy rather than part of a "complex of sociocultural experiences" (Dyson and Freedman, 1991: 4).

One possible explanation of this is that while in general literacy theory has moved towards a focus on context and sociocultural practices, much of the research on gender and literacy in the U.S. has remained rooted in theories of essentialized and categorical differences between female and male students drawn from psychological studies (Gilligan, 1982; Belenky et al., 1986). In other words, much of this research rests on the assumption that males as a group and females as a group must experience education differently because they belong to two naturally different categories of humans. But the problem with this line of research is that it ignores both the similarities between the ways in which many male and female students experience literacy (or other school activities) and the ways in which these experiences can vary within each category. Thus, gender and literacy research in this tradition often overlooks sociocultural factors like race and class and their impact on literacy learning, and often leads to theories of categorical "differences" that are implicitly or explicitly deemed "natural" and therefore unchangeable. In particular, the over-reliance and misinterpretation of Carol Gilligan's (1982) theory that males and females have different moral reasonings and thus different "voices" has led to a view of gender that is ultimately incompatible with, and perhaps antithetical to, more complex theories of literacy.

Literacy as a Contextualized Social Practice

Sociocultural theories of literacy insist that contextual factors such as place, time, and community and social structures such as ethnicity and gender are essential to the understanding of literacy. As earlier chapters have noted, Street (1984: 95) calls this the "ideological" perspective on literacy which views literacy "in terms of concrete social practices and...ideologies in which different literacies are embedded." Thus, literacy is never an "autonomous" skill, but always holds political and ideological significance and must be understood within the framework of culturally constructed systems and practices. Additionally, literacy is not unitary, but rather a general category of social practices, loosely tied to reading and writing, that hold different purposes, meanings, and values in different settings.

This contextualized view of literacy—and particularly of school-based literacy—can be seen in the work of Heath (1982) and Dyson (1995). Heath examines the way in which the community-based language and literacy practices of two towns—Roadville and Trackton—impacted the experience of their children at school, contextualizing her study with background information on the history of the area, the two communities, and the prevalent attitudes towards life, work, and education held in these communities. She looked specifically at the function of "literacy events" in each community, and found that patterns of reading and writing in each community were connected to patterns of using space and time, demonstrating that the practice of literacy was integrally tied to other practices and values. But students from both communities used (and valued) language and literacy differently to their teachers, who came from middle-class urban backgrounds. For instance, Trackton students were not used to indirect directives, identification questions, or "school" modes of turn taking. Their dialect, too, was not understood by the teachers, and often the teachers assumed that the students were not polite. Heath demonstrates that the mismatch between school and community language and literacy practices can make some students less successful in school than others.

Through her study of an elementary school class, Dyson (1995) shows how students are *not* free to use language (written and oral) to portray themselves in any way they like. Dyson points out that words are embedded with socially constructed meanings that serve to define not only what a child can say, but what he or she can *be* in the world. Literacy serves to embed students in a particular place—based on relationships governed by race, gender, and other factors—in this web of hegemony and ideology. The students she observed used characters and elements of speech from cartoons, such as the Teenage Mutant Ninja Turtles, in the plays that they wrote and acted in order to gain power and prestige in their peer group. This led to their "writing themselves" into powerfully raced and gendered roles in order to form alliances with popular students. A focus on individuality and student "voice" in children's writing, Dyson warns, can lead to blindness towards these workings of power and children's reproduction of gender, race, and class discourses.

Sociocultural theories of literacy, then, provide a tradition of research on literacy that focuses on the contextualized values, skills, and worldviews that surround the acts of reading and writing. Research in literacy has broadened to include not just empirical moments of literacy practices, but of the ways in which literacy works more symbolically and discursively to create relations of power between people.

This study also extends the notion of literacy (and gender, as discussed below) to the level of the individual. Like Camitta (1993), I view literacy as reflective of sociocultural values but also as reflective of individual interests, life experiences, and values. If literacy is viewed as merely a social construct, then we cede all power to social forces and institutions and ignore individual agency. Individuals like Keri and Paula come to literacy practices with unique backgrounds and personal desires as well as group affiliations, socially shaped worldviews, and cultural values. The study of individuals and their literacy practices, then, can lead us to understand the affiliations, values, and beliefs that form the basis of the relationship between literacy and other social practices (Baynham, 1995).

Gender and Literacy

In order to understand how gender and literacy interact with each other, we must view gender—like literacy—as a social practice constituted through social interaction. Theories of practice foreground the importance of social interaction, context, and interconnectedness—the same qualities Dyson and Freedman called for in their studies of literacy. A focus on practice provides a connection between "personal life and social structure" by focusing on "what people do by way of constituting the social relations they live in" (Connell, 1987: 61–62). Because social relations are at the center of the relationship between the individual and society in theories of practice, neither personal life nor social structures can be static or reproductive; each can influence and transform the other through social practice. Additionally, because many communities, like schools, often welcome new individuals who may engage in social practices in new ways, opportunities for continuity and displacement are always created (of course, as Gee suggests, this change may also be generated out of great struggle and discord as members of the community reconfigure their shared beliefs and assumptions about the world; see Gee 1996). The focus on social interaction and practice, then, allows researchers of gender to ask not what the roots of gender or gender differences are, but how interpersonal relations are organized around gender, including the way in which they often reflect a symbolic male/female dichotomy.

Orellana (1995: 1) writes, a "social practice view of gender suggests that the meanings we attach to being male or female... are shaped through social practices.... Those meanings can change over time and across cultures, situations, and contexts; while we are always either male or female, the fact of being male or female can have different implications and varying degrees of salience across a range of situations, and in interactions with other social categories." This theory adds a stronger sense of historicity and context and a more complete understanding of the possibilities of transformation of gender practices (and structures and representations) through literacy. Connell (1987) further proposes that gender be seen as a constantly evolving social process that is linked to other social processes, and that always reflects a relationship of power. This vantage point suggests that individual students and teachers have the power to determine how they will practice gender through literacy while recognizing that this creation is shaped and limited by structural and discursive forces.

Many researchers of gender and literacy note that literacy and gender can be seen as both social and personal practices. Steedman's (1982) classic study of a story written by three 8-year-old girls demonstrates how the girls both took up and challenged the gendered subject positions through articulating, in their story, the values and future they envisioned for themselves. In the story, the girls questioned values and practices of heterosexual love and marriage, mothers' desire for and resentment of children, mothers' loss of freedom, and the ways in which girls become women. Steedman looks at the story as a sociological and historical artifact, and argues that it reveals the children's view of the social processes that shaped their lives and their power to make sense of these processes theoretically by understanding contradictory themes through narrative. Using Vygotsky's theories of language and writing, Steedman argues that the girls created the meaning of the events in their story through writing it. In this way, the girls' story can be seen as practicing gender through literacy by both internalizing and resisting the social positions open to them as working-class girls.

Davies (1993) also explores the intertwining practices of gender and literacy by showing the ways in which primary school children are influenced by, resist, and "take up" discourses of gender through reading and writing in school. She argues that individuals express various forms of masculinity and femininity which available sociocultural discourses and sociohistorical contexts make open to them. Though she attempted to teach the students she studied to critically analyze the discourses of masculinity and femininity they read in books, Davies found that the students were, for the most part, unable to see that they were controlled by these discourses. She argues that students' resistance to this notion was caused, in part, by the Western assumption of individuality and free choice. The students viewed these assumptions as both "free choices" and "natural."

What this theory of practice adds to the study of literacy and gender, as Orellana points out, is the notion that the division of all people into the categories of male and female comes to hold different meanings in different contexts and communities, and that this division can change. "Gender is produced (and often reproduced) in differential membership in communities of practice," write Eckert and McConnell-Ginet (1992: 95). Ultimately, viewing gender as the process of *creating* differences through social interaction can lead us to a fuller understanding of the ways in which literacy—as social interaction (Dyson, 1995)—often organizes practice "in terms of, or in relation to, the reproductive division of people into male and female" (Connell, 1987: 140).

As students use literacy to make sense of and to grant meaning to the fact of being male or female, they also make sense of other social categories such as race, class, and culture (Gilbert, 1992). The social practices and interactions open to the girls of Steedman's study, for example, were not only shaped by their position in society as girls but also as members of the working class (see also Cherland, 1994, and Finders, 1997, for studies of literacy, gender, and social class). Similarly, Paula, and Keri's school-based literacy practices were tied to their positions as first-generation Americans, their class background, their academic and social positions, and their racial/cultural group affiliations.

Methodology

This chapter is based on a larger six-month ethnographic study of an eleventh-grade English class at Montana High School,[1] an urban high school in California. The student body at Montana High School was about 40 percent African American, 24 percent Asian (mostly Chinese, Korean, and Japanese), 24 percent white, and 10 percent Latino at the time of the study. The school draws students from the middle-class, mostly white and Asian neighborhood that surrounds it as well as from a nearby city (Rockville) that is mostly African American and has high rates of poverty.

I chose Montana High School as the site of my research for two reasons. First, because of my extended involvement with the school as a girls' basketball coach and my personal relationships with teachers in the English department, I could gain access to the school easily and use my background knowledge of the school to inform my study. Secondly, and more importantly, I chose Montana because of its reputation as an urban school that successfully educates a diverse student population. The teacher of the class I observed, Mr. Brown, was recommended to me by others in the English department as an excellent teacher and a teacher-researcher. His thoughtful and informed perspective on class activities provided valuable insights into the students' literacy and gender practices.

Data Collection and Analysis

Montana High School operates on a block schedule which means that each course, like eleventh-grade English, meets for a 90 minute "block" each day for one semester of the school year. Thus students only take three to four courses at a time and move to entirely new courses for the second semester of the year. I observed Mr. Brown's English class three times a week for the entire semester it met, January to June 1999, taking fieldnotes during all observations. After six weeks, I chose seven focal students (including Paula and Keri) for closer observation. In hope of providing new perspectives on existing theories of gender and literacy, I selected focal students who were representative of the ethnic and class diversity of Mr. Brown's class, representative of a range of academic achievement, representative of different immigration patterns, and representative of different extracurricular activities and visibility/popularity levels. Of these factors, ethnicity, class, and popularity were the most salient for theoretical reasons. Existing research and my own initial observations demonstrated that the practice of gender is strongly influenced by the practice of ethnicity, class, and popularity (Connell, 1987; Finders, 1997; Thorne, 1993; Willis, 1977). Each focal student was interviewed two to three times about his or her views on literacy, gender, the school community, and their English class. Additionally, I collected all of the focal students' writing assignments for the class.

After I chose focal students, I also began to audiotape all class discussions so that I would have accurate records of students' conversations in class. I continued to take fieldnotes while audiotaping in order to record non-verbal data, "unofficial" asides, and my observational and theoretical comments. When students worked in small groups, I observed and audio-recorded a group in which one or more of my focal students was a member. In sum, I audiorecorded and transcribed twenty-nine class meetings totaling of 43.5 hours of class.

I used a multilevel framework to analyze the ways in which gender is practiced in the eleventh-grade honors English class at Montana. This model was influenced in part by DiPardo's (1993) analysis of literacy practices and the discourse of multiculturalism at the college level as well as by Acker's (1992) work on institutions as gendered. Fairclough's (1992) Critical Discourse Analysis methodology also shaped my framework. The framework takes the interactional practices of gender as its focus and looks at the forces that shape and represent those practices—forces such as institutional constraints, student background, literacy tasks, and individual goals and desires. My central question in the study was, "How is gender practiced through literacy in the classroom?" I coded all forms of data (fieldnotes, transcripts, interviews, and writing samples) using the five core themes that emerged from this question:

1. GENDERED INSTITUTIONS. This term refers to descriptions or practices that reveal the gendered structure of institutions, like Montana High School. An institutional practice was considered gendered when it represented itself as such explicitly (as in the "Battle of the Sexes Rally") or when it implicitly made distinctions between males and females.

2. GENDERED DISCOURSES (I.E., COMMONLY-HELD, SOCIOCULTURAL ASSUMPTIONS). Prominent discourses that arose were the value of a (white

male) "canon" of classic literature; the importance of preparing high school students for literary analysis in college; the assumption of universality of human experience; the belief that equality, individuality, and choice are characteristics (and excellent ones, too) of life in the United States; and finally, the understanding that "gender" means "female."

3. THE HIERARCHY OF GENDER. This core theme takes its label from Connell's (1987) view of gender as a hierarchical power structure with males holding power over females. More specifically, Connell (1987: 140) asserts that males who emphasize their masculinity are at the apex of this structure, and men who act less "hegemonically masculine" are below them. Below these men, women who emphasize their femininity are privileged.

4. GENDER, ETHNICITY, AND SOCIAL CLASS. Here I use the term "ethnicity" to refer to the ways in which students identified themselves, how they practiced, and how they were perceived as belonging to a particular ethnic group. Students' expertise at literacy practices was judged by other students in part on their gender and ethnicity. This appeared in student interviews and student interaction, particularly in small groups.

5. NEGOTIATIONS OF GENDER BORDERS. This core theme addresses the representation and active practice of masculinity and femininity as separate, dichotomous spheres. It takes its wording from Thorne's (1993: 65) notion of the continual construction of "borders" between masculinity and femininity and includes the patrolling, crossing, and negotiating of this border. Laughter during whole class discussions, practices of homophobia, representations of characters, and written arguments are examples of such negotiations. These negotiations not only positioned students as practitioners of gender, but also demonstrated ways in which they manipulated and questioned gender as a defining category of society and their lives.

Participants

Both Paula and Keri were originally chosen as focal students because they represented the range of academic ability, popularity, ethnicity and class backgrounds of the students in Mr. Brown's class. Additionally, I chose Paula as a focal student because she seemed to be able to practice gender in ways that were both hegemonically masculine and emphasized feminine. Though Paula dressed quite femininely, had long, styled hair and aspired to be (and became) the prom queen, she also came into class each morning talking about professional sports and players. Her practice of gender called into question theories that more popular students often emphasize traditional practices of masculinity (if they are male) and femininity (if they are female). I chose Keri as a focal student in part because I was surprised that a student with such strong academic skills (straight As) and critical thinking skills would rarely speak in class. Though Keri focused on feminist issues in nearly all her written assignments, she was representative of a large group of female students in the class who rarely shared their views and took up leadership positions infrequently. Both Paula and Keri spoke and wrote openly about practicing gender out of school and in school, and both tied these experiences to their literacy practices.

Findings

Keri and Paula shared similar views about the place of women within the hierarchy of gender at the level of society, in their homes, and at the school, but each negotiated this view, and their place within it, in distinct ways through their literacy practices. While Paula often took up leadership positions in class by contributing to whole class discussions or leading small groups, Keri (as mentioned above) most often abdicated leadership positions and left them to male students in the class. However, in almost all her written work, Keri focused on the subordinate position of women in society and argued forcefully that women should be treated equally to men. Additionally, both students' practices of gender seemed to change throughout the semester as a result of their reflections on the literature that they read.

Keri

The only time that I heard Keri share her views on women's position in society verbally with others in her class was during the first week of school when students were asked to bring in an important object from their childhood to share with the rest of the class. Students brought in many different things, from photos, to stuffed animals, to baseball gloves. The following is an excerpt from my fieldnotes describing the object Keri brought in—a scarf—and how she explained it to the rest of the class.

> Keri, who is sitting to my left, presents a scarf. She tells the class that, as many of them may know, in the country she comes from [Iran], women have to cover their heads [she circles her face with her hands] all except their faces. When she was little, she and her brothers used to run home from school so they could go out and play. Every day she'd see her brothers running out the door and then her mother would pull her back in and make her put on a scarf. She hated wearing

scarves, and she would try to run out the door before her mother could catch her. [Students laugh.] But usually she did. She even sometimes sneaked out the back door. [She pauses a lot and her voice is quiet. She seems very nervous.] Sometimes when her mom didn't catch her, her brothers would make her go back in to the house and put on the scarf. [She is twisting the scarf around with her hands.] The day that we got on the plane to come here—to America, she says, my mother and I ripped off our scarves and threw them on the ground. Keri starts crying. She is not sobbing audibly, but there are tears rolling down her face and her voice is quivering. Everyone waits in silence to see if she is going to continue. I am crying, trying not to let the tears roll down my face. Keri sits down, and Ms. Nguyen goes to Mr. Brown's desk, pulls out two Kleenexes, and brings them back to her.

Keri's presentation of the scarf questioned the gender borders in place in Iran by showing mandated scarf-wearing to be unfair, undesirable, and oppressive. She questioned a custom that served to conceal women and symbolically confine them to private, unseen realms of society. She also shows how her mother and her brothers acted in ways to police this border. At the same time, though, Keri presented the United States as an unequivocal place of freedom and opportunity for women. When I asked Keri about this in an interview, she said she felt that women had far more freedom in the U.S. than in Iran, and she described the freedoms this way:

Keri: In my country right now, when I talk to my cousins, and one of my cousins just came to America just like, six months ago, she is like so different now, because when she came, at first she was so shy, she wore her scarves still in the street. And so, it was, it was really weird 'cause when I looked at her, I'm like, "Why was, would I be like that if I were in Iran?" 'Cause, she, she had still, I don't know why, but she still wore her scarf here. I guess she was kind of reluctant to take it off, you know. I was like, "Just take it off! Let's go out." And she didn't even talk about boys or anything, she didn't talk about going out with her friends. Her life was basically staying at home, taking care of the house, cleaning up, and going to school which she couldn't go further than high school. Then she came here, and she's just, now she's just going crazy, and she was partying, and we're taking her out, and everything. So and my parents, for some reason now that they're here, they're letting me do all this stuff. And, I just feel a lot happier here, because I could, I can do all these things. Without like being afraid of what's going to happen.

AG: Do you feel as if there are any other limitations or pressure here that weren't true in Iran? For instance, a lot of women, particularly teenage girls here feel pressured to wear make-up and um, you know, spend more time on their appearance. And some women in the U.S. find that kind of oppressive, too. You know, like they *have* to spend all this time altering their appearance.

Keri: Actually, I really want to do this because it's fun. And my mom kind of, um, because she couldn't do this, be kind of like, wear make-up and stuff when she was a kid, she's always like, "Oh, why don't you wear a skirt! Or Why don't you wear this?" And she tries to like basically, relive her life through me. I don't know if that's what she's trying to do, but she's always like, "Oh, let's go get your hair colored and do all this stuff." And I don't really mind because it's really fun, because she pampers me. It's not really a pressure at all. I am too happy to even care. I'm just too h- I'm just happy being here and doing all this stuff, doing it to notice the bad stuff.

Even though Keri critiqued the gender borders in Iran that confined women to the home and did not allow the same educational and public opportunities as men, in initial interviews she did not offer the same critique of the U.S. Instead, she presented the "freedom" given to her as a female in the U.S. as the freedom to go out, party, talk about boys, wear make-up, and color her hair. These "freedoms" are practices that, while perhaps not available choices in Iran, strongly reinforce gender borders that separate and exaggerate differences between males and females and that often position females as objects of sexual desire in the U.S.

Later in the semester, however, (and in part due to the English unit on the novel, *The Bluest Eye*, by Toni Morrison) Keri began to question gender practices and borders in the school and within U.S. society. In her final reading log entry for *The Bluest Eye*, Keri also demonstrated her changing views of beauty and the "freedom" of altering her physical appearance. She wrote, "Beauty is truly the most destructive idea in the history of human thought. For it always ends up causing a person to become envious, self-conscious, and depressed. And when you somehow become beautiful, then you always have to worry about being more beautiful than anyone else." When I asked her if the presentations about beauty had changed her views of beauty, she explained:

Because you know when they [other students] said that the girls try to be like this ideal, I don't know, skinny person and all that stuff, I realized that I was doing all that stuff. I, I didn't actually think about it, I didn't think I was doing, you know, trying to be that perfect girl, but I guess that was what I was doing because I bought all that make-up, I do all this hair stuff, I exercise and everything so I can lose the weight and be skinny and that kind of stuff. And I'm sure that a lot of girls also noticed because they used to say, you know, "I'm doing this for *me* because I want to be beautiful." You know? That's partly true, but I don't know, I'm willing to admit that it's not for me, it's just trying to be what society wants me to be, trying to fit in.

Breaking away from her earlier position that the U.S. provided her with freedoms and choices that she did not have as a female in Iran, Keri began to see that the "choices" open to her as ways of altering her appearance were not free choices at all, but ways in which broad sociocultural gender borders were maintained. The "freedoms" of wearing make-up and wearing different clothes, Keri came to realize, were ways in which girls were pressured to desire particular representations of beauty and perfection. Rather than seeing the U.S. as a place of unbridled freedom for women, Keri started to recognize, question, and critique the structures that supported gender borders and the dominance of men in the U.S. as well as Iran.

Although Keri used school-based literacy practices to question gender borders and the hierarchy of gender in her life and in the literature read for school, she hesitated in sharing these views with others in her class. For instance, during a discussion of *In Dubious Battle*, a novel by John Steinbeck, it was suggested that the birth of a child in the opening chapters served to symbolize the birth of the strike that makes up the core of the novel's plot. In the scene describing the child's birth, Mac—a labor organizer—intimidates an old midwife into leaving her patient and pretends in her stead to know how to deliver a baby in order to gain the trust of the other workers in the labor camp. While none of the students questioned this interpretation directly, Keri revealed her opinion of this scene in an interview:

> Well, I just thought, I don't know, it just kind of made me mad because it's a really mean thing to do, you know, if you don't know anything about it, but all he was concentrating on was trying to like get good with the guys and have them trust him and stuff. And he would actually risk someone's life just to do that. And I thought that's not really a good thing to do. So I just got kinda pissed off when he did that.

Keri's response shows that she finds Mac's actions morally questionable, and although she does not directly challenge the privileging of men's labor over women's, she does interrogate the implication that Mac's action was somehow justifiable. However, in parallel to the public masculine/private feminine dichotomy of labor that partly constitutes the hierarchy of gender in the U.S.—and even more dramatically in Iran, as seen in Keri's story of her scarf—Keri did not share this view publicly with the class, but rather, only privately with me. Like many of the girls, she "chose" not to participate in whole class discussions and only in some small group discussions. This meant that her interpretation of literature, which often called into question women's oppression, was rarely—if ever—heard.

When I asked Keri why she and other female students didn't speak more in class, she theorized that the girls were shy and intimidated by male debaters. Members of the Debate Team were primarily white and Asian males. Their high status was defined by the school through course titles and competitions, and they were granted particular privileges and advantages within and through the school culture. Keri observed,

> I could talk if it's something that means a lot to me, but most of the stuff it's, it's not really something that I really care about. But other girls, I don't know, maybe they also don't have feelings about it or, or 'cause a lot of my friends in this class, they're just shy, they don't want to get embarrassed or anything.

Seemingly like most female students in this class, Keri was more comfortable questioning gender practices by means of her writing, rather than through class discussions. Small group work, however, seemed to afford an arena in which Keri and other girls were more apt to disrupt the hierarchy of gender through their interaction with others by taking up leadership positions. In her *In Dubious Battle* presentation group, Keri did this by organizing the work of the group and providing literary analysis. The group work begins like this:

Keri: Okay, I didn't hear the question
Zoe: [reading from the assignment sheet] "In great literature, no scene of violence exists for its own sake. How does a violent scene in this novel contribute to the meaning of the book? Choose a violent scene."
Andy: That shouldn't be hard to do.
Keri: How about when Joy dies? That like started the strike.
Andy: Yeah
Zoe: I think that the most violent scene is the ending. That part about ( ).
Keri: I didn't think —
Andy: ( )
Keri: We, are we going to act this out?
Andy: Hey, Keri, could you hand me my binder? The binder?
Keri: Okay, let's talk people! Think it's going to ( ). Just pretend it's not here. [referring to the tape recorder]
Sean: Oh, we do this today? Uh-oh
Keri: No, we set it up today.
Sean: Oh
Zoe: Okay, what do you guys want to talk about in our presentation?
Keri: Um, I guess we could say that, 'cause at the end he started doing like he after Jim died he kept, he tried to use that to keep the strike going. That could

be his death was like, if he hadn't have died maybe the strike wouldn't have gone on, but it might go on.

Throughout this small group work Keri positioned herself as a leader and as a capable student by directing the conversation and offering analytical perspectives. But at the same time, she interjected comments that lessened the power in these positions by making claims for her ignorance, asking questions of the other students, or by valuing others' comments over her own. Later in this discussion, she remarks, for example: "I like your other one, the little kid one, but I don't know" and "Okay, you know big words. I can't read them." Other students' reactions to her show ambivalence towards her position as a leader and as an academic; while no one contradicts or challenges her attempts to organize the group, both Sean and Andy respond to her questions by changing the topic, demonstrating that her position as a leader is not seen as authoritative.

Keri did take up leadership and knowledgeable positions in the discussion, but she did not do so to the same extent when her group presented their findings to the rest of the class: she did not introduce the group or answer questions from other students, she limited herself to one turn at talk, and she did not introduce any new ideas. Like many of the girls I observed in this class, she seemed to feel more comfortable and was more often called upon to take up leadership positions within the contexts of small groups rather than whole class discussions or presentations.

Paula
Perhaps because of her widespread popularity, Paula was more comfortable speaking out in whole class discussions than most of the other female students in Mr. Brown's class. By publicly voicing her opinions, Paula rejected the hierarchy of gender that was created in the classroom when male students more often took up leadership positions in class or positioned themselves as students more skilled than female students. Paula also questioned the prevailing practices of gender she encountered in school and out-of-school by explicitly raising these topics in various literacy activities—including class discussions and her writing assignments.

During a small group presentation connected to the reading of *The Bluest Eye*, Paula questioned notions of beauty, their connections to ethnicity, and the way in which they had worked in her life to define her as female. Her monologue is notable not only because she explicitly questions the gender borderwork accomplished by the internalization of ideals of beauty, but also because she takes the floor for far longer than she did at any other point in the course, suggesting that this was a topic about which she felt strongly and personally. I have quoted from her monologue at length in order to do justice to the complex interweavings of literacy with in-school and out-of-school issues of gender. Paula says,

> Society's perception of beauty causes ( ) to concentrate on, on, on a physical definition of beauty. Um, that's just how our society is, and that's me, just because I find myself getting caught up in the media. And society also, because I come to school everyday, "Oh, I have to dress nice, oh, I have to wear make-up and everything," but I just want to share with you guys, like how recently, last year, I discovered I didn't wear make-up for one day, and I was just like, "Well, I'm so ugly, oh, my god, no one's going to talk to me," but everyone treated me the same. So I was like, "Oh, so maybe it's not the way I look, maybe they like me as a person." ...I feel like society, I mean, not many people are comfortable with that because we are brainwashed when we are younger to think, "Oh" you know, "Baby dolls. Be perfect. Pretty hair, a slim waist" you know, ( ) blond hair, pretty eyes, you know, slim waist, and I don't feel like I fit into the criteria, but at the same time, I don't feel like I'm ugly. Because, you know, I had a Barbie when I was younger, but I knew that was the Barbie it wasn't me, and I can't, I realized like at fifteen that that's not, but, so I, it never caught me like I was ugly... So, like the Asian aspect of everything. When I was younger, I used to be really pale, and I looked like I was Chinese or something because I was just a lighter skin tone, and I was always told that I was a cute. But, it was just like a few years ago, when I went to visit like my family in Los Angeles and I had like totally changed from when I was younger, I got darker, you know, and I'm not as skinny as most Cambodian girls are, they were just like, "Whoa! What happened to you?" [A few disbelieving laughs come from students.] And they were, they told me, they were like, "Do you ( ) for the fact that you were light-skinned, now you're not cute any more!" And I was, that hurt me, but at the same time I was like I don't care 'cause you know whatever. 'Cause when I think about it now, it's just like my culture has this image too and it's just like I don't fit it. But I don't feel like I am an outcast or anything like that, because it's just, I've been Americanized, and you know, that's what the American culture has taught me in some ways, for the fact that to be, to be yourself, to be an individual, and not to just follow, not to just fit like this perfect person. And, so, a lot of people, a lot of people in my culture would say that I'm not Cambodian enough for the fact that my family has like made our own little, you know, life for ourselves, that we're like Americanized, but so, yeah.

Paula's presentation demonstrates the many ways in which the notions of beauty and gender she brought to class influence her literacy practices. She shows how ideals of beauty have operated in her life at a social and at a personal level and, as raced and classes concepts; she has felt the pressure to define herself and her worth through cultural ideals of feminine beauty like those represented in the media (supermodels) and girls' toys (Barbies). At the same time, the gender borders created by feminine ideals of beauty have entered her life in complex and personal trajectories. Because she is an ethnic minority, because she has dark skin, and because her home culture is Cambodian, Paula notes that she has internalized a desire to achieve and measure herself by particular upper-class, white ideals of beauty that are difficult to resist but impossible to achieve.

Like Keri's view of the hierarchy of gender created by ideals of beauty, however, Paula's monologue is not unilaterally critical or transformative. Although Paula notices the ways in which representations of female beauty and worth have affected her life and others, the solution she provides depends on a discourse of individuality and modernity that exhorts females to resist this by being "individuals" and "yourself." Additionally, when her initial critique of U.S.-based ideals of beauty shifts to Cambodian culture, she then posits U.S. culture as one that has "taught" her this—"to be yourself, to be an individual, and not to just follow, not to just fit like this perfect person." For the most part, however, Paula's presentation concerning beauty ideals questioned the gender borders surrounding beauty that are ritualized at societal levels and internalized at the personal level. Paula, like Keri, seemed to be more aware of and critical of the way in which gender operated in the classroom, in literature, and in the school because she felt her home culture—Cambodian—was very oppressive for women. Her heightened awareness of the ways in which gender practices are structured and represented seemed to lead her to question them more often than many other students in the class. Paula's presentation, like Keri's presentation of her scarf, suggests that school-based literacy practices can be used to critique and transform gender practices.

Paula did not limit her analysis of gender borders and the hierarchy of gender to oral literacy practices such as verbal discussions of literature. In writing, as well, she often questioned the symbolic representation of gender in the literature the class was assigned to read and study. Paula's essay on *Death of a Salesman*, for example, questioned the hierarchy of gender by disrupting the discourse of universality in the essay question set by the teacher. Thus, in her essay on the theme of immortality in American literature, Paula struggled to fulfill the literacy task assigned to her in light of her interpretations of literature as comprising classed, raced, and gendered texts. The assignment asked the students to use a quote from Arthur Miller—"Above all, perhaps a need greater than hunger or sex or thirst is a need to leave a thumb print somewhere on the world"—to draw connections between *Death of a Salesman* and other American literature. Paula had read *Narrative of the Life of Frederick Douglass, An American Slave* by Frederick Douglass and *The Awakening* by Kate Chopin and sought to compare these two texts to *Death of a Salesman* in her essay. However, she found this difficult to do when the theme of immortality implicit in "leaving a thumbprint on the world" did not seem to apply to Douglass's or Chopin's work. In fact, Paula found that Douglass and the protagonist of *The Awakening*—Edna Pontillier—seemed to have very different goals in life from Willy Loman, the protagonist of *Death of a Salesman*. Rather than seeking immortality, Douglass and Pontillier seemed to be trying to break free of the bounds of race and gender that restricted their lives. In an excerpt from her final essay, Paula wrote:

> Douglass didn't desire fame or fortune. He wanted the right to be able to live and breathe at his own pace. Freedom, was his goal. He didn't lead a life of lies and dishonesty. What you saw, was what you got. Douglass struggled for his freedom for himself. The world could not have stopped him if it was coming to an end. He was determined and prepared for all the odds against him. In the end, his freedom proved his determination. The Dream benefited him and others around him. Whereas, Willy Loman's death brought him and his loved ones heart ache and pain....
>
> Another success story happened in *The Awakening* by Kate Chopin. A woman living her life for another person and not knowing why. She was brought up in a society where women did as they were expected and didn't say a word otherwise....
>
> Success and being successful is valued in so many different ways. Today, success is still being redefined from generation to generation.

The themes of Paula's essay demonstrate how her non-academic experiences came to bear upon her interpretation of literary texts. Rather than arguing that the theme of immortality runs through all of American literature, as most students in the class did, Paula points out salient differences between the lives and goals of Willy Loman, a middle-class white male, and Frederick Douglass, a black man born into slavery, and Edna Pontillier, an upper-class white woman. As someone who faced discrimination in her life as both a female and as a Cambodian-American, Paula was not able to discount the ways in which the practices of gender and race influenced the characters' goals and motivations. Douglass "didn't desire fame or fortune. He wanted the right to be able to live and breathe at his own pace. Freedom, was his goal." And Pontillier was represented as a woman trapped by gendered social expectations, as "a woman living her life for another person and not knowing why. She was brought up in a society where women did as they were expected and didn't say a word otherwise." In the conclusion to her essay, however, as Paula strives to fulfill the explicit and implicit expectations of the writing assignment. She changes her prevailing argument to claim that Loman, Pontillier, and Douglass are all examples of characters in American literature who strive for "success," even though "[success] is valued in so many ways." (Of course, the notion of "success" is problematic here since both Pontillier and Loman kill themselves in the end).

Paula's roles in small group work were also tied to the notions of gender and ethnicity she brought to class. Her Cambodian background seems to have led Paula to see herself as allied with other marginalized groups in society and within the school—most notably African-American students. Indeed, when she worked in small groups Paula was consistently more likely to take up a leadership role when the others in her group were African American rather than white or Asian. Paula explained to me in an interview how she chose to position herself in a group of all white female students (in which she was fairly silent) and a mixed-sex group of African American students (in which she was the leader).

AG: What made the difference (in how much you participated in these groups)?

Paula: It was because I did feel like I was needed in that [Bluest Eye] group. Because, maybe you saw, all the colored people are like there. It was like the minority group. And I just felt like we just, I felt like I wanted this to be good, where people, you know, like know that like we're actually thinking in the class also because they barely say anything in the class. I wanted them to you know put some have some input in the class and just like I was trying to just encourage them you know just to think more, and just like "What do you want to say?" I mean, in the other group, I had like Jane with me and stuff? And I didn't feel like, I didn't feel intimidated by her where I didn't have to say anything, I just felt like mmmm, I just felt like we both know we want to (say) and it's going to come out anyways, you know? Like I didn't have, no-one was going to hold anything back ( ). But when I was in my other group, I just felt like they were just holding a lot back because they just didn't want to say anything.

As a student of Cambodian descent, Paula identified herself as a minority student within the school and as a member of a marginalized group within the class. She felt that other students in the class viewed the minority students as unthinking, and it had not escaped her notice that these students rarely spoke in class. At the same time, however, when I asked Paula why she did not participate as much in this small group discussion as others, she said repeatedly that she "chose" not to because she knew the other students would get the work done. Drawing upon a discourse of personal choice, Paula represented the dynamics of the group work as equitable and power-free. But Paula was a strong leader in the *Bluest Eye* group later in the semester and in other groups, perhaps because she felt the pressure to demonstrate her capabilities as a minority student. Thus Paula's out-of-school, gendered, and raced experiences influenced not only how she interpreted literature, but also how she positioned herself as a participant within the literacy activities of the class. That Paula could recognize (gender and ethnic) inequities in particular groups and situations, and work to change them, but not others, demonstrates the complex and often conflicting nature of the ways in which inequities emerge through literacy.

Conclusion

If we return for a moment to *Refuge*, Keri's essay based on her interview with Paula, this piece of academic writing appears not only as an artifact of the students' literacy practices but also of the gender practices they bring to the classroom. In *Refuge*, Keri uses writing to represent the interests she and Paula share as women growing up in non-American home cultures where women are expected to be particularly subservient to men. Keri's representation of Paula also eschews the positions in which Paula is most often seen in school—that of homecoming princess and "Miss Popularity"—and instead positions her as a female in a particularly sexist world and culture. Keri's account of the interview disrupts the naturalness of the form of femininity she and Paula are pressured into taking up in their home cultures, and shows how they are both negotiating types of femininity in their lives. This shows a recognition of gendered power relations and willingness to contest them that I saw in both students' oral and written literacy practices.

While the out-of-school gender practices of Paula and Keri came to bear upon their literacy practices in very meaningful ways, they were not always positive. Both students were less likely to challenge the hierarchy of gender that existed in the class and in U.S. society through their actions—by, for instance, regularly taking up leadership positions in whole class and small group literary discussions. This reinforced the general pattern in the class in which female students were more likely to do more of the silent work (like homework) while male students were more likely to do public work (like speaking up in class discussions). This public/private dichotomy reflects the gender hierarchy found in U.S. society at large (Connell, 1987).

The relationship between the practice of gender and literacy is symbiotic, however, so while gender practices shaped literacy practices in Paula's and Keri's lives, their in-school literacy practices were also shaping their analysis of gender practices. This can be seen in the way that reading *The Bluest Eye* and hearing her classmates talk about ideals of beauty changed Keri's view of what it meant to be a "free" woman in the U.S. In another example, Paula originally requested to be partnered with Keri for the interview activity because, she explained to me, Keri's presentation of the scarf made her want to get to know Keri better. The literacy activity that prompted Keri to talk about her life in Iran as a girl sparked Paula's interest in talking to Keri about their home cultures in more depth. Literacy activities thus provided ways in which social practices that were *symbolically and structurally* tied to masculinity or femininity (in varying degrees) could be questioned and transformed.

The practice of literacy in this English class—within serious societal and institutional constraints—provided opportunities for different forms of masculinity and femininity to be held, questioned, and negotiated. Women and men (real and fictional) could be, and sometimes were, represented in ways that called into question the ways in which they practiced masculinity and femininity. Thus literacy was both a *means through which* students practiced gender and a *practice* that represented gender actively.

The literacy practices of Keri and Paula, in particular, demonstrate that students' out-of-school gender practices and representations of gender came to bear on their academic literacy tasks in real and significant ways. Language arts classrooms thus hold the possibility of serious critical thinking about (and transformation of) socially endorsed gender practices and male- dominated hierarchies of gender. At the same time, literacy practices can serve only to reinforce these practices and hierarchies. Ultimately, by looking at how students bring their notions of gender to bear upon literacy, both through what they do and through how they represent others, can we begin to use academic literacy as a way in which to transform students' lives.

Note

1.   Pseudonyms are used for the school, location, and the participants in this study.

Works Cited

Acker, J. (1992). Gendered institutions: From sex roles to gendered institutions. *Contemporary Sociology*, 21 (5), 565–569.

Baynham, M. (1995). *Literacy practices: Investigating literacy in social contexts*. London: Longman.

Belenky, M., Clinchy, B., Coldberger, N., and Tarule, J. (1986). *Women's ways of knowing: The development of self, voice, and mind*. New York: Basic Books.

Camitta, M. (1993). Vernacular writing: Varieties of literacy among high school students. In B. Street (Ed.), *Cross cultural approaches to literacy* (pp. 228–246). Cambridge, UK: Cambridge University Press.

Cherland, M. R. (1994). *Private practices: Girls reading fiction and constructing identity*. London: Taylor & Francis.

Connell, R. (1987). *Gender and power*. Stanford, CA: Stanford University Press.

Davies, B. (1993). *Shards of glass: Children reading and writing beyond gendered identities*. Cresskill, NJ: Hampton Press.

DiPardo, A. (1993). *A kind of passport: A basic writing adjunct program and the challenge of diversity*. Urbana, IL: National Council of Teachers of English.

Dyson, A. (1995). Writing children: Reinventing the development of childhood literacy. *Written Communication*, 12 (1), 4–46.

Dyson, A. and Freedman, S. (1991). *Critical challenges for research on writing and literacy: 1990–1995*. Berkeley, CA: National Center for the Study of Writing.

Eckert, P. and McConnell-Ginet, S. (1992). Think practically and look locally: Language and gender as community-based practice. *Annual Review of Anthropology*, 21, 461–490.

Fairclough, N. (1992). *Discourse and social change*. Cambridge, UK: Polity Press.

Finders, M. (1997). *Just girls: Hidden literacies and life in junior high*. New York: Teachers College Press.

Gee, J. (1996). *Social linguistics and literacies: Ideology in discourses*. London: Falmer.

Gilbert, P. (1992). The story so far: Gender, literacy and social regulation. *Gender and Education*, 4, 185–199.

Gilligan, C. (1982). *In a different voice: Psychological theory and women's development*. Cambridge, MA: Harvard University Press.

Heath, S. (1983). *Ways with words: Language, life and work in communities and classrooms*. Cambridge, MA: Cambridge University Press.

Orellana, M. (1995). Good guys and "bad" girls: Gendered identity construction in a writing workshop. Paper presented at the Annual Meeting of the American Educational Research Association, San Francisco, April.

Steedman, C. (1982). *The tidy house: Little girls writing*. London: Virago Press.

Street, B. (1984). *Literacy in theory and practice*. Cambridge, UK: Cambridge University Press.

Thorne, B. (1993). *Gender play: Girls and boys in school*. New Brunswick, NJ: Rutgers University Press.

West, C. and Zimmerman, D. (1987). Doing gender. *Gender & Society*, 1 (2), 125–151.

Willis, P. (1977). *Learning to labor: How working class kids get working class jobs*. New York: Columbia University Press.

Response to

"Negotiating Gender"

Barrie Thorne

ver three decades of extensive immigration have transformed the social and cultural landscape of California, which has received more immigrants than any other U.S. state. According to recent statistics, one fourth of all California residents were born in another country, and a third of school-age children and youth speak a language other than English at home. Driving along streets in Oakland or Los Angeles—peppered with commercial signs in many different languages— one sees striking juxtapositions of culture. Taxi drivers and others who explain the "new California" to recent arrivals are prone to reciting comparisons that dramatize the magnitude of demographic change, such as, "In Los Angeles there are more Iranians than anywhere but Tehran and more Mexicans than in Mexico City; more Vietnamese live in Orange County than anywhere but Vietnam."

There is much to be discovered about the ways in which people from different backgrounds craft relationships and identities in the multicultural settings of urban California and elsewhere. Amanda Godley has undertaken such an exploration in a detailed ethnography of an ethnically diverse eleventh-grade high school English honors class. Her chapter focuses on two students—Keri, who migrated with her family from Iran, and Paula, a first-generation Cambodian American—whose lives have been shaped by the new immigration and who share experiences with one another and with the rest of their class. Their families' trajectories of migration and settlement, and the American popular culture and school-centered worlds in which both girls are immersed, constitute a jangling mix of gendered meanings and practices. Godley uses concrete examples from classroom observations and taped discussions, interviews, and student essays to document these girls' emotion-laden efforts to sort out multiple, sometimes contradictory constructions of gender and to determine how they want to live, and to be.

The chapter opens with a striking example of juxtaposed cultural forms: an excerpt from an essay by Keri, who describes her classmate Paula as "Miss Popularity, homecoming princess, the all-star basketball player." These words evoke the American teenage culture of Archie comic books or the television series, *Beverly Hills 90210*. But Paula is also seen, and sees herself as Asian; although born in the U.S., she presumably grew up speaking Cambodian at home. She has felt the pressure of Barbie beauty ideals (blonde, white, impossibly slender), with Cambodian-American twists. In a classroom presentation, she says that she doesn't match up to either ideal, since she is "darker" and "not as skinny as most Cambodian girls." By that point in the school year Paula has come to question appearance-obsessed and racialized ideals of femininity, in part through reading and discussing Toni Morrison's novel, *The Bluest Eye*.

Keri is also preoccupied with issues of the body and beauty, and commercial products figure centrally in her experiences. I was struck by the descriptive snapshots of Keri and her mother—when she was young and they lived in Iran, her mother and brothers securing a scarf over Keri's hair, ignoring her resistance; mother and daughter throwing off headscarves together when they left for the U.S. and, in Paula's teenage years, how the mother continued to engage with her daughter's appearance, encouraging her to use make-up and to color her hair.

These snippets of life history, developed in the context of a literacy-focused high school class, are as much about North Americanization, the reworking of ethnic identities, and experiences of racism, as they are about gender. But ethnicity, gender, age, religion, and other categories of social placement and identity inflect one another, and their organization and meanings vary by context. When I explain this approach in my women's studies courses, I often scan the classroom, looking for someone who is wearing plaid. I then invite everyone to focus on one color—like navy blue—in the overall design and trace the way it crosses other lines and patches of color, reconfiguring into a complex whole. Like a navy blue line in a multicolored plaid field, gender never stands alone; it is always constituted along with other strands of identity and modes of social placement.

In part because they are from immigrant families and have moved between cultures, Keri and Paula are aware that gender relations and femininity may be constructed in varied ways. They portray Cambodian and Iranian gender practices as oppressive to women, in contrast with North America—a place of "freedom" and "choice"—although as the semester progresses, they grasp some of the forced and commercialized nature of these seeming "choices." Their multiple cultural roots and future opportunities to read and dialogue across lines of difference may lead Keri and Paula to even more nuanced understanding and evaluation of hybrid and changing forms of "ethnic" and "American" cultures. Hung Thai (1999) and Nazli Kibria (1999) have found that second-generation Vietnamese, Chinese, and Korean American college students continually revisit issues of identity. Some use their ethnic backgrounds as a basis for critical reflection on American cultural practices such as the emphasis on self-sufficient autonomy at the expense of family and community.

Mr. Brown, the teacher of English 3H, encourages students to actively engage with one another and with issues of cultural difference and inequality. Some of the classroom moments of sharing and critical consciousness resemble the desegregated, constructive "communities of difference" that Fine (1997: 248) describes from research in schools in the Northeast. After years of documenting the patterns of racial, class, and gender segregation and inequality that characterize much of U.S. high school life, Fine decided to highlight sites of constructive practice and the "discourses of possibility" they bring to view. Structured inequalities are also basic to daily life in the school Godley studied, with white boys monopolizing leadership positions and class discussions, and African Americans, and girls of varied backgrounds, tending toward silence. But her study also contributes to discourses of possibility by showing that literacy practices can become vehicles for bridging and learning from difference and for developing critical consciousness.

Works Cited

Fine, M. (1997). Communities of difference: A critical look at desegregated spaces created for and by youth. *Harvard Educational Review*, 67, 247–284.

Kibria, N. (1999). College and notions of "Asian American:" Second-generation Chinese and Korean Americans negotiate race and identity. *Amerasia Journal*, 25, 29–52.

Thai, H. (1999). "Splitting things in half is so white!" Conceptions of family life and friendship and the formation of ethnic identity among second generation Vietnamese Americans. *Amerasia Journal*, 25, 53–88.

CHAPTER TEN

Spoken Word: Performance Poetry in the Black Community

Soraya Sablo Sutton

n this chapter, I explore the role that performance poetry (spoken word) plays in literacy development in the African American community. I argue that spoken word, as a literacy event, builds solidarity within the black community while increasing the literacy skills of both the poet and the audience. I also make a case for the implications that this non-school literacy practice has for traditional school-based literacy.

In the midst of our desperately dot.com society, where it is no longer necessary to leave your home to go to the grocery store, or ever to speak with another live person face-to-face, I discovered one section of the community where human contact is not, in fact, obsolete. While the rest of us are busy downloading our daily dose of information overload, a cadre of young African American men and women are creating their own versions of chat rooms in cafés, clubs, and community centers across the United States. With performance poetry—or spoken word—human contact is a prerequisite. Poetry is, after all, ultimately about creating a connection between the poet and the listener. Although the poets must compete with sound bits and commercial breaks for moments of the collective consciousness, when they are successful at capturing those few moments the potential for effecting change is great.

Background

In this study, I conceptualize performance poetry or spoken word as a literacy event according to the definition offered by Heath who writes, a "literacy event is any occasion in which a piece of writing is integral to the nature of participants' interactions and their interpretive processes" (1988: 350). Specifically, performance poetry is a written literacy event which is experienced by the audience by means of an oral performance.[1] Thus, the spoken word genre challenges the argument proposed by scholars such as Ong (1967, 1982) and Goody and Watt (1963) who suggest that once written literacy is introduced into a society, the members of that society will no longer rely on oral forms of communication. Spoken word not only relies on oral performance—the oral actually takes precedence over the written.

In response to this dichotomization of orality and literacy, several theorists contend that most often the two exist simultaneously within a culture. According to Kaschula, "'the great divide' between literate and oral societies...should not be over-emphasized. There exists rather an interaction between the written and the oral. The introduction of writing has by no means led to the extinction of oral poetic forms" (1991: 120). Echoing this sentiment of the simultaneous function of oral and written forms of literacy, Major adds that "poetry is, after all, a form of music made out of words. So a written tradition, based on an oral one, evolved side by side with that continuing oral tradition" (1996: xxxii).

As my study demonstrates, the oral performance aspect of spoken word is crucial to the transmission of the message and the connection that the poet makes with the audience. Although many of the poets publish and distribute their work in written form, they continue to do oral performances because they value this personal connection and feel it could not be accomplished solely by the use of written conventions. As Smitherman states, as a "literary genre, poetry, both traditionally and now, is written to be recited, even in a sense 'sung.' Thus poetry is the form that can most effectively go where black people are at, for it combines orality, music, verbal performance, and brevity" (1977: 180).

In addition to challenging the division between orality and literacy, I contend that becoming literate involves far more than simply learning to manipulate written language. I argue for a definition of literacy which is in line with the work of Paulo Freire, who writes,

> To acquire literacy is more than to psychologically and mechanically dominate reading and writing techniques. It is to dominate these techniques in terms of consciousness.... Acquiring literacy does not involve memorizing sentences, words, or syllables...but rather an attitude of creation and re-creation, a self-transformation producing a stance of intervention in one's context. (1988: 404)

The poets and the audiences who participate in spoken word are becoming increasingly literate because of the consciousness-raising potential of this activity. They are learning that they have the power to acquire this "stance of intervention [in their own] context" that Freire speaks of. Rather than simply accepting the injustices that plague their daily lives, these poets and the audience members challenge stereotypical representations of their community, redefine their cultural identity on their own terms, and work at becoming agents of change in their own environment.

It is important to understand, as well, that the contemporary spoken word movement did not develop in a vacuum. There is a rich poetic tradition in the African American community that is rooted in resistance and constant struggle for everyday survival. In the following section, I provide an overview of the role that oral tradition and spoken word have played in the African American community throughout history.

History of Oral Tradition Among African Americans

Despite the pervasiveness of written literacy in western society, African Americans have maintained a strong history of oral tradition. In fact, the majority of cultural transmission in the black community continually takes an oral form. According to Smitherman, this tradition can be traced back to our roots in Africa. As she notes, the "African American Oral Tradition is rooted in a belief in the power of the Word. The African concept of *Nommo*, the Word, is believed to be the force of life itself. To speak is to make something come into being" (Smitherman, 1994: 7). Through signifying, call and response, and church sermons, African Americans learn to value the creative use of oral language for the purpose of socialization and cultural survival. As Smitherman elaborates,

> In Black America, the oral tradition has served as a fundamental vehicle for gettin' ovuh. That tradition preserves the Afro-American heritage and reflects the collective spirit of the race. Through song, story, folk sayings and rich verbal interplay among everyday people, lessons and precepts about life and survival are handed down from generation to generation. (Smitherman, 1977: 73)

Black children learn early on that they must be literate in the communication styles of their culture, such as being able to hold their own in ritualistic word-play know as "the dozens"—a form of signifying.[2] Performance poetry or spoken word is but one manifestation of this oral tradition.

In addition to functioning as a tool for socialization, historically oral tradition and spoken word have also functioned as powerful mechanisms for transmitting a collective worldview and for calling the community to action. During the Civil Rights Movement, for example, a group of poets emerged as cultural voices attempting to re-define African American identity. These artists—who formed the Black Arts Movement of the 1960s—included influential poets such as Amiri Baraka, Sonia Sanchez, Addison Gayle Jr., Larry Neal, and Haki Madhubuti (formerly Don L. Lee). These poets, writers and artists attempted to move people to action through creative expression. Amiri Baraka describes the poetry of that time as,

> The rhythmic animation of word, poem, image, as word-music.... This form came out of the revolutionary sixties Black Arts Movement, from way back beyond sorrow songs and chattel wails. Where we created the word as living music, raising it off the still Apollonian, alabaster page.... Our art describes our past, the middle passage, Slavery the struggle of the Afro-American Nation! For Democracy, self-determination and the destruction of national oppression and capitalism. (Baraka, 1996: xiii)

The poetry of the Black Arts Movement reflected the political climate of the time: "These poets and their artistic compatriots grew disenchanted with...the reality of American culture and society and the possibility of any kind of meaningful assimilation by blacks. They instead turned exclusively to the black community for inspiration and sustenance, and took on roles as teachers and exhorters, often articulating the rage of the black masses with frightening accuracy" (Harper and Walton, 1994: 2). Through their words, these poets attempted to "heal black folks through the evocative power of art, and transform their suffering into constructive political action" (Smitherman, 1977: 177). A particularly influential group of poets during the 1960s was *The Last Poets*. Describing their efforts to serve as an artistic complement to the politics of black power, members of the Last Poets explain that their

> mission was to pull the people up and out of the rubble of their lives. These courageous, articulate, artistic scribes knew deep down, that poetry could save people. They knew that if Black people could see and hear themselves and their struggles through the spoken word, that they would be moved to change. They knew that if they took a stand for Black people and exposed their deepest fears and fires that America could ignore them no more. (Oyewole et al., 1996: xxvii)

In this chapter, I hope to demonstrate how the contemporary manifestation of the African American oral tradition—the spoken word movement of the past decade—also functions as a community tool for action.

Major (1996) calls the nineties another Renaissance time due to the resurgence of black poetic expression. Following in the footsteps of Amiri Baraka and Sonia Sanchez, we have young poets like Saul Williams, Jessica Care Moore and D'Knowledge who have gained national attention in their attempt to revitalize spoken word in the black community. As evidenced by its historical origins, this genre of literate production has tremendous potential to effect social change in the community. It exists as an authentic cultural representation, produced for and by community members. One might argue that the spoken word movement of the 1990s represented a call for an internal as opposed to external revolution. Rather than trying to provoke the audience to organize a march or boycott, many of the poets with whom I spoke explained that the first step toward any form of positive change was through self-examination or personal reflection among their audience. The poets believe that if people can get closer to their own sense of "truth" by finding their voice, they can learn to deal with each other more truthfully.

Through a process of self-examination and truth telling, poets and the audience are able to learn more about themselves and their social context. This places them in an optimal position for making a change in their lives. Poet Audre Lorde calls this function "poetry as illumination." She writes, the

> quality of light by which we scrutinize our lives has direct bearing upon the product which we live, and upon the changes which we hope to bring about through those lives. This is poetry as illumination, for it is through poetry that we give name to those ideas which are—until the poem—nameless and formless, about to be birthed, but already felt. (Lorde, 1984: 36)

Each of the poets in this study confirmed that poetry serves this illuminating function in their lives. Many even reported that writing poetry helps them to articulate feelings and issues which are so personal that they cannot talk about them with friends or family. Poetry helps them deal with these issues by giving voice to their experiences.

One of the reasons why poetry is such a powerful tool for communication and change is because of its potential for creating a space for identity development and its ability to connect the poet with the audience on a very personal level. The poets in this study deliberately make reference to everyday issues in their poetry such that any person sitting in the audience can take what they have said and apply it to their own experience. In this way, the poets are not only naming their own reality, but they are also naming the reality of each person who comes out to hear them speak.

One way to conceptualize the strong connection that exists between poet and audience is through the concept of dialogue. On several levels, one could argue that there is a dialogue going on when a poet takes the stage. First of all, there is the element of call and response which is typical of the African American oral tradition. Smitherman explains how call and response works,

> The idea is that constant exchange is necessary for real communication to take place. Scholars refer to this style of talk as "Call-Response." It has been ritualized in the Traditional Black Church, particularly in the back-and-forth exchange between the preacher and the congregation during the sermon. But even outside the church, whenever African Americas *conversate*, Call-Response abounds.... The only wrong thing you can do in a black conversation is not respond at all because it suggests that you *ain't wit* the conversation. (1994: 8)

In this way, the audience actually becomes an integral part of the performance, as they interject periodically to show support and acknowledge that they understand where the poet is coming from. If the audience fails to respond, the poet will often stop in the middle of a poem to make sure her message is being heard. "Check-ins" such as, *You know what I'm saying?* facilitate audience response and ensure that the connection is never lost.

On another level, dialogue is occurring in the Bakhtinian sense of the concept. Bakhtin maintains that every utterance is always a response to something that has previously been said and anticipates what will be said in the future.

> Not only does an utterance call forth or provoke a new word, it creates itself in anticipation of that response. Thus each word is doubly oriented; it looks back to the word it is answering and forwards to the anticipated word it will partly determine in advance. Words are thus borderzones between self and other.... Any utterance, no matter how weighty and complete in and of itself, is only a moment in the continuous process of verbal communication. (quoted in Morris, 1994: 13)

In the case of spoken word, the poets approach the stage with the purpose of responding to particular social issues which are significant in their lives and the lives of community members. The audience thus responds directly to the poet through call and response and begins a new dialogue with their peers as they discuss the poet's performance and the issues that were raised.

Spoken Word in this Black Community

The poets in this study draw on cultural elements of the African American community, use familiar language and references to make connections with the audience. They approach writing and performing poetry in a similar fashion as described by poet June Jordan, who notes,

> poetry is not a shopping list, a casual disquisition on the colors of the sky, a soporific daydream, or bumpersticker sloganeering. Poetry is a political action for the sake of information, the faith, the exorcism, and the lyrical invention, that telling the truth makes possible. Poetry means taking control of the language of your life. Good poems can interdict a suicide, rescue a love affair, and build a revolution in which speaking and listening to somebody becomes the first and last purpose to everyday social encounter (in Muller, 1995: 3)

The spoken word artists I encountered are cultural workers who have a vested interest in creating connections among themselves and those in their community. They take their craft very seriously and are afforded due respect by their audience. Despite numerous negative societal forces, which they face on a daily basis, these poets are determined to work for change through the sharing of their selves and their words. Moraga rightfully refers to contemporary black poets as magicians, attempting to infuse a community with hope in an improbable context.

> These "young, gifted and Black" artists and thinkers are the survivors of an education bent on securing their silence, their acquiescence, their inferiority complexes, and ultimately their suicides.... The young magicians are women of color / sisters / poets / warriors / writers who have learned to transform the "gray concrete" of urban despair to "yellow brick roads" of imagination, opportunity and future. (quoted in Forman, 1993: xvi-xvii)

A group of "young magicians" who transform their realities and connect with their community through the art of spoken word is the focus of this chapter.

Methodology

The Setting

On any given night of the week in this northern California city, you can walk into a local club or community center and find a crowd waiting to hear a poet perform. As you enter the dimly lit room, the aroma of brandy and incense permeates the air. A tall, muscular man releases the red velvet rope and you enter "The Basement" (a pseudonym). Small white candles flicker in blue glass containers on each table and loud conversation and laughter can be heard over the smooth sounds of the live jazz band playing on stage. As it gets closer to 10 o'clock, the room becomes a bit more crowded, and soon there is no place to sit. Just then, the host approaches the stage and announces that the poetry will begin momentarily. In a low, deep voice he says:

> You are experiencing the Blue Candle, this is a stage to promote spoken word and positive expression in the black community. We have poets, singers, we have rappers, jazz artists who come and sit in. It's just a positive place to come and express yourself and get some things off your chest right here in the community. That's why it's been put together, it's been goin down for about a year and a half now for those of you who this is your first time.

For ten weeks, I attended poetry readings at three different urban locations in the northern California Bay Area. This chapter reports findings from just one of these sites that I call, The Basement. The poetry readings took place exclusively at night. Most began between 7 and 10 o'clock and lasted beyond midnight at times. The readings took the form of open microphone—or "open mic"—sessions, which occur several times a week in this community and are open to any poet in the house who wants to get on stage. Poets who wish to read that evening simply put their name on the list as they enter the club. I also observed poetry performances that were advertised in advance and featured specific poets.

The Basement is located on the west side of a predominantly African American community called Mosswood. The west side has a reputation for high crime and equally high unemployment rates. The Basement hosts open mic sessions every Tuesday evening, and regular patrons know it's important to get there early in order to get a seat.

The Poets

At each poetry reading between five to ten poets perform their work in front of an audience of anywhere from fifteen to seventy-five community members. Over the course of my data collection, I noticed that there were several poets who were regulars at the open mic sessions. They were well-known by the audience and always received a positive reaction to their readings. From this group of regulars, I chose three poets as my focal subjects for this chapter. They were also part of a larger study I conducted that comprised five poets in all. I conducted interviews with these three poets and obtained written copies of their poetry as well as audio recordings of their performances. These poets are all African American, ranging in age from the mid-twenties to early thirties. They are natives of this community, and each of them performs at a variety of locations several times per month. The following is a brief introduction to each of the poets.[3]

Damu is a tall brother with a thin face and dreadlocks that fall just below his ears. He wears baggy jeans and an extra large shirt that hangs loosely on his lanky frame. Damu has lived in Mosswood all his life, but he has traveled extensively. He gets much of his inspiration for his poetry from the different places where he has visited. Upon first meeting Damu, you have to stand very close to hear his soft, unassuming voice. However, when he gets on stage, there is no mistaking his ability to command the crowd and hold the audience's attention as he takes its members on a journey with his poetry. Damu performs regularly at The Basement as well as at several other clubs in the community.

Roxanne is known as a "Blue Candle Player" because she performs almost every week at The Basement. In fact, due to her popularity at this club, she has become known as "the first lady" of The Basement. Roxanne has been writing poetry since she was about 12 years old and has an extremely strong stage presence. She often crowns her short, black hair with a large red or black velvet hat and wears horn-rimmed glasses. Like Damu, Roxanne also lives in Mosswood. She works as a child care specialist at a residential treatment center for drug-addicted mothers and their children. Roxanne has performed "everywhere," according to her.

Branden is a 26-year-old, light-skinned brother with freckles and a crooked smile. He has short, twisted dreadlocks and a goatee. Branden was born and raised in Mosswood and currently lives in the home where he was raised most of his life. Branden performs about once a week at open mic sessions at Johnnie's—another popular poetry venue in the area—and has been a featured poet on numerous occasions. About every other week Branden makes an appearance at The Basement. Like Roxanne, he is well-known and respected within the spoken word community as one of the most talented poets around. He has been writing poetry since he was in high school and plans to write a novel. Branden currently works as an elementary school teacher. Each of the poets has his or her own unique style of writing and performing. Although it is impossible to do them justice within this study, I have attempted to represent them and their work as accurately and completely as possible.

Data Collection and Analysis

For ten weeks I attended open mic sessions that featured poetry readings. This amounted to a total of 17 observations, each lasting two to three hours. Prior to beginning this work, I was familiar with a few of the sites already and had attended poetry readings with friends over the past two years. I always made an effort to introduce myself to the poets after the performance and explain my research project to them so that they would become familiar with me, and we could begin to develop a rapport. All of the poets who I spoke with were very willing to talk with me and share their work. After I determined who my focal poets would be, I began recording their performances and transcribing selected poems. I also obtained written copies of their poetry to compare with the oral versions I collected. After spending about a month visiting local poetry spots, taking field notes, and getting to know some of the poets, I began interviewing them. Some of the interviews were taped at the actual poetry readings, in between sets with jazz playing in the background. Other times I met the poets at local cafés or in their homes.

Over the course of my study, I collected volumes of poetry from each focal poet. From this collection, I chose one or two poems from each which I considered to be "signature pieces"—poems representative of their work that helped illuminate some of the more salient issues that emerged from their interview responses and my observations in the field. Throughout the next section, I will refer periodically to specific portions of these poems in order to illustrate particular points or arguments (see also the appendices for this chapter).

I examined the data from the interviews to discover recurrent themes. From this information I determined that the following areas were salient issues around which I could organize my analysis. The first is that of *motivation*. I was interested in finding out what the driving force was behind these poets' writing. I examined the data for evidence of why the poets were so committed to spoken word. This line of inquiry led me to discover that the poets made a clear distinction between the type of spoken word that they are doing now and the type of poetry they were exposed to in school. Consequently, I first focus on an analysis of the differences between in-school and out-of-school literacy. In an attempt to characterize non-school literacy, I present on two emergent themes: the *function* poetry plays in the lives of the poets, and the ways the poets were able to create a *connection* with their audience through spoken word. In addition, the specific themes the poets themselves discuss in their poetry are analyzed, and, use the words of the poets themselves to tell their stories of what spoken word means to them. I conclude this analysis with a discussion of the implications of my study for school-based literacy.

Findings

Writing In and Out of School

The majority of the poets in this study reported negative experiences with writing in school. They first experienced poetry in a traditional school-based literacy form which often meant exposure to poems they considered irrelevant to their daily lives. According to Damu, even though he always had a love for writing, he never felt that his passion was nurtured while he was in school. He recalls becoming frustrated and bored with assignments that had no connection to his life. Describing his high school experience, Damu recounts, "I would be sitting in class and it got to the point where I'd be like cutting school... I have to write about the stuff *I need* to write about. And I got in trouble, I end up going to continuation school.... so, I never really wrote in school, I just wrote for myself [at home]."

Upon entering college, Damu hoped to find the freedom to express himself through his writing, but unfortunately, he ran into even more obstacles with regard to his use of Black English and his choice of topics. As Damu explains,

> I took a creative writing course and I got judged a lot for my grammar, but my grammar was how I write...I was being judged on like a Shakespearean scale, but I'm talking about things that's happening today not in the sixteenth century...it was like my choice of words, my phrases, my sentences, sometimes even my topic. And they wanna change things and it's like, yeah this is grammatically correct, but it would change the whole composition, so it's like, I ran into artistic differences.

As with Damu, Roxanne has always had a love for writing; however, she also ran into difficulties writing in school-based, standard English classes. Describing the strategy she used to get through her college English courses Roxanne explains, "I was never good with practical grammar...so I would always write my papers about characters who either had ghetto language or southern slurs, you know, and that's how I covered up me having to present grammatically correct papers" (laughs). Roxanne also believes that because she attended an historically black college, many of her professors were more open to her writing in Black English.

Those poets who were exposed to poetry within the school setting, found it alienating and uninspiring because it had little to do with their daily lives. As Branden describes, "in English class in high school you go over poetry, but they went over like I guess like, ahh Edgar Allan Poe, all that kind of stuff.... I don't know if it was because of the language of the times, I don't know if it was because I just didn't want to be there, but it

was like, I was not diggin it." Even when Branden's teacher tried to propose an analogy between rap music and the poetry of Edgar Allan Poe,
Branden reports that he was "not trying to hear that," because he had
already been turned off by the genre of poetry to which he was being
exposed. The English teacher who succeeded in capturing Branden's
attention was the one who, as he recalls, "showed me the beauty of the
English language and what I could do with the language." This was his
ninth-grade teacher, who encouraged creativity and allowed students to
focus on their lived experiences as inspiration for their writing.

Once theses three poets began experimenting with literacy in non-
school settings, however, they soon realized that writing did not have to
be a totally irrelevant and useless activity. In fact, many of them would say
that now writing poetry played an essential role in their daily lives. In contrast to the poetry most of them were presented with in school, spoken
word is, by definition, relevant to their lived experience. This falls in line
with Smitherman's definition of black poetry. She contends that it "must
be functional and relevant to the lives and daily struggles of black people"
(Smitherman, 1977: 179). Following this line of thought, poetry becomes
a tool for identity development and self-reflection.

Damu views the spoken word genre as "an area for people who just
wanna do the art but don't wanna be judged or criticized." After years of
being told that his writing was inferior, Damu finds solace and creative
freedom in his poetry. He loves to write, and spoken word is one area
where he does not constantly have to be in fear of the teacher's disap-
proving red pen. Making a similar point, Roxanne states that each spoken
word artist has the right to define his or her poetry on his or her own
terms. She takes offense to people who try to say her work is not true
poetry because it does not follow a traditional, school-based format. She
explains simply that a poem "is what the writer says it is." Expressing a
similar view, Damu points out that because he is not restricted by the
standards of school-based literacy, he can ensure that everything he writes
is accessible and relevant to members of his community. He describes his
poetry as "a little bit intricate, a little bit intellectual you know, simply
because I'm always trying to progress, but it's not anything complex or
exclusive, you know, if you got eyes, ears, and a mouth you can relate."

The poem by Damu presented in this chapter is an excellent example
of his poetry. It is indeed easy to relate to and is directly relevant to issues
in the community. *Internationally Negro* is a poem Damu wrote while visiting Cuba (see Appendix A). This trip enabled him to reflect on the idea

of global interconnectedness among people of color. It opened up a world of possibilities of which he was not previously aware. In his own words,

> there was Black folks there that looked just like me and they were really intelligent but they were making like eight dollars an hour out there and here I am in the United States of America, and you know, I got TV, bathroom, but at the same time, they have more of a spiritual connection than we do out here in the States. We're more on the materialism, where they don't have any materialistic items...but they black like I'm black but you know we're kinda like pieces of the puzzle.

Through his poem, Damu hopes to extend this idea of global black identity to his audience. He recognizes that within his community, people are being killed because of what street they live on. His perspective on interconnectedness sheds new light on what he considers a very narrow-minded attitude. He explains, "I really wish people would get rid of this like local-ass attitude about I'm from eastside, westside, you know what I'm sayin? We all came on boats, period. Point blank. You know, came from Africa. The rest is just things they use to divide us, so it's like you're internationally Negro." Damu hopes that this point comes across clearly to his audience, and he writes,

> I'm so far from those cellular phones
> beeper tones
> all-American Negroes
> being placed in my face on a daily basis

He explained to me that he is not trying to put his community down, but rather he wants to acknowledge that we are all part of a bigger picture.

Branden also recognizes the importance of writing poetry which will give the audience something to think about. Recognizing the fact that he was turned off by poetry which he felt lacked authenticity, Branden makes an effort to ensure that his audience will not be alienated by his work. He feels that as a poet, he has some degree of responsibility to bring issues to the table for the audience to consider. Commenting on some of the popular rap artists who confine their lyrics to money, cars, and women, Branden feels that these rappers could be using their influence to bring a more positive message to the community. As he states, "with the power that [rappers] have, [they] need to start trying to build some bridges instead of trying to do this same old stupid shit." By means of his poetry, Branden attempts to build bridges for his community.

The following section discusses specific characteristics of spoken word as a non-school literacy event beginning with the function it plays in the lives of the poets.

The Function of Spoken Word in the Lives of these Poets

One thing all of the poets I studied agree upon is that spoken word is always about telling the truth. Branden contends that the only way to truly learn the craft of poetry is by making an effort to learn more about your own identity. He states that the better you know yourself, the better your poetry will be. In addition to learning to tell their truth through poetry, many of the poets commented that poetry functions in their lives as a way to get things off their chest. Roxanne claims that writing poetry gives her peace of mind. She even acknowledges that if no one ever came out to hear her perform, she would continue to write. Therefore, although her poetry may serve as a learning tool for the audience, ultimately she writes for herself. In addition, however, Roxanne recognizes that she has a responsibility to share her gift of poetry with her community. Just as she has benefited from writing the poem, her audience can benefit from hearing it. She recalls that this was a lesson she learned early on in her career as a poet.

> There was a time in my life when my mentor told me that my craft doesn't belong to me.... She was like... the things that you say are so powerful that they can become an empowering tool for others.... It doesn't belong to you. Once it comes out and it spills on the paper, you have to give it away. And that's when I started getting into doing performances.

In addition to functioning as a form of truth telling and helping poets to discover more about themselves; poetry can also be a source of pride and empowerment for the poets as they redefine their reality on their own terms. Branden points out that he gains a sense of pride from producing poetry. He states that he continually surprises himself when he is able to complete a piece of which he is particularly proud. He states, "a lot of times after I finish I'm like amazed or kinda surprised at myself that something like that could come out of me." Branden and the majority of the poets in my larger study never had the opportunity to experience that sense of satisfaction with school-based literacy activities.

In his poem entitled *E.S.O.*, Branden expresses pride in his community by painting a picture from an insider's perspective (see Appendix B). He writes,

there's no better place to see such a display
of grown folks at play there's
no otha place to see folks ride and side
except for on the eastside.

In these few lines, Branden is describing a typical weekend afternoon in Mosswood, where you can find groups of young African Americans hanging out and socializing. In contrast to the constant negative portrayals presented in the evening news of his hometown and the people who live there, Branden presents an image of a community which he loves and claims as his own, and even refers to himself as "the great folk/street hero." Spoken word gives him the space and power to define not only his sense of self, but also his community. Like the other poets in this study, Branden uses his poetry to celebrate aspects of black life which are often devalued, misunderstood, or simply ignored. Any audience member who hears this poem cannot help but be filled with the same sense of pride that Branden experiences.

Orality and the Audience Connection

All of the poets with whom I spoke agree that the oral aspect of their performance enables them to make a crucial connection with their audience which is far more powerful than the written text alone could ever achieve. Damu explains that he hopes the audience leaves his performances with a sense of awareness and a sense of connection with the poet. He feels that spoken word is essentially about human interaction. Poets craft their message by means of their voice tone, speed, volume, and pitch. In turn, the audience interprets that message. This quality of orality can be informed by James Gee's discussion of the importance of prosodic cues in verbal interaction. Gee claims that the act of writing down an oral text results in the loss of crucial prosodic cues that relate directly to meaning. He notes that when the oral becomes written,

> we have lost most of the prosody of the text, the way in which the speaker's voice rose and fell in pitch, the way in which she lengthened and shortened her syllables, the way in which she speeded up and slowed down her rate of speech, and the places she hesitated and paused. These matters constitute the overall rhythmic organization of the text, and they are crucial to how the speaker expressed her viewpoint, attitude and the deeper sense she was trying to make above and beyond the literal meaning of her words and sentences. (Gee, 1991: 106)

Although the quote from Gee refers to conversation rather than spoken word, I believe that his point about the importance of prosody is absolutely relevant to spoken word. Gee's argument supports the claim that verbal performance is just as important, if not more so, than written versions of the poems. In fact, I found that the poets I observed would often deviate from the written text during their spoken word performance. For instance, I have heard Branden perform his poem *E.S.O.* many times and each time he may place a different stress on particular words, speed up or slow down at certain parts, raise or lower the volume of his voice for emphasis, even add words here and there. As he explains, "I think that's the beauty of it because… it's the same poem but, sometimes it can be interpreted different ways just by saying one or two words a different way."

Most of the poets felt that in order for them to take full advantage of the oral experience of spoken word, they could not come to the stage with a written document at all. They reported that they prefer to perform their poetry from memory because it allows them the freedom to experiment with not only linguistic variation—of the kind Gee alludes to—but also physical variation, such as using eye contact, body gestures, and facial expressions to draw the audience into the experience.

What the Poets are Writing About

Each of the three artists in the study reported here begins from a place of absolute relevance when writing their poetry. The topics of their poems range from sociopolitical issues, to economics, to sexuality, through to interpersonal relationships among African Americans. The consistent goal of their performance is always to find a way to create a connection with their audience.

In addition to creating a connection, Roxanne's poetry can also be described as a call to action. However, unlike much of traditional black poetry—which often includes a great deal of irony, humor, and sarcasm— Roxanne's words are very direct and to the point. In *Hate/Hate/Hate: How African Americans Treat Each Other*, Roxanne reveals the complex factors that contribute to the quality of life in her community (see Appendix C). She first notes the social and economic factors that negatively affect African American life. She writes:

> ghetto soil is unfertile land
> planted by america's hands to enslave
> so-called the *free* black man… see
> our groceries be
> a dolla mo' and
> each corner bearing a liquor store with its

nicotine sticks and false fingertips and
economically keeping us under massa's whip
teaching us to
hate
hate
hate

This theme of documenting injustice in the community can be seen in several of the poets' work. For instance, both Damu and Branden point out the constant police presence in their neighborhoods. However, the interesting thing is that both poets not only comment about the problem that many African Americans face with law enforcement, they also describe strategies to avoid the police. Because they are aware of the problem they can attempt to take steps to prevent it. Damu writes in *Internationally Negro*,

and a warrant for your arrest in the pocket of your local cop
who supplies your drug spot
and arrests you for sellin' rocks
am I soundin like that old clock
of the same story
another Negro gets clocked then shot, popped
yeah, you know that plot
the one that won't be featuring me
'cause I'll be some place
some where
with
some body

Damu's experience in Cuba gave him a global perspective that enabled him to envision himself rising above problems concerning the local police. Later in his poem, Damu suggests that much of the social inequality African Americans experience is woven deeply into the fabric of American society.

when in doubt about the views that I now represent
please refer to section four of your fourteenth amendment
that's that part that documents that black folks are bein' pimped
and legally ensures that the U.S. of A. will always be exempt
from all reparations that exceed the amount of zero

Rather than simply complaining about injustice, Damu uses his poetry to offer a critical analysis of his situation. Even though Branden's poem *E.S.O.* has primarily a celebratory tone, he also includes a warning to his fellow

African Americans about the problem with the police (in the following poem, "one time" is a slang term used to refer to the police). He writes,

> but
> watch out now cuz
> one-time is cruisin these streets of the
> E. S. O.
> but I ain't trippin cuz I'm in S.A.'s 5 .0 and
> if Mr. Piggy wanna fool with me
> I'm puttin the pedal to the flo' cuz
> I gotta go
> gotta go
> but I'll be back to take
> my place
> as the great folk
> street hero

Although Branden acknowledges the police presence in his community he also makes certain to point out that they will never succeed in diminishing the love and pride which he holds for his own community.

The poetry of the spoken word artists not only validates the experiences of community members by documenting injustice such as police brutality. It also points out the self-destructive behavior of African Americans which at times contributes to the negativity in the black community. So, in addition to simply making a connection with the audience, the poets hope to bring issues to the table and leave the audience with something to think about. However, Branden makes the crucial point that the poet must be careful not to be perceived as talking down to the community or of "being too preachy." As he explains, "it's a fine line in this game—you don't wanna be preachy, but you gotta come with something relevant." In order to accomplish this goal of being "teachy but not preachy," the poets often use rhetorical devices which serve to disarm the audience. These devices include humor, familiar dialect, and references to everyday matters to which people can relate.

For instance, Roxanne effectively points out some negative aspects of African Americans' behavior, but she does so in such a way that clearly acknowledges her own role in perpetuating the problem. In *Hate/Hate/Hate*, Roxanne comments on the futility of the lives of many African American males:

> I pretend not to see them
> but I see the gathering of fine black men
> haven't found the king within their souls

they stroll like
soldiers off duty
posted on somebody's property that
they don't own
they roam with
pagers and cellular phones and
call themselves taking care of business
they practice potential mug shots on each other

In this way, spoken word holds up a mirror to some of the not so positive aspects of the community. Later in the same poem, Roxanne deals with the demise of the black family.

we laugh in the face of a queen who has five in her tribe
we laugh cuz
ain't no daddy in sight
we laugh because
warriors not men enough
they run after making kingdom come
we laugh 'cuz
she thought he could
be right
we laugh 'cuz
he's who he's always been
and that's
gone with the
same wind that blew him in
we laugh
'cuz he ain't just her baby's daddy
but he's our daddy
and he's our sons
and he's our brothers too
and we laugh
to keep from crying

Paying close attention to not coming across as "preachy," Roxanne uses the pronoun "we" rather than "you." This signifies her direct connection with the community and the problems it faces. Through her poetry, Roxanne both holds a mirror up to African American men, pointing out that they need to take responsibility for their children, while she also notes how pathologically this problem is handled in the black community. Roxanne gets to the heart of the issue, pointing out the pain that often exists beneath laughter.

Finally, spoken word poetry strives to provide the audience with a sense of hope. In addition to presenting an honest portrayal of some of the negative aspects of the community, much of the poetry also leaves the audience feeling that they have the power to transcend this negativity. In Roxanne's ironic poem entitled *American Me*, she takes a critical look at America as a capitalist society (see Appendix D). She describes what she thinks it will take for African Americans to get ahead within this system. Her plan is one of assimilation (or rather infiltration) while still maintaining her cultural identity. She writes:

> I'mma pretend I'm with this miseducated scheme
> and lead you to believe I
> too quest the American dream
> I'll get the job, the promotion,
> and the president's position
> I'mma fool you all for the
> recognition cuz see
> that's when I'mma put my plan into full effect
> I'mma spread the word to refuse your welfare check
> If you're Black
> come work for me
> cuz see I got full benefits and social securiteeee
> I'mma buy up all your stocks and boooonds
> put the proceeds in the black community
> ain't that where they belong?

Although the structure and syntax of this poem suggest it is directed at mainstream white America, it is actually a call to action for the African American audience. Each time I saw Roxanne perform this poem the listeners were on their feet, high-fiving each other, faces filled with pride because their experience has been validated and their hope restored.

Conclusion: Implications for School-Based Literacy

This project confirms my belief that non-school literacy practices can play a crucial, empowering role in the lives of those who participate in them. The poets, with whom I had the honor of speaking, effectively utilize non-school literacy to redefine their lives, to reach out to members of their communities, and even to call people to action. Although each of these poets has a very distinct and unique style, they share in common the fact that they use spoken word to reflect on their lives and to tell the truth about the most wonderful, endearing aspects of their community. In this way they make visible the lives and culture of a people who so often remain silenced or ignored. In addition, the poets use their craft to critique the not-so-positive elements of their lives, and call attention to the systematic injustices that work to prevent their progress, while at the same time pointing out what African Americans can do to improve their own situation. They hold up a mirror to community members and point out the ways in which their own negative behavior contributes to their situation. However, this message is always delivered with love because the poet comes from the very community he or she is critiquing.

Spoken word is a powerful tool that could possibly be incorporated into the classroom in conjunction with a critical pedagogy curriculum. Due to its recent commercial popularity—appearing in movies such as *Love Jones* and *Slam*—students would most likely recognize spoken word as an authentic cultural representation which could be used as a tool for literacy development. Preliminary evidence of a successful intervention project that incorporates popular culture into the classroom can be found in Mahiri and Sablo's (1996) study. Mahiri and Sablo concluded that non-school literacy practices tend to be perceived as more authentic by the students and therefore more relevant to their lives.

Clearly the introduction of any form of non-traditional literacy in the classroom will be met with some resistance. Bringing spoken word into the schools would require that we reconceptualize both the form and the function of legitimate literate production. We would need to broaden and challenge our conception of literacy to include its social nature, incorporating both the oral and written aspects of literacy, drawing directly on the lives and experiences of the students, and recognizing the importance of taking a political stance against social injustice.

More research is warranted in this area to discover just what it would take to incorporate spoken word effectively within the confines of the traditional English class. In any case, we cannot dispute that the potential for presenting students with a powerful and authentic literacy experience exists.

APPENDIX A

INTERNATIONALLY NEGRO
BY DAMU

I think of all the places I would rather be
all the time
but there's a few times when I would rather be
where I am
and God damn
this is one of them
you see,
rain falls while I sweat because of the heat
as my toes relax in the sand
sweatin' from the concrete
I can hear the beat of the earth
when I close my eyes to listen and I'm listenin'
to the sounds of freedom
that some men will never hear again
while feelin' warm kisses
from the Caribbean's wind.
It's got me fallin in love again with
Revolutionary thoughts
in a peaceful setting
like a moment in life
that's not worth forgetting
is the moment I'd die for

I'm being blessed with the chance of living more
just a ghetto celebrity on tour,
inhaling the breeze of the Caribbean shore
from Oakland to Cuba
I went through Mexico so
I guess I'm what you call
Internationally Negro

A international Negro from the "O"
feeling the beat of the next country's tempo
I'm so
hot as fuck in my cut-off shorts
well it's the ironic freedoms of my U.S. passport
reminding me that I'm a stolen import
who's been exported into consciousness
I'm loving life with the help of god's gifts
living proof that black gods do exist
and yes it don't stop
as cars drive by bumpin' the newest hip hop

and community corner stores for your every block
and a warrant for your arrest
in the back pocket of your local cop
who supplies your drug spot
and arrests you for sellin' rocks
am I soundin' like that old clock
of that same story

another Negro gets clocked then shot, popped
yeah, you know that plot
the one that won't be featuring me
'cause I'll be
some place
some where
with
some body
Internationally Negro
Internationally Negro

amiga or amigo
I'm watchin' tropical sunsets with tropical people
I'm so far from those cellular phones
beeper tones
all-American Negroes
being placed in my face on a daily basis
co-signing a constitution written by racists, so
when in doubt about the views that I now represent
please refer to section four
of your fourteenth amendment
that's that part that documents
that black folks are bein' pimped
and legally ensures that the U.S. of A.
will always be exempt
from all reparations
that exceed the amount of zero
so I ain't got no choice
but to be internationally Negro

I can't wait and procrastinate
in the States for my chance to be equal
when
I'd rather sip tea by the Nile
with the world's first people
perfecting the original race to relax and parlay
I'm livin the lifestyle of the Negro who got away
from that *Juice, Menace to Society*, I got to *Set It Off* reality
got me decolonizin' minds well into the next century
makin' sure my friends and family are free

free from those checks,
those checks that keep you in check
by makin sure you're dependent
on which ever way the man
lets you go
I'm independently, internationally Negro

APPENDIX B

E. S. O.
BY BRANDEN

There's nothin like a good day
in the east bay
talkin about when the sun is out
not a cloud in the sky
the sun be beamin hiiiigh but
its real mild out
that's perfect cuz
that's when black folks get wild out
I mean wild as in havin fun
outside in this California sun
where folks run not walk
so they can post up and talk with
members of the opposite sex and
nobody's plexin cuz
there's enough to go around
cuz folks be comin from waaaay outta town
to this town
to chase a skirt
or maybe just flirt but
watch out now cuz
one-time is crusin these streets of the
E. S. O.
but I ain't trippin cuz I'm in S.A.'s 5. 0 and
if Mr. Piggy wanna fool with me
I'm puttin the pedal to the flo' cuz
I gotta go
gotta go
but I'll be back to take my place
as the great folk
street hero
there's no betta place to see such a display
of grown folks at play there's
no otha place to see folks ride and side
except for on the eastside
the O

APPENDIX C

Hate/Hate/Hate: How African Americans Treat Each Other by Roxanne Hanna-Ware

Hate
Hate
Hate
How african americans treat each other
Hate
Hate
Hate
How african americans treat each other

I pretend not to see them
but I see the gathering of fine black men
haven't found the king within their souls
they stroll like
soldiers off duty
posted on somebody's property that
they don't own
they roam with
pagers and cellular phones and
call themselves taking care of business
they practice potential mug shots on each other
but smile wide as Babylon drives by
in his black and white ride
cuz he be Big Daddy Pimp who gets his props
and don't give a damn about the Black man
his simp, his trick, that's been played since the time
of the Transatlantic slave trade

I pretend not to see them
but I see the gathering of apparently strong Black men
and with my american sigh
((sung)) *oh say can you see...*
playa you bein played!
they play cops and robbers for real
in between drug deals
and prison time and unemployment and welfare lines
angry men and women who haven't learned to be free
haven't been taught that from the penitentiary

hate hate hate
how african americans treat each other
see ghetto soil is unfertile land
planted by america's hands to enslave
so-called the free black man

when do men get to practice being kings at home
raising their children to be proud descendants
that roam streets paved with sweat and tears of
forefathers four hundred years of freedom cries and
his story lies about the alibi that made and keeps america rich

see
our groceries be
a dolla mo' and
each corner bearing a liquor store with its
nicotine sticks and false finger tips and
economically keeping us under massa's whip
teaching us to
hate
hate
hate

how african americans treat each other
we laugh in the face of a queen
who has five in her tribe
we laugh cuz
ain't no daddy in sight
we laugh because
warriors not men enough
they run after making kingdom come
we laugh 'cuz
she thought he could be right
we laugh 'cuz
he's who he's always been
and that's
gone with the same wind that blew him in
we laugh
'cuz he ain't just her baby's daddy
but he's our daddy
and he's our sons
and he's our brothers too
and we laugh
        to keep from crying

hate hate hate
how african americans treat each other
see I know the darker of brother
he was the other one the street chose to be its son
the girls called him black and ugly
and the boys called him black-ass nigga
so he figured he get him a colored girl's dream
to fill his pockets with profits and pride
and give him a dip in his pimp stride

and make him a baaad mutha
black sheep
when he got grown enough he left home
and never came around to dry the tears his mother weeps
found him a woman croonin her with
giiirl, you so fiiiine,
     so fiiine!
he done found him another woman croonin her with
look at that behiiind,
     damn that's a big ole behind!
he be found him another woman croonin her with
look at them wide hips
make me wanna kiss those big sweet lips
and each woman asking him
which other woman he have been with
and now he croonin her with
who the fuck you think you talkin' to black bitch

hate hate hate
how african americans treat each other
he say he don't love her but he does
just don't know how to
she say she love him but hate his ugly ways
and some say she was a pretty young thang once
but lost her smile when she lost her teeth
lost her sparkle from a black eye that
fashion fare didn't make a shade to cover
she was
looking to be his lover
was looking to be his significant other
but truth be told she was just his significant ho
but he strolled and he sold cuz
he'd been taught well to
hate hate hate

wonder why there's anger well
anger is
ain't never getting enough respect
wonder why there's crime
community residents ignoring more education
who's gon' stand and raise their hand up high and try to be the
black man or black clan
his-story lies about tomorrow
you can't borrow the jewels
the ancestors left as treasures
you got to measure up to your own
and be
kings and queens of your own throwns

and be
soldiers that win your own wars
and do somethin'
you never done before like
love one another
and don't ignore your daughter
or your son
or each other
you ain't got to be at war with your brother
and break down that wall of
hate

don't let the fate america has for the darker color be
how african americans treat each other
I said
don't let the fate america has for the darker color be
how african americans treat each other

APPENDIX D

AMERICAN ME
BY ROXANNE HANNA-WARE

You ask me if I was angry
for what happened back then
the raping of my motherland
but what of slavery that still exists today
Free at last! who's to say...
see I work as hard as you for lesser pay
Equal Rights... Well that's a laugh
because see if we're so equal then where's my cash

So I'mma enter your work place in full disguise
with silky permed hair and color contact eyes
trying my best to look just like you and be your friend
African
white-washed
American

See I'mma pretend I'm with this
miseducated scheme
and lead you to believe I
too quest the American dream
I'll get the job, the promotion,
and the president's position
I'mma fool you all for the
recognition cuz see

that's when I'mma put my plan into full effect
I'mma spread the word to refuse your welfare check
If you're Black
come work for me
cuz see I got full benefits and social securiteeee
I'mma buy up all your stocks and boooonds
put the proceeds in the black community
ain't that where they belong?
and if you feel like I ain't paying you enough
to support you and your kids?
Well, I think you told me
where the unemployment office is
     In fact, I'll just fire you
and employ a whole new crew
and see, they'll happen to be all black folks too
my silky hair, you'll soon be shocked when I arrive
still business-suited but
with nappy locks
I know my nappiness tends to offend you
well that's cool cuz see
your moose-straggly-thin-shit offended me too
Don't worry about me sneaking doing this
you know my people have always been loud
so when we comin
I'll make sure we're yellin
I'm Black
and I'm proud!
When I'm rich I won't quite be done
Cuz see I'm gonna build me a school for black folks called
"How to come and get you some!"

See, you asked me if I was angry
for what happened back then
The raping of my motherland
Well, that's when I was African
See, I plan to own your houses
I plan to own your businesses
Hell, I may even plan to own
you
Don't be angry though
just remember
I'm American too

Notes

1. Throughout this chapter I use the terms *spoken word* and *performance poetry* interchangeably; however, it should be made clear that *spoken word* is a particular type of poetry. It is not the poetry found in the traditional academic canon, however. Rather, it is a poetry that is written for, by, and about urban community members. It is poetry which is written to be performed orally in front of a live audience.
2. Smitherman (1994: 206) defines signifying as the "verbal art of ritualized insult, in which the speaker puts down, needles, talks about (signifies on) someone to make a point or sometimes just for fun. It exploits the unexpected, using quick verbal surprises and humor and it is generally characterized as nonmalicious and principled criticism."
3. The poets' actual names have been used at their request.

Works Cited

Baraka, A. (1996). Foreword. In A. Oyewole, U. Hassan, and K. Green (Eds.), *On a mission: Selected poems and a history of the last poets*. New York: Henry Holt.

Forman, R. (1993). *We are the young magicians*. Boston, MA: Beacon Press.

Freire, P. (1988). The adult literacy process as cultural action for freedom and education and conscientization. In E. Kintgen, B. Kroll, and M. Rose (Eds.), *Perspectives on literacy* (pp. 398–409). Carbondale, IL: Southern Illinois University Press.

Gee, J. (1991). *Sociolinguistics literacies: Ideology in discourse*. London: Falmer.

Goody, J. and Watt, I. (1963). The consequences of literacy. *Comparative studies in society and history*, 5, 304–345.

Harper, M. and Walton, A. (Eds.). (1994). *Every shut eye ain't asleep: An anthology of poetry by African Americans since 1945*. Boston, MA: Little, Brown and Co.

Heath, S. B. (1988). Protean shapes in literacy events: Ever-shifting oral and literate traditions. In E. Kintgen, B. Kroll, and M. Rose (Eds.), *Perspectives on literacy* (pp. 348–377). Carbondale, IL: Southern Illinois University Press.

Kaschula, R. F. (1991). New wine in old bottles: Some thoughts on the orality literacy debate, with specific reference to the Xhosa Imbongi. In E. Sienaert, N. Bell, and M. Lewis (Eds.), *Oral tradition and innovation: New wine in old bottles?* Durban: University of Natal Oral Documentation and Research Center.

Lorde, A. (1984). *Sister outsider: Essays and speeches by Audre Lorde*. Freedom, CA: The Crossing Press.

Mahiri, J. and Sablo, S. (1996). Writing for their lives: The non-school literacy of California's urban African American youth. *Journal of Negro Education*, 65 (2), 164–180.

Major, C. (Ed.) (1996). *The garden thrives: Twentieth century African American poetry*. New York: Harper Perennial.

Morris, P. (Ed.) (1994). *The Bakhtin reader: Selected writings of Bakhtin, Medvedev, Voloshinov*. London: Edward Arnold.

Muller, L. and the Poetry for the People Collective. (Eds.). (1995). *June Jordan's poetry for the people: A revolutionary blueprint*. New York: Routledge.

Ong, W. (1967). *The presence of the word*. New Haven: Yale University Press.

——— (1982). *Orality and literacy*. New York: Methuen.

Oyewole, A., Hassan, U. B., and Green, K. (1996). *On a mission: Selected poems and a history of the last poets*. New York: Henry Holt.

Smitherman, G. (1977). *Talkin' and testifyin': The language of black America*. Detroit, MI: Wayne State University Press.

———. (1994). *Black talk: Words and phrases from the hood to the amen corner*. Boston, MA: Houghton Mifflin.

Response to

"Spoken Word"

June Jordan

heories abound. Mostly they soar and circulate without empirical trial and assessment. This has always been true. But in spheres of life and death significance such as medicine or public education we need to reject traditions of theoretical flight unless they test well on the grounds of real-life application and results.

Sablo Sutton does us a great service here with her analysis and documentation of spoken word performance poetry in the black community. She confronts theoretical constructs that would define literacy as something written rather than something lived: The black poet and his/her black community in an alive, out-loud engagement. She proves herself more generous and intellectually more sophisticated than those theorists who insist upon an either/or formulation of literacy; Either it's written down or it's never written down; either it's based upon words on a page or it's based upon success or failure on a stage.

Citing various opinions, Sablo Sutton illuminates a non-exclusive model; she centers her research and findings on three black poets who write their poems—yes—and who, also, assume, and depend upon, alive and out-loud presentation of their poetry for their validation.

As she reports, her research on spoken word in the black community revealed that "the oral performance aspect of spoken word is crucial to the transmission of the message and the connection the poet makes with the audience." In order to understand the specific cultural meaning of this written-oral dynamic, Sablo Sutton offers a pertinent history of verbal black art from the 1960s forward. Thirty-five to forty years ago, black poetry erupted from the streets and captured—and shaped—the revolutionary spirit of The Civil Rights Movement. This was not classroom poetry. These were words to feed a people under the heel and the gun of violent white resistance to black struggling for equality. These poems were neither learned nor known at school. They were memorized and chanted and painted on walls and sidewalks, and the poets found themselves carrying the proud burden of public utterance for an invisible multitude of "second-class citizens."

Today's black spoken word derives from that awesome precedent of the poet and his or her people reaching towards commonly defined survival. But Sablo Sutton identifies one very important difference: "the contemporary spoken word movement did not develop in a vacuum. There is a rich poetic tradition in the African American community that is rooted in resistance and constant struggle for everyday survival..., rather than [in] trying to provoke the audience to organize a march or boycott, many...stated that the first step to any form of positive change...was through self-examination or personal reflection." This is a huge difference that Sablo Sutton examines with characteristic thoroughness and care: What does it mean, or not mean?

Further, she shepherds us through a host of scholars stumbling their way towards wanna-be useful concepts of literacy and verifiable dialog. For example, she opens our minds to expanding ideas about "call and response," by citing Bakhtin's claim that

> each word is doubly oriented, it looks back to the word it is answering and forward to the anticipated word it will partly determine in advance. Words are thus borderzones between self and others.

In other words, "call and response" is, actually, response and then call and then response.

However, and most importantly, Sablo Sutton persuasively delivers the empirical grounds for her judgments and thoughts. She lets us join her ten weeks of on-site inquiry at The Basement, an Oakland, California, jazz club where black poets attempt to earn the trust of an audience that attempts to reward, or redirect, the poet standing right there. She introduces us to three poets, in particular, and lets us listen to their artistic and political hopes, as well as to their relevant personal histories, and their distinctive poems.

After all of this, Sablo Sutton integrates her discoveries with her summoning premise that "spoken word, as a literacy event, builds solidarity in the black community, while it increases literacy skills of both the poets and the audience."

Sutton concludes with a compelling appeal to build on her work, and, thereby, "ascertain how best to incorporate spoken word" into the classroom/ written-down literacies that, otherwise, fail to acknowledge, and to protect, the living/dialogic literacy embodied by African American children in our public schools.

CHAPTER ELEVEN

What They Do Learn in School: Hip-Hop as a Bridge to Canonical Poetry

Ernest Morrell and Jeff Duncan-Andrade

As English teachers at an urban public high school in California, we bore witness daily to students who showed high intellectual abilities but were failing or significantly under-achieving academically. After seeing this for several years and with hundreds of students, it became obvious that the problem was not with the students or their intellectual capacities, but, rather, with the school's ability to help them reach their academic potential. We noticed, for example, that many students could critically analyze complex and often richly metaphoric hip-hop music that they listened to and then effectively articulate that analysis to others. Yet, most of these students were failing to exhibit the same analytical skills in class with regard to canonical texts. Through observation and study, we hypothesized that hip-hop music could be used as a vehicle for these youth to develop academic literacy skills that we felt could also transfer to other "literary texts." The pedagogical and curricular implications became clearer as we began to explore further how teaching hip-hop music as a literary genre could help scaffold and develop the academic literacies of youth who have often been labeled as "non-academic" or "semi-literate."

Through description and analysis of a curricular intervention that incorporated hip-hop texts along with canonical poetry texts, this chapter demonstrates a number of effective ways to reach urban youth and help them develop their analytical skills. It also delineates how this pedagogical approach can facilitate a more critical consciousness in these students. Following the reasoning of several literacy theorists (Ferdman, 1990;

Freire, 1970; Freire and Macedo, 1987; Street, 1993), and the findings of literacy researchers like Lee (1993) and Mahiri (1998), we argue for a broader definition of school-based literacy that encompasses cultural values, self-awareness, and the development of critical consciousness.

This chapter is divided into eight sections. The first is on critical literacy, critical pedagogy, and cultural identity, and it argues that students can be highly motivated to learn when course material is presented in the context of more authentic cultural frames. In the next section on hip-hop music as the voice of youth resistance, we develop additional arguments for how rap music is one such cultural frame for many urban youth. We also discuss the literary qualities of rap texts, their worthiness for serious academic study, and their viability for use in scaffolding other complex literary concepts. After presenting our methods, we provide a section on the poet in society where we describe and discuss the intervention model we created that incorporates and links popular culture texts to the study of mainstream canonical texts. The next three sections provide the classroom vignettes through which we make an analysis of this curricular intervention subsequent to drawing conclusions for teaching and learning in the final section.

Critical Literacy, Critical Pedagogy, and Cultural Identity

New Literacy Studies theorists (e.g., Barton and Hamilton, 2000; Ferdman, 1990; Gee, 1996; Street, 1984, 1993) have argued that social and cultural contexts have significant implications for the processes of becoming literate. Often, the failure of urban students to develop particular forms and practices of academic literacy stems from perceptions of inaccessibility of the school curriculum. Ferdman (1990: 187) argues that this inaccessibility is an outcome of the failure of schools to bridge effectively contrasting home and school cultures of urban youth. He noted that:

> Literacy involves facility in manipulating the symbols that codify and represent the values, beliefs, and norms of the culture—the same symbols that incorporate the culture's representation of reality.

Students who are not from the dominant culture in a society often struggle to merge their culturally coded representations of reality with those reflected in the school curriculum. In contrast, Ferdman noted that students whose culture is valued or promoted through literacy instruction in schools will be more inclined to obtain a high level of literacy than those students whose cultural frames are not. Implicit in Ferdman's argument is the idea that the lack of consideration given to the cultures and cultural values of children who are members of ethnic minority groups leads to unequal educational achievement based on ethnicity.

Beyond these discontinuities, Freire (1970: 47) noted the importance of using literacy as a vehicle to critical consciousness among people who are oppressed. A key element of Freire's work is that literacy must initially be taught in the language of the people:

> Critical and liberating dialogue, which presupposes action, must be carried on with the oppressed at whatever the stage of their struggle for liberation. The content of that dialogue can and should vary in accordance with historical conditions and the level at which the oppressed perceive reality.

Later, Freire and Macedo (1987) discuss the importance of reconstituting a radical view of literacy in conjunction with radical pedagogy that revolves around naming and transforming those ideological and social conditions that undermine the possibility of community and public life organized around imperatives of a critical democracy. An emancipatory theory of literacy points to the need to develop an alternative discourse and critical reading of how ideology, culture, and power work within capitalist societies to limit, disorganize, and marginalize the more critical and radical everyday experiences and commonsense perceptions of individuals. Literacy, then, is part of the process of becoming more self-critical about the historically constructed nature of one's experience (Hull, 1993). To be able to name one's experience is part of what it means to "read the world" and to begin to understand the political nature of the limits and possibilities of life within larger society. To be literate is not to be free; it is to be present and active in the struggle for reclaiming one's voice, history, and future. As part of the discourse of narrative and agency, critical literacy suggests using history as a form of liberating memory. History means recognizing the figural traces of untapped potentialities as well as sources of suffering that constitute one's past. A radical theory of literacy needs to be constructed around a dialectical theory of voice and empowerment.

Freire argues that pedagogy should help to impart or uncover the literacy in oppressed people. When challenged by a critical educator, students begin to understand that the more profound dimension of their freedom lies exactly in the recognition of constraints that can be overcome. In the process of becoming more critical, people can discover for themselves that it is impossible to deny the constitutive power of their consciousness in the social practice in which they participate. Radical pedagogy is dialectical and has as its goal the enabling of students in the critique the hegemonic practices that have shaped their experiences and perceptions in order to free themselves from dominating ideologies, structures, and practices.

Freire used Popular Culture Notebooks in São Tomé and Príncipe in order to create exercises that validated the experiences of the learners. The reader's development of a critical comprehension of the text and the sociohistorical context to which it referred was an important factor in Freire's conceptions of literacy and critical pedagogy. He also argued strongly for the use of the native language as a prerequisite to the development of any literacy campaign that purports to serve as the means to a critical appropriation of one's own culture and history.

An extension of this argument to our own project suggests that students' language must not be viewed as subordinated and antagonistic to the dominant language. Rather, for the critical educator, language like that of hip-hop music and culture is culturally authentic and also, as we show in this chapter, a viable bridge between popular culture and the school culture. Given its literary substance, social critique and cultural relevance to urban youth, hip-hop music provides a salient cultural frame for developing literary.

Hip-Hop Music: Urban Youth's Voice of Resistance

"Just as F. Scott Fitzgerald lived in the jazz age, just as Dylan and Jimi Hendrix were among the rulers of the age of rock, it could be argued that we are living in the age of hip-hop" (Farley, 1999); Farley argued that the creative people who are talking about youth culture in a way that makes sense happen to be rappers and that youth are responding in many ways. Hip-hop artists sold more than 81 million CDs, tapes, and albums in 1998, more than in any other genre of music. Although hip-hop got its start in black America, more than 70 percent of albums are purchased by whites. Taking the lead from urban youth cultural and language styles, major corporations are adopting advertising schemes and creating products such as lines of clothing, and personal care and personal image goods, along with other consumables that cater to the "hip-hop generation." Even mainstream Hollywood, exemplified in the case of Warren Beatty's *Bulworth*, is dealing provocatively with issues related to hip-hop. Although the music is largely criticized by politicians, religious groups, and some women's groups, its proponents claim that it is here to stay because it truly represents the vibrant voice of youth and points to problems that this generation and many other Americans face in daily life.

Hip-hop music emerged as a representative voice of urban youth partially because it is a genre created by and for them. Powell (1991: 245) noted:

> [Rap] emerged from the streets of inner-city neighborhoods as a genuine reflection of the hopes, concerns, and aspirations of urban Black youth in this, the last quarter of the 20th century. Rap is essentially a homemade, street-level musical genre.... Rap lyrics concentrate primarily on the contemporary African American experience.... Every issue within the Black community is subject to exposition in the rap arena. Hit rap tunes have broached touchy subjects such as sex, sexism, racism, and crime.... Rap artists, they contend, don't talk that love stuff, but [rather] educate the listeners.

Baker (1993: 33) discussed the genre of rap music and gangster rap in particular as having an "anti-establishment expressivity that has scarcely been matched." His work also called attention to the prophetic nature of rap artists in their analysis of urban communities:

> [Rappers] had been prophetic with respect to tensions between black urban youth and metropolitan police authorities. It was precisely the type of jury-exonerated violence against the black Rodney King that urban rap had in mind when it claimed that police justice was but another name for young-black-male victimization. And the fiery violence of the spring of 1992 in Los Angeles was just the kind of "armed response" that N.W.A. had prophesied in its versions of the strength of "street knowledge" recorded on *Straight Outta Compton*.

Indeed, during and immediately following the Los Angeles Insurrection of 1992, many rappers were called on to appear on talk shows, to be interviewed by news media, and generally speak as the representative voice of urban youth. In his 1993 album *Predator*, Ice Cube, a former rapper for N.W.A., proclaimed himself a prophet of the urban dilemma. Indeed, in an interview with bell hooks for *Spin* magazine in 1993 (cf., hooks: 1994), Ice Cube describes the purpose of his music in terms of helping whites to better understand the historical and ongoing dimensions of racism directed at blacks. He alludes directly to the educational purpose of his music—that he is not only trying to entertain, but to inform. His joking referral to the "Ice Cube library"—the music CDs he has produced—indicates that he feels his music is worthy of careful study. It is clear that many rappers consider themselves to be educators with at least a portion of their mission dedicated toward raising the consciousness of their communities. The influence of rap as both resistance and re-education for urban youth permeates the work of artists like Lauryn Hill, Pras and Wyclef Jean of the Refugee Camp, Public Enemy, Nas and Mos Def. They all endeavor to bring an accurate, yet critical depiction of the issues and conditions of urban youth.

Giroux (1996: 1) takes a much less celebratory view of the impact of hip-hop culture on working-class urban youth, but, nevertheless, agrees that it is a worthy topic of study in urban schools. His work addresses the crisis confronting youth he labels a "generation under siege," enmeshed in a culture of violence coded by race and class. He notes the negative connotations of youth culture promoted in popular media that propel youth toward mistrust, alienation, misogyny, violence, apathy, and the development of fugitive cultures. These same media, he contended, have commercialized the working-class body and criminalized black youth. Critical pedagogues, he argued, must consider elements of popular culture such as hip-hop music as a serious site for social knowledge to be discussed, interrogated, and critiqued. Whether the power in its messages can be used for good or ill, few can dispute the impact of hip-hop culture in the lives of working-class, urban youth. Giroux promotes a synthesis of critical pedagogy and cultural studies to gain a critical understanding of how youth are being constructed differently within a hip-hop culture that is simultaneously oppressive and resistant and that represents violence as a legitimate practice in defining youth identity.

Mahiri (1998) builds upon New Literacy Studies theorists and critical pedagogical perspectives to contend that teachers could become sources of resistance to the ideology and practices of cultural domination and exploitation that permeate institutional structures in society by working to better understand and build on the authentic experiences of students who have been marginalized by the educational process. He argues that this could be achieved through the creation and implementation of counterhegemonic curricula. His work examines African American youth popular culture as a site where young people have forged a common identity manifested in dress, language use, music, video games, sports and common heroes. Mahiri argued that elements of youth popular culture such as hip-hop music potentially could act as unifying and equalizing forces in culturally diverse classrooms, and that certain of these elements could also provide motivation for learning traditional subject matter as well. In another work, however, Mahiri (1996) identifies a number of problematic issues and cautioned against thinking that rap music would be an easy fit in traditional school curricula and classroom communities.

Methods

In the context of the conceptual foundations outlined above, our teacher research and curricular intervention was planned and implemented to address the following questions:

1. In what ways can the utilization of elements of popular culture in the curriculum contribute to the pedagogical objectives of developing critical and analytical skills in under-achieving urban youth?
2. If these skills can be demonstrated in student critiques of popular culture texts, in what ways or through which pedagogical strategies can these skills transfer to student critiques of canonical literary texts?
3. Can this curricular approach increase students' political awareness and critical analysis of the personal, commercial, and ideologically charged messages and images communicated to them through the various media of popular culture, as well as through canonical literature?

Data collected throughout the unit of work included observations, field-notes, videotapes of student preparation and presentations, interviews, and copies of all written work. Our research was facilitated by the fact that as co-teachers of this unit we were able to interchange our roles in leading instruction and attending to the collection of data. When analyzing the student work, we focused on literacy events in which students were dialogically engaged with a hip-hop text or a canonical poetry text. As mentioned in earlier chapters in this book, Heath (1983: 350) defines a literacy event as "a communication act that represents any occasion in which a piece of writing is integral to the nature of participants' interactions and their interpretive processes." In this study we expanded this definition to include communicative acts in which *any text* (including visual and audio texts) is integral to the nature of participants' interactions. This allowed us to consider hip-hop music in its various forms as being textual.

In our analysis, we looked for evidence of critical and analytical skills that are valued by K-12 and postsecondary institutions. At the same time we were attentive to literacy events in which the students demonstrated awareness and/or analysis of themes, messages, or images that revealed intentioned subject positions and coded power relations with respect to different people in society. To aid our analysis, we consulted the literature of critical, social, and literacy theories, as well as texts about strategies and competencies for college writing, state curriculum frameworks, and commentaries from university professors and administrators regarding the qualities and attributes of successful students.

Ultimately, we chose to look for examples of students appropriating the tools and language of literary analysis when discussing both hip-hop texts and canonical texts. Specifically, we coded the data for instances of the use of literary theory and terminology and a willingness to deconstruct or problematize the texts. Furthermore, we looked for instances where students were able to construct and support an argument and defend it against opposing arguments. We also focused on whether and how students were able to make segues between the hip-hop texts, the canonical texts, and their own lives. Finally, we analyzed the data for examples of students politicizing the texts by relating textual issues to contemporary social problems and to their personal lives.

In this chapter we have focused on two key classroom occurrences: presentations and group discussions. Presentations were formal events during which small groups took over a portion of the class in order to collectively answer and dialogically draw out implications of a central question or issue that had been posed for analysis. Whole class group discussions occurred after each of these formal presentations in semi-structured question and answer sessions. For description and analysis of the students' literacy practices inside these two class activities, we selected three vignettes that illustrate the kinds of arguments, analysis of issues, and textual connections that the students were able to make. The first two vignettes—"Cell Therapy" and "Coleridge and Nas: Imagine a Better World"—occurred during formal presentations. The third— "Don't Shoot the Messengers"—occurred during the whole group question and answer session following a particular presentation. These vignettes are presented following a brief description of the intervention unit itself.

The Poet in Society: A Description of the Unit

There were several objectives for this unit that combined our simultaneous agendas of tapping into popular culture and facilitating academic and critical literacy development. We needed to cover the poetry of the Elizabethan Age, the Puritan Revolution, and the Romantics that were all part of the district-mandated curriculum for twelfth-grade English. In addition to a critical exposure to the literary canon, we felt it important to extend the issues and ideas presented in poetry and song into themes for expository writing. Other objectives were to develop oral and written debate skills, to develop abilities to work in groups, to develop skills in formal public presentations, to develop note taking skills, and to develop abilities to both critique and write in different poetic forms such as the sonnet, the elegy, and the ballad.

We began the unit with a general overview of poetry and also attempted to define poetry and the role of the poet in society. We emphasized the importance of understanding the historical period in which a poem was written in order to more deeply appreciate the poem. In our introductory lecture, we laid out all of the historical/literary periods that would be covered in the unit (Elizabethan, Puritan Revolution, Romantics, and Metaphysical Poets from England, and the Civil War, Harlem Renaissance, Civil Rights Movement, and Postindustrial Revolution in the United States). It was our intention to place rap music and the postindustrial revolution right alongside these other historical periods and poems so that the students would be able to use a period and genre of poetry they were familiar with as a lens with which to examine other literary works, and also to encourage the students to re-evaluate the manner in which they viewed the texts from popular culture.

The second major portion of the unit was the group presentation of a poem and rap song. The groups were commissioned to prepare a justifiable interpretation of their poem and song with respect to its specific historical and literary period and to analyze the linkages between the poem and song. There were eight groups for this portion who were, after a week of preparation, each given a day to present to the class and have their arguments critiqued by their peers. The groups were assigned as follows:

	Group Poem	Song
1.	"Kubla Khan," Coleridge	"If I Ruled the World," Nas
2.	"Love Song of J. Alfred Prufrock," Eliot	"The Message," Grand Master Flash
3.	"O Me! O Life!" Whitman	"Don't Believe the Hype," Public Enemy
4.	"Immigrants In Our Own Land," Baca	"The World Is a Ghetto," Geto Boys
5.	"Sonnet 29," Shakespeare	"Affirmative Action," Nas
6.	"The Canonization," Donne	"Manifest," Refugee Camp
7.	"Repulse Bay," Chin	"Good Day," Ice Cube
8.	"Still I Rise," Angelou	"Cell Therapy," Goodie Mob

Other poems used for this unit were: "Let America Be America Again" by Langston Hughes and "Elegy Written in a Country Churchyard" by Thomas Gray.

In addition to the group presentations, students were asked to produce an anthology of ten poems that contained an elegy, a ballad, a sonnet, and a poem that described a place with which they were familiar. The title of the poem was to be the place that was featured. The students were asked as well to write a poem that conveyed a mood, a poem that dealt with a political, social, or economic problem that was important to them (racism, teen pregnancy, drug abuse, police brutality, poverty, homelessness, etc.), a love poem, a poem that celebrated a particular facet of life (first date, summertime, graduation, etc.), and two open poems that dealt with whatever subjects the students chose and that were written in any style they desired. Following the group presentations, we held a poetry reading in which each student selected five of his or her original poems to read for the class and on which to give brief comments. As an additional assignment to be completed outside class, students were asked to pick any song of their choice and write a five- to seven-page critical essay on it. They were also required to submit a transcription of the song.

Cell Therapy

Welcome to Room 330 at East Bay High.[1] It is a room with no windows, no heat, and little air. It has no computers or other technology except for the telephone. The wooden desks that fill the rows are all, from what we've been told, older than us, the teachers. The carpet has brown duct tape stretching across it to prevent the snags from ripping. On the chalkboard is a potpourri of information on topics ranging from the impending essay assignment, to the group projects, through to general college preparation and study tips. The walls are littered with *Time Magazine* pictures of the Million Man March, and the student uprising at Tiennamen Square. There are also posters of Malcolm X, W.E.B. DuBois, and famous women, Asian Americans, and Latinos. There are posters that have been created by students for past projects, famous movie advertisements, signs from marches and protests, and a section titled, In the News, for posting current event items. One wall is dedicated to literature and pictures related to college. This wall contains college newspapers and banners in addition to guidelines for admission and tips for college essays. There are four bookshelves located at different points in the room holding novels and anthologies that we have picked up over the years. In short, this is more to us than a classroom. It is a refuge and a home that we have tried to imbue with a spirit and a culture that stands in direct opposition to the many of the school's other constraints. On this particular day, Room 330 was abuzz with energy as the students were presenting their hip-hop/poetry projects. As the bell rang to start class, the four student leaders are assembled in the front of the class. As the bustle dies down, one can detect a hip-hop beat in the background. The beat is emanating from a small CD player on the floor as Cham begins to speak. She glances down at her notes and then gives a big smile to the class as she begins:

> Cham: First we would like to analyze the title. Cell, we think, means two things. One is a small room in a prison. Or, it could mean…a cell in your body. Therapy means treatment for a disease. Cell Therapy is like treatment for your mind, your body. Something is going wrong. (You can hear Goodie Mob rapping lightly in the background as students begin to make notes from her comments.)
>
> Phan: Like cell, meaning jail. Or your mind or your brain cell (points to her temples) meaning jail therapy.
>
> Evan: You know cell therapy could be actual physical treatment…

The group shows a facility with the language and the tools of analysis by beginning their presentation with the multiple possible meanings of the title. The concept of holding simultaneous multiple meanings is an important one to students and scholars that engage in similar types of analysis. The remainder of the student presentation analyzes the lyrics within the dual context of the rap artists attempting to purify adulterated brain cells and attempting to alleviate the social ills that lead many urban youth into jail cells because of the adulteration of their brain cells. Next, the members of this group attack the beat of Goodie Mob's "Cell Therapy":

> Phan: Okay, we want to talk about the beat first. (Phan turns around and points to the CD player, which is still thumpin' Goodie Mob) It's really different, it's like a haunting music, it creeps up on you and then it goes boom, you know? (Cham reaches down to turn the music up a notch) So, it's kinda like, it goes on here to talk about the New World Order he's saying that this world is going to creep up on us and it's going to hit us in our face pretty soon.
>
> Brad: It creeps up on us like a fog in San Francisco. I associate fog with mystery and the world is creeping over us like an undercover mystery in a sense.
>
> Cham: What I noticed was the way that they rap the song. The way that they came…uh…if you listen to the rest of the songs on the album they don't sound like this. They don't sound as aggressive. He's like, you better listen up before this and this happens.
>
> Phan: You know like it's preaching. We have to listen to them, you know before it blows up in our face and we don't expect it.

The students (as teachers) embrace the notion that the beat should also be analyzed as text. Not only are the words important to the overall message of the song, but also the beat itself communicates. Phan describes the beat as haunting and relates the themes in the beat to those of the actual text. The rapper-poets are warning against a New World Order that is colonizing the minds of urban youth. According to Phan, the beat underscores that message. Whether or not one agrees with her analysis, it is difficult to dispute that it is, in fact, analysis. The group has taken the title and the beat to establish the context for their interpretation of the text. They are constructing an argument and defending this argument by means of "textual" evidence. The group does not summarize; rather, they synthesize their understanding of the text and their emergent theory of its ultimate purpose. They have stated that they believe the purpose of the text to be critical, informative, and to deliver a social message to young urban listeners. For example, Evan argues:

> All right, we're gonna hit the first stanza, but we're not really gonna go line-by-line (reads the first stanza). Okay, it starts with, "When the scene unfolds." Basically, we're in the midst of a new world order. A repercussion of the new order is that it's brought on people like young girls getting pregnant. We see that now, but it's going to be more widespread. It's also saying, "Sega ain't in this order, them experimenting in Atlanta, Georgia...United Nations overseas." We interpreted that, as far as Sega...we think that technology is really great now. We look at Sega Saturn, Nintendo 64, and the Internet and we say, "Technology just can't get any better than this." But what he's trying to say is that Sega is nothing compared to the technology they'll be using to take our minds over.

Evan has initiated the textual analysis portion of his group's presentation. He announces that they are not going to "go line by line" through the lyrics; instead, they will discuss the pertinent themes of each stanza as they relate to their overall argument. Evan does, however, read the first stanza and shows his understanding of the schema of literary analysis, where one does often engage the text line by line. He shows a willingness and ability to apply this schema to a hip-hop text and to deviate from that schema in a way that serves to strengthen his analysis.

Evan also demonstrates a willingness to read his world onto and into the text. Taking the Goodie Mob line, "Sega ain't in this New World order," Evan utilizes the group's lived experience with video games to underscore his point. Video games represent entertainment and diversion to the students in the class. The games are only a simulation and do not represent reality. Evan contends that Goodie Mob's message is that, in the new world order, the same technology will be used, but not as a game. In this order there will be real winners and losers who will not gain infinite second chances with the push of a reset button.

Finally, Evan and his entire group, show a willingness to politicize the text in relating it to everyday urban issues. Evan concedes that young girls in his community are getting pregnant in large numbers. "We see that," he proclaims. His reading of the text is not only informed by his experiences, it informs his experiences as well, because Evan is now discussing a contemporary social phenomenon within the context of an orchestrated world order that has multiple repercussions for the urban poor.

Coleridge and Nas: Imagine a Better World

Jawan, who has been waiting patiently with his hands behind his back while Pamela and Alice explain Coleridge's "Kubla Khan," takes the paper that he has been concealing and begins to "read" the text, which is Nas's "If I ruled the World." He says,

> I kind of felt like [Nas] was trying to imagine a world where...blacks didn't have problems and was treated like everyone else. Like when it say (Jawan takes the packet with the rap texts and searches for a line. Everyone in his group has now switched from the textbook to the packet of supplemental poems and raps) when he talks about imagining smoking weed in the streets without cops harassing you and going to court with no trial, he's kinda saying imagine life without anybody bothering you or whatever. (Jawan lets the paper fly as he gestures with his hands to bring his point home) When he's talking about people bothering him, he's talking about white people.

As Jawan pauses, Pamela looks over his shoulder at the paper as both search the text for clues to support the argument that Jawan is making:

Teacher: I know that Nas doesn't have line numbers, but try to give us a general sense of where you are reading.

Jawan: I think when he says: "imagine going to court with no trial/ lifestyle's cruising blue behind my waters/ no welfare supporters/" he talking about people worrying about their struggle in everyday life, not worrying about their kids getting killed. Like I know my mom, she be worrying every night. Sometimes she can't even get to sleep for worrying or whatever.

Jawan has taken his paper and rolled it up, and as he talks about his mother a smirk comes across his face either from pain or embarrassment. Whatever the source, this particular portion of the song has struck an emotional chord with him. We knew Jawan's mother for the three years that he was in high school and knew that she did in fact worry about his safety—so much so in fact that she had seriously considered taking him out of school and sending him to live with relatives on several occasions. It is important to note that, at this point, Jawan is reading his world onto and into the text to inform his interpretation and analysis.

This is not just about presenting an argument for a song for a grade; this is about imagining a better world for urban youth. This is a point that resonates with Jawan, his family, his classmates, and his community; and, as it does, it also brings emotion into the analysis. This reading of Nas and the juxtaposition against another romantic, Coleridge, allows the students in this group to read their world into the nineteenth-century British text as well and to understand how Coleridge also is imagining a better world than the one he is now confronted with. The issues that Coleridge and Nas are talking about are similar, and looking at Coleridge through the lens of Nas through the lens of this urban East Bay community have brought that point home in a way that both serves as a useful literary analysis and also informs the lived experiences of the students. It is a chance for Jawan to push the understandings of his classmates on these two texts, but it is also an occasion to share a troubling part of his life. Finally, it is important to consider that Jawan felt it an appropriate segue and a useful example to amplify his interpretation of the Nas text.

James, a counterpart of Jawan, adds to the discussion:

> This point in the song is about…imagine you're out in the street and you're just getting harassed by police. In this world, there would be no cops harassing you. Not just for smoking weed, but just being there. (James' voice also fills with emotion as he lifts his hands in desperation and leans in toward the student-audience as he makes the point.) I felt that snakes represent not just the whites, but society in general. Some snakes tend to wrap around you and hold you…it's like society will hold you and strike like a cobra. You take example of Michael Jackson…he was big and society loved him, then they struck and said that he molested a kid. Society tends to do that to us…people of color, they can't wait to strike and bring us down.

James takes the metaphor that Nas uses of the snake to analyze both the society that Nas is describing as well as his own. In describing the danger of the snake and the way that snakes have of grabbing hold and striking, James uses the pronoun *us* rather than *they* which he would have to use if his analysis remained solely located in the song. He also extrapolates from Nas' text to issue a condemnation of society in general that tends to "strike and bring students of color down." The group continues with its analysis of the Nas song:

Pamela: Like when it says "days are shorter and nights are colder," that's the way that the world is now, but that is not the way that he wants it to be. I don't think that the nights are any colder than they've ever been, but it's like [James] said, because you are up at night worrying, you get to experience that the nights are actually cold. I guess that would make your days shorter too because you worry about stuff.

James: Like when he's talking about black diamonds and pearls, he could be talking about...like white diamonds and pearls are expensive and people tend to think that white pearls are better than black pearls just like society thinks that white people are better than black people and he wants to make things totally opposite. It's like weddings and funerals. Weddings are supposed to be happy occasions and people usually wear white. A funeral is a sad occasion and everybody wears black. Why is that? (James hunches his shoulders in a shrug) It's just a stereotypical view of society that white is always going to be better than black. It's something good, then people wear white, it's something bad, and people wear black, that's just the way that society looks at it (As he makes this last statement he pounds his hand into his paper with the same rhythm that he pronounces the words) Black diamonds and pearls could also mean the children.... If you look into the chorus part when they say walk right up to the sun, they are not talking about the (points to the sky) the sun that is making that heat, the son is our future.

Alice: It could also be like the son, S-O-N, like the Son of God.

James: Yeah, it's not the sun, S-U-N. If you look in this thing (he waves the packet text), you will never see sun, S-U-N, because it's like the son, Son of God, because we're all like the Sons of God.

Jawan: (Holds up his hand to be recognized in his own group before speaking) Yeah I think it's like the sons are the children and take them to school and the sons, the children, will enlighten them because it's the next generation.

The members of the group are also able to consider multiple interpretations of the text as James, Alice, Pamela, and Jawan all offer slightly different perspectives of the meaning of such phrases as "black diamonds and pearls" or "walk right up to the son." When providing his interpretation, for example, James gives examples of the way that the color black has negative connotations in the English language and is usually associated with sadness, evil, or death. James relates the semantic with the physiological and psychological in making the political statement that society extends its negative connotations of black to those whose complexion is darker as well. He also implies that people of color have internalized some of these assumptions as well. Here both James and Nas imagine having a world where things black were considered of value, such as diamonds and pearls.

Don't Shoot the Messengers

This group, for its presentation, has engaged in an analysis of T.S. Eliot's "The Love Song of J. Alfred Prufrock" and Grand Master Flash's "The Message." During the question and answer period, Jermaine and Vuong are asked to sum up the relationship between the two texts:

> Jermaine: Like we said before, they both have messages that are to society. You can interpret it two ways, uh… both of them are not just speaking to people that's around them, they're speaking to everyone…
>
> Vuong: The line that I want to point out is, "No I am not Prince Hamlet, nor was meant to be/ Am an attendant lord, one that will do/ To swell a progress start a scene or two,/ Advise the prince; no doubt an easy tool." It's like, he's not the one that is going to do the revolutionary acts. He won't go out there and revolt, but he'll advise you on what you need to do. Because Hamlet was someone that…he lost his throne, I mean, he lost what's rightfully his because his father was killed by his uncle. He wanted revenge to take his throne. He's saying to the lower class I can help you, but I'm not going to be the one that takes up that throne because I am already someone that has power. I am the attendant lord I can help you right now if I wanted to…
>
> Minh: So the two poems connect because they both put out a message saying that this is what's going on, you're in this position and they're in that position. Do something about it together, or else you'll be buried in your own problems. Take pride in yourself and have a long perspective…

Jermaine, Vuong, and Minh all answer the question in different ways, but each draws a similar Marxian correlation between the hip-hop text and the canonical text. Both Jermaine and Minh see Eliot and Grandmaster Flash as playing a proactive role in society through their poetry. Both also see poet's message as directed toward the working class in opposition to elite classes who have created—through their opulence and greed—the oppressive conditions that are at the center of each text. Vuong, however, does not see Eliot as a revolutionary character. He uses Eliot's reference to Prince Hamlet as evidence of the role of the poet as an advisor rather than a revolutionary. Vuong still arrives at the same Marxian analysis, though, as he critiques Eliot for aligning himself with the bourgeoisie. Following Minh's response, the group is hit with a barrage of questions from the class:

> Brad: In the "Love Song of J. Alfred Prufrock," I'm asking about the yellow fog and yellow smoke, I want to hear your reasoning that it's representing the writer of the poem

Minh: First, we said that it represents industrialism. Then we looked at the verbs "rub" and "slipped" which represent work in industrialism

Minh, in his response to Brad's question, draws upon a historical criticism correlating Eliot's critique of the yellow fog and smoke that were permeating his world with the rise of industrialism in the early part of the twentieth century. He also holds on to his Marxian analysis relating Eliot's choice of verbs with the cause of the proletariat who were increasingly exploited during the rise of industrialism:

Phan: I just wanted to know why you thought it was significant about the women coming and going talking of Michelangelo. I know you talked about it being rich women, but I don't see why he mentioned it so many times.

Vuong: It's kind of, in the sense... it's a message right. Never mind what's happening to you, but look at what these people (raises his hand and his paper toward the ceiling) up at the top are doing. You're laboring, but what are they doing? Some people don't even realize it. They're just laboring. In "Native Son," Bigger Thomas' mom, all she did was work, work, work. She knows they're up there, but she didn't really care what they were doing. She just knew she had to work.

Jermaine: What he's saying is that the working class people are not questioning why they don't get to come and go talking about Michelangelo.

Minh: People don't really care about what's going on, they're just chillin'. So that's what you gotta focus on, 'cause people are gonna come and go and not help you.

Again, Vuong, Jermaine, and Minh respond to Phan's question with a Marxian critique. Vuong makes an analogy to "Native Son," a text the class had read prior to the poetry unit. Jermaine and Minh extrapolate from the text, from the themes of the course and, to some degree, from their own lived experiences as working-class urban youth. Jermaine actually uses the term *working class*, although Eliot never does in his poem. Minh employs the pronoun *you* when answering the question rather than *they* or *the poor* which would seem more appropriate given that the fictional poem was written over seventy years ago. His answer indicates that he sees Eliot as speaking directly to him and the class, sending a message across generations to raise consciousness and encourage revolutionary praxis:

Orlando: Do you think, from the introduction, that he's relaying some divine message and he's the poet like Dante? Because some guy named Guido da Montefeltro he's talking to Dante the poet. You know, if he could do it all over again, he would like calm down. But he can't and since people do not return from these depths of poverty, he can

Jermaine: answer their questions without fear of notoriety or being looked upon unfavorably.

I think that you can obviously see that [Eliot] was worried about the notoriety. Mr. Prufrock, the character in the poem, he was definitely worried about the notoriety. It says in the third from the last stanza: "Shall I part my hair behind? Do I dare eat a peach?/ I shall wear white flannel trousers and walk upon the beach./ I have heard the mermaids singing each to each./ I do not think that they will sing to me." If you read the footnote at the bottom, it says that the sirens would attack those who were adventurous, those who had a lot of notoriety. I think he was worried about the notoriety because he said, "they won't sing to me.' So he's saying, should I try to bring an uprising? If I don't bring an uprising, I won't get notoriety, they won't sing to me.

Both Orlando's question and Jermaine's response are evidence of fine textual readings. Orlando tunes into a footnote to the poem, adding his own class critique to Dante's text in anticipating how Eliot is applying it to his own poem. Jermaine chooses a stanza of his own to show the ambivalence of Eliot's protagonist, J. Alfred Prufrock, who was deciding what to do with the overwhelming secret he carries throughout the poem. Although Prufrock never reveals his secret, Jermaine is convinced that secret was powerful enough to start an uprising or at least raise the critical consciousness of all who became privy. Jermaine and Orlando have synthesized their own theories and critiques with the actual text and even gone so far as to include annotated references to support their comments. They also continue to read their worlds into the text, keeping at the forefront of the discussion the very real issues of poverty, oppression, and social transformation.

Conclusion

The unit was consistent with the original goals of being culturally and socially relevant, critically exposing students to the literary canon, and facilitating the development of college-level expository writing. The positioning of hip-hop as a genre of poetry written largely in response to post-industrialism was a concept with which the students were able to relate. The issues of joblessness, poverty, rage, and alienation all had resonance with the urban youth culture of which the students were a part. It also helped to facilitate the transition to understanding the role individual poets may have played in their own societies. As one student, Orlando, responded in an interview:

I think it helped me, because like I appreciated hip-hop like already. And, so now, I can appreciate poetry as well...y'all did a great job relating both of them...

The students were able to generate some excellent interpretations as well as make interesting linkages between the canonical poems and the rap texts. For instance, group two talked about how both Grand Master Flash and T.S. Eliot looked out into their rapidly deteriorating societies and saw a "wasteland." Both poets were essentially apocalyptic in nature as they witnessed death, disease, and decay. Also, both poems talk about a message, indicating the role of a poet in society as a messenger or prophet. Group six discussed the role allegory plays in their two poems where both John Donne and the Refugee Camp use a relationship with a lover to symbolize the love and agony the poets feel for their societies.

The unit reflected basic tenets of critical pedagogy in that it was situated in the experiences of the students, called for critical dialogue, critical engagement with texts, and related the focus texts to larger social and political issues. However, some criticisms we need to make were that students should have had a greater role in selecting the hip-hop texts that were included in the unit. As one student—Walter—observed:

The group presentations, putting the poem and the song together is a pretty good idea. I think that made us get pretty deep into the songs. Also, I think it would be kinda cool if the students would recommend songs. For analyzing, like (he points to the board) you know, in that format. Because, I think that there are a lot of artists out there, smaller time artists that really aren't recognized. They really have a lot to say as opposed to like Foxy Brown. I don't know, you could get a lot deeper than some of the mainstream stuff.

This student was not only excited about the juxtaposition of the rap and canonical texts, but saw the potential of critically engaging with the content of the hip-hop songs. His judgment of the value of hip-hop texts was not determined by record sales or popularity (what he critiques as "mainstream"), but by the depth of the lyrics and the message. Learning to critically analyze popular media as Walter has done is an empowering skill that will serve him well as a citizen in a democratic society, as well as in the post-secondary academy where such talents are highly valued.

Finally, the students were not only engaged and able to use this expertise and positionality as subjects of the postindustrial world to make powerful connections to canonical texts, they were also able to have fun with learning about a genre of music and literature with which they were familiar. As the unit was culminating and the students are working independently on assembling their poetry unit portfolios, the classroom buzzes with energy following the final poetry readings. As students were working to meet the deadline for critiquing each other's work and assembling their packages, we asked Jermaine for some final comments:

> I guess for me, what I got out of the poetry unit as a whole was this was probably the best thing that I've done in my whole years of school. That's what I do. I rap, I emcee or whatever. It's hard right now. I think it's hard right now sometimes for rap to get the respect that it deserves. Like, in a lot of cases, people don't always look at rap as...serious music. My thing is that I want to take rap to the level where it can be accepted by all people on all types of levels in different countries, because it is in different countries right now. No one thinks of it as Shakespeare or whatever. Shakespeare is a great writer, but no one thinks of it as Shakespeare or whatever. How come in every classroom, it can't be required? How come, on the AP [college course credit] tests, there's not rap songs that you have to look at and analyze as serious work, as actual serious work that somebody put their feelings into? Just as there are weak emcees, there are weak writers and people don't buy those books just as people don't buy those tapes or whatever. It's the same thing with rap or whatever. You get the better writers, and the better writers sometimes sell more, you have your bestsellers or whatever, you know what I'm saying. You might have your Grisham, or you might have your KRS One. You might have your...uh...who else writes excellent books...uh...you might have your Amy Tan, and you might have your Bahamadiah or whatever. So, it's like the same or whatever. So, I just want to say that this was a good, no a great unit. Every teacher should approach this unit in the same fashion that you guys did to open up and expand your mind or whatever. A lot of people don't understand certain aspects of rap, but they don't want to ask that next question. They might not listen to rap or whatever. Or they just might think that rap is garbage. It's not garbage. It's like actual music from like actual people.

Jermaine's comments powerfully reflect many of the goals and aspirations we had in the design and implementation of this classroom unit. In the future, we plan to re-engage and analyze the written data, conversations, and presentations for evidence of critical literacy events as well as proficiency according to the state frameworks and what is considered outstanding scholarship in postsecondary institutions. The goal is to show that the students engaged in both critical, intellectual work, and work that has currency in the academy and that will help them navigate the gatekeeping mechanisms that often preclude them from access to higher education and economic empowerment. Ultimately, however, hip-hop music should be able to stand on its on as a worthy subject of study in the academy rather than just being a bridge to something more "acceptable" like canonical texts.

Note

1. East Bay High is an urban, multicultural school of nearly 2200 students located in a large Northern California city. The ethnic breakdown of the campus is approximately 40 to 45 percent Asian/Asian American (Chinese, Vietnamese, and Southeast Asian), 35 percent African American, 15 percent Chicano/Latino, and 5 to 10 percent other immigrant groups (e.g., Bosnian, African). Less than 1 percent of the student population is white American. At East Bay High standardized test scores lag far behind state and national norms. The school regularly scores in the twentieth and thirtieth percentile on major standard assessments such as the SAT 9, the CAP, and CLAS assessments and the median SAT score, and for the past five years has been below 800, which would place an individual student in the tenth percentile nationally. According to the most recent state educational data 57.9 percent of the school population is eligible to receive Aid for Dependent Children (AFDC), and only one classroom is wired to the internet. The focal class selected for this study is an accurate cross-section of the school with respect to ethnicity, socioeconomic status, and academic performance.

Works Cited

Baker, H. (1993). *Black studies, rap, and the academy.* Chicago: University of Chicago Press.
Barton, D. and Hamilton, M. (2000). Literacy practices. In D. Barton, M. Hamilton, and R. Ivanic (Eds.), *Situated literacies: Reading and writing in context.* London: Routledge.
Farley, C. (1999). Hip-hop nation: There's more to rap than just rhythms and rhymes. After two decades, it has transformed the culture of America. *Time*, 153 (5), 55–65.
Ferdman, B. (1990). Literacy and cultural identity. *Harvard Educational Review*, 60 (2), 181–204.
Freire, P. (1970). *Pedagogy of the oppressed.* New York: Continuum.
——— and Macedo, D. (1987). *Reading the word and the world.* Westport, CT: Bergin & Garvey.
Gee, J. (1996). *Social linguistics and literacies: Ideology in discourses.* London: Falmer.
Giroux, H. (1996). *Fugitive cultures: Race, violence, and youth.* New York: Routledge.
Goodie Mob. (1995). *Cell therapy. Soul food.* New York: LA FACE.
Heath, S. B. (1983). *Ways with words: Language, life and work in communities and classrooms.* Cambridge: Cambridge University Press.
hooks, b. (1994). Sexism and mysogyny: Who takes the rap? *Zmagazine*. February. eserver.org/race/misogyny.html (accessed December 10, 2002).
Hull, G. (1993). Critical literacy and beyond: Lessons learned from students and workers in a vocational program and on the job. *Anthropology and education quarterly*, 24 (4), 308–317.
Ice Cube. (1992). *The predator.* New York: Priority Records.
Lee, C. (1993). *Signifying as a scaffold for literary interpretation: The pedagogical implications of an African American discourse genre.* Urbana, IL: National Council of Teachers of English.
Mahiri, J. (1996). Writing, rap, and representation: Problematic links between text and experience. In G. Kirsch and P. Mortensen (Eds.), *Ethics and representation in qualita-

tive studies of literacy (pp. 228–240). Urbana, IL: National Council of Teachers of English.

———. (1998). *Shooting for excellence: African American and youth culture in new century schools*. New York: Teachers College Press.

Nas (1996). *It was written*. New York: Columbia Records.

Powell, C. (1991). Rap music: An education with a beat from the street. *Journal of Negro Education*, 60 (3), 245–259.

The Refugee Camp. (1996). *The score*. New York: Columbia Records.

Street, B. (1984). *Literacy in theory and practice*. Cambridge: Cambridge University Press.

———. (1993). *Literacy in cross-cultural perspective*. Cambridge: Cambridge University Press.

"What They Do Learn in School"

Jeannie Oakes

Seeking both traditional and radical outcomes, critical educators Ernest Morrell and Jeff Duncan-Andrade juxtapose Samuel Taylor Coleridge with Nas; T. S. Eliot with Grand Master Flash, and Walt Whitman with Public Enemy in their twelfth-grade English class. They draw on new literacy theorists to ground their approach to poetry in the argument that academic failure among urban youth can be traced—at least in part—to social and cultural discontinuities between home and school. Morrell and Duncan-Andrade make the case that (a) traditional course material will be more easily and willingly learned when it is placed within the context of more authentic cultural frames; (b) the cultural authenticity and literary merit of hip-hop music make it such a frame for urban youth; and (c) the analytic skills learned through the frame of hip-hop can be transferred to canonical poetry, and, thereby, foster tradition-al academic literacy learning. Going beyond a narrowly utilitarian objective of transmitting the dominant cultural canon (or at the least, the typical spin placed on that canon by high school curricula) and echoing Freirean theories, they also assert that this pedagogy can promote eman-cipatory ends: "a broader definition of school-based literacy that encom-passes cultural values, self-awareness, and the development of critical consciousness." Morrell and Duncan-Andrade hope their students will both read the canonical word and read the world of their own experience in ways that prepare them to struggle to reclaim their "voice, history, and future." Following Mahiri, these two teachers hope to become for their students, "sources of resistance to the ideology and practices of cultural domination and exploitation."

Critical researchers as well as teachers, Morrell and Duncan-Andrade render their propositions problematic and then document, analyze, and tell the story of their urban students' interweaving of hip-hop and the canon. And, indeed, they provide evidence that their students displayed both (a) critical and analytic skills that are valued in K-12 and postsecondary education; and (b) awareness and analysis of themes, images, and the like that revealed "intentioned subject positions" and "coded power relations." Scaffolded by masterful teaching, these urban young people used the language and tools of literary analysis to unpack, discuss, and manipulate the symbols of urban youth culture. Importantly, these teachers did not make the common "nativist" error of presuming that their students' race and social location necessarily made the students experts in hip-hop—that "their" culture in all its complexity and richness is somehow transmitted to them by dint of their demographics. Rather, by learning a critical "reading" of hip-hop (which is different from magically receiving an intuitive understanding of a critique-filled countercultural literature), the students constructed critical tools that allowed them iteratively to reframe and own a more informed cultural amalgam. In brief, these students appear to have gained a measure of "critical capital" or a critique that enables them to draw from multiple cultural traditions and leads them to a measure of mastery over how they understand their own social locations.

Masterful pedagogy connected the students with "their" culture and transformed these connections into a larger social critique, and all the while scaffolded their use of critical and analytic tools to parse the lines and stanzas of Coleridge and Eliot. The students even enjoyed it! Yet, as I read this careful work, I am struck by the existential absurdity of it all. These were determined, talented teachers and admirably persistent twelfth-graders; after all, they were still in a school where huge numbers of their teachers and student peers had dropped out. And, here they were, together, using hip-hop to slog their way through the poetry of the Elizabethan Age, the Puritan Revolution, the Romantics, and "contemporaries" like T. S. Eliot (as worthy as it may be), and to master such forms as the sonnet, the elegy, and the ballad. Why? To delight in the beauty and meaning of the poetry? Probably not. To promote cultural unity by sharing the rich heritage of literate Anglo-Americans? Not likely. To acquire knowledge they need to succeed in twenty-first century occupations? Hardly.

Beyond the absurdity, I am struck by the sheer injustice. At the end of the unit, one student—Jermaine—asks, "How come, on the AP tests, there's not rap songs that you have to look at and analyze as serious work, as actual serious work that somebody put their feelings into?" Now, hip-hop would probably not be my choice of content for more equitable AP tests, nor are AP tests my choice of indicators of academic literacy. However, Jermaine's question goes to the heart of the sociology of knowledge and power.

The answer is that these teachers and students grappled with this material because they had to. Not only was it the district's mandated curriculum. In Bordieu's formulation, these canonical poems and conventional ways of analyzing them are part and parcel of the cultural capital required to mark these students as intelligent. The definition and understandings of intelligence that pervade schooling, like all meanings, are products of the cultural contexts in which they have been constructed. In all societies, the meanings that dominate are those constructed by elite groups. In culturally diverse societies, elites and the meanings they construct reflect the dominant culture. Because of these elites' political, economic, and social power, their culturally based definition of intelligence becomes "common sense." Accordingly, an ideology of intelligence makes the particular cultural capital—the culture, lifestyle, and ways of knowing of the white, wealthy, and thus most powerful—not only be seen as more valuable than others, but as a function of biologically determined ability. Put bluntly, the canon is smart; hip-hop is not, and there is nothing culturally or politically neutral about the distinction. The "critical capital" these students gained appears potent, even thrilling to this observer. But these triumphs in the classroom only point to what cannot be accomplished in the classroom alone.

Being smart matters in no small part to these teachers and students because it has exchange value. For a high school student, being smart—that is, reflecting the dominant meanings of intelligence—is of great consequence, particularly for those with little economic or social capital that might compensate for a less than stellar mastery of the required twelfth-grade English curriculum. What other chance do they have to acquire credentials that certify them as serious enough, as smart enough, as good enough to leave impoverished and disparaged neighborhoods, at least temporarily, for college. (Of course, once there, absent great athletic talent, they will slog their way through more poetry of the Elizabethan Age, the Puritan Revolution, the Romantics, and "contemporaries" like T. S. Eliot—and their equivalents in the other high-status disciplines that comprise the high-status undergraduate curriculum—for the privilege of remaining outside impoverished and disparaged neighborhoods as adults.)

For me, the question remains: Can this pedagogy (or any pedagogy, for that matter) enable students to "pass" as knowledgeable, comfortable, and deserving members of the dominant culture with their mastery of the high-status canon or to gain access to the power and privilege that comes from being able to do so? Amassing cultural capital that counts—either a genuine "taste" for Coleridge and Eliot (not likely even in classrooms of the privileged), or (more likely) a grudging tolerance for this cultural rite of passage required of those who will inherit their parents' upper middle-class lifestyle and privilege—seems far removed from these urban students transferring their analytic skills from Public Enemy and Ice Cube. Certainly, we are wrong to expect that gifted teachers will correct macro patterns of social inequality in the micro-worlds of classroom curriculum instruction.

Even so, Morrell and Duncan-Andrade make clear that teachers must try to do no less, and that Jermaine and his peers deserve no less. Without such teaching and learning, we can't get beyond well-intentioned, ill-fated efforts to provide urban students with access to elite academic knowledge. Indeed, this theme runs throughout the issues raised and research reported in this book as a whole. Without such research, teaching and learning we won't push society to tackle more important work: re-defining whose culture and way of life counts as worth knowing and worth living.

Contributors

Chapter 1

JABARI MAHIRI is an Associate Professor of Education in the division of Language, Literacy, Culture and Society in the Graduate School of Education at the University of California at Berkeley. Dr. Mahiri is also the director of the Center for Urban Education funded by the Spencer Foundation. His most recent book is *Shooting for Excellence: African American and Youth Culture in New Century Schools*.

Chapter 2

PEDRO A. NOGUERA is the Judith K. Dimon Professor of Communities and Schools at the Harvard Graduate School of Education. Dr. Noguera's research focuses on schools' responses to social and economic forces within urban environments. His most recent book is *Confronting the Urban: How City Schools Can Respond to the Forces of Social Inequality*.

Chapter 3

PETER COWAN is an Assistant Professor in the Department of Language Education at Indiana University. His research interests include Latino visual discourse as a form of subaltern knowledge; exploring how English-language learners learn to write in English in school; and how preservice Language Arts teachers are prepared for teaching in multicultural urban classrooms. Dr. Cowan's most recent publication, "'Drawn' into the community: Reconsidering the artwork of Latino adolescents" appeared in *Visual Sociology*.

JOSÉ DAVID SALDÍVAR is Professor and Chair of the Department of Ethnic Studies at the University of California at Berkeley. He has also been the Chair of the American Cultures Program at the same university. Dr. Saldívar's most recent book is *Border Matters: Remapping American Cultural Studies*.

Chapter 4

WAN SHUN EVA LAM teaches in the Department of Teacher Education & Curriculum Studies at the University of Massachusetts, Amherst. Dr. Lam's research is on the relationships between identity and literacy development in the transnational context of internet-based communication. Among her recent publications is a book chapter with Claire Kramsch titled, "Textual identities: The importance of being non-native," in *Non-Natives in English Language Teaching*.

CLAIRE KRAMSCH is Professor of German and Foreign Language Education and Director of the Berkeley Language Center at the University of California, Berkeley. Dr. Kramsch's research areas include applied linguistics and second-language acquisition, as well as language pedagogy. One of her books, *Context and Culture in Language Teaching*, won the MLA's Kenneth Mildenberger Prize for Outstanding Research Publication in the Field of Foreign Languages and Literatures.

Chapter 5

BETH LEWIS SAMUELSON is a Ph.D. candidate in the division of Language, Literacy, Culture and Society in the Graduate School of Education at the University of California, Berkeley. Her interest in research on unschooling is connected to her own high school education in a tiny boarding school in the Equateur Province of the Congo. She has published a review titled, "Language and literacy diversity in the United States," in *TESL-EJ*.

CAROL D. LEE is an Associate Professor of Education and Social Policy in the Learning Sciences Program of the School of Education at Northwestern University. Dr. Lee's research focuses on the design of curriculum that draws on forms of cultural capital to support literate problem solving in response to literature. She is the author of *Signifying as a Scaffold for Literary Interpretation: The Pedagogical Implications of an African American Discourse Genre*, and she is co-editor, with Peter Smagorinsky, of *Vygotskian Perspectives on Literacy Research*.

Chapter 6

JENNIFER SEIBEL TRAINOR is an Assistant Professor in the English Department at the University of Pittsburgh. Dr. Trainor is the winner of NCTE's Promising Researcher Award, and she is also a member of the National Writing Project. She has published in the areas of labor practices in composition, literacy, and critical pedagogy. Her most recent publication is titled, "Constructions of whiteness in education for social change," in *College Composition and Communication*.

ANDREA ABERNETHY LUNSFORD is a Professor of English and Director of Stanford's Program in Writing and Rhetoric. She is also on the faculty of the Bread Loaf School of English. Dr. Lunsford has designed and taught undergraduate and graduate courses in writing history and theory, rhetoric, literacy, and intellectual property. She has written or co-authored thirteen books, including her most recent work, *Everything Is an Argument*.

Chapter 7

TONY MIRABELLI received his Ph.D. from the Graduate School of Education in the division of Language, Literacy and Culture at the University of California, Berkeley. Dr. Mirabelli is currently the Tutorial Coordinator for the Athletic Studies Center of the University of California, Berkeley.

STUART TANNOCK is a Lecturer in the Graduate School of Education at the University of California, Berkeley. He also works closely with the Center for Labor Research and Education there. Dr. Tannock's research and teaching interests focus on labor movement organizing and education, workplace and labor market ethnography, the sociology of youth, and the political economy of higher education. His most recent book is *Youth at Work: The Unionized Fast-Food and Grocery Workplace*.

Chapter 8

JANE STANLEY is the Assistant Director of the College Writing Program at the University of California at Berkeley. Dr. Stanley is presently writing about the history of composition instruction and the rhetoric of remediation at that institution.

GESA E. KIRSCH is Professor of English at Bentley College. Her research and teaching interests include composition studies, ethics, feminism, qualitative research, and women's roles in higher education. Dr. Kirsch was formerly the Associate Executive Director for Higher Education with the National Council of Teachers of English. Her most recent book is *Ethical Dilemmas in Feminist Research*.

Chapter 9

AMANDA GODLEY is an Assistant Professor in the School of Education at the University of Pittsburgh. One focus of her research is on the ways in which gender is practiced through literacy activities within and beyond schools. One of Dr. Godley's recent articles with Jennifer Seibel Trainor is "After Wyoming: Labor Practices in Two University Writing Programs."

BARRIE THORNE is Professor of Sociology and Women's Studies at the University of California, Berkeley. She also co-directs the Center for Working Families. Dr. Thorne is the author of *Gender Play: Girls and Boys in School*, and is co-editor of *Feminist Sociology: Life Histories of a Movement*.

Chapter 10

SORAYA SABLO SUTTON received her Ph.D. from the Graduate School of Education in the division of Language, Literacy, and Culture at the University of California, Berkeley. A central focus of her research has been on literacy issues—and specifically those concerning students of color in urban schools. One of Dr. Sutton's recent articles with Jabari Mahiri is "Writing for Their Lives: Non-School Literacy of Urban, African American Youth."

JUNE JORDAN was a Professor of African American Studies at the University of California, Berkeley. A prolific poet, novelist, essayist and political activist, Professor Jordan is the author of 26 books. One of her books which chronicles her work in stimulating and sustaining the writing of poetry at various levels is *Poetry for the People*.

Chapter 11

ERNEST MORRELL is an Assistant Professor in the School of Education at Michigan State University. He recently received an American Educational Research Association Post-Doctoral Fellowship for his research on academic and critical literacy development through engaging popular culture. Dr. Morrell has a forthcoming book on this topic.

JEFF DUNCAN-ANDRADE is Director of Teachers as Agents of Equity and Change in the Graduate School of Education at the University of California, Los Angeles. Dr. Duncan-Andrade's research examines how high school students' sport involvement can be used to facilitate their academic success. Initial findings from this work have been reported in several newspaper articles and highlighted in a National Public Radio special.

JEANNIE OAKES is Professor of Education and Associate Dean in the Graduate School of Education and Information Studies at the University of California, Los Angeles. Dr. Oakes also directs UCLA's Institute for Democracy, Education and Access (IDEA), which brings UCLA's research capacity and commitment to bear on pressing public issues in Los Angeles and in California. Her latest book is *Becoming Good American Schools: The Struggle for Civic Virtue in Education Reform* (with Karen Hunter Quartz, Steve Ryan, and Martin Lipton).

Index

About the Editor

Jabari Mahiri is Associate Professor of Language, Literacy, and Culture and co-director of the Center of Urban Education in the Graduate School of Education at the University of California at Berkeley. He has been Senior Fellow of the Annenberg Institute, an Executive Committee Member of CCCC (Conference on College Composition and Communication), and a high school English teacher in the Chicago public schools. Dr. Mahiri is the author of *Shooting for Excellence: African American and Youth Culture in New Century Schools*, as well as a number of journal articles on the language and literacy development of urban youth.

Colin Lankshear, Michele Knobel,
& Michael Peters
General Editors

New literacies and new knowledges are being invented "in
the streets" as people from all walks of life wrestle with
new technologies, shifting values, changing institutions,
and new structures of personality and temperament emerging
in a global informational age. These new literacies and
ways of knowing remain absent from classrooms. Many education administrators, teachers, teacher educators, and academics seem largely unaware of them. Others actively
oppose them. Yet, they increasingly shape the engagements
and worlds of young people in societies like our own. The
New Literacies and Digital Epistemologies series will explore this terrain with a view to informing educational
theory and practice in constructively critical ways.

For further information about the series and submitting
manuscripts, please contact:

Michele Knobel & Colin Lankshear
Montclair State University
Dept. of Education and Human Services
3173 University Hall
Montclair, NJ 07043
michele@coatepec.net

To order other books in this series, please contact our
Customer Service Department at:

(800) 770-LANG (within the U.S.)
(212) 647-7706 (outside the U.S.)
(212) 647-7707 FAX

Or browse online by series at:

www.peterlang.com